Apology to Apostrophe

Apology to Apostrophe

Autobiography

and the Rhetoric of

Self-Representation

in Spain

James D. Fernández

Duke University Press   Durham and London 1992

© 1992 Duke University Press
All rights reserved
Printed in the United States of America
on acid-free paper ∞
Library of Congress Cataloging-in-Publication Data
appear on the last printed page of this book.

Contents

Acknowledgments

I thank the two anonymous readers for Duke University Press who made some very helpful suggestions on this manuscript. Parts of my argument on Santa Teresa appeared in Spanish in my article published in *MLN:* "La *Vida* de Teresa de Jesús y la salvación del discurso." An abbreviated version of chapter 2 has appeared in the *Revista de estudios hispánicos*. Both references appear in this book's list of works cited. I thank the editors of those journals for permission to reprint. Salvador Carrasco took on the formidable task of translating quotations from foreign languages into English with his characteristic rigor and intelligence. I am also grateful to both the Frederick J. Hilles Fund of Yale University and the Program for Cultural Cooperation Between Spain's Ministry of Culture and U.S. Universities for their generous support of this publication.

This project originated as a doctoral dissertation written at Princeton University, under the direction of Luis Fernández-Cifuentes. His influence and example have been far too important and pervasive to be accurately reflected in a few endnotes. After studying the texts of so many autobiographers who routinely repudiate their schooling, it gives me great pleasure to acknowledge my profound indebtedness to this exemplary adviser, teacher, scholar, and friend.

My friendship and dialogue with Sylvia Molloy, José Muñoz

Millanes, Arcadio Díaz Quiñones, and Carlos Alonso have been invaluable. I thank them for their advice and their comments on different drafts of this book. I am also grateful to a whole series of outstanding teachers; in particular to Raúl Rodríguez and Robert Russell.

Another "source" that could never be adequately acknowledged in endnotes is the community of readers in which I lived while a graduate student. The commitment, honesty, intelligence, and enthusiasm of my classmates have given me a glimpse of what Hispanism could be. I especially thank Antonio Vera-León, Benjamín Muñiz, and Humberto Huergo for the warmth and intellectual vigor they shared with me. Bo Conn is a one-of-a-kind friend and reader.

My parents, brothers, and sister have given me the unconditional love and support I needed to complete this project. I hope that the earnestness of my efforts honors the memory of my beloved grandparents.

Finally, I dedicate this book to Marisa Carrasco who *lived* this project with me; not as guardian of any safe haven but rather as a joyful and loving *compañera de viaje*.

Introduction

Para ser sujeto, hay que estar sujeto.
To be a subject, you have to be subjected.

—*Anonymous*

Unautobiographical Spain?

"Spaniards don't write autobiographies." This cliché is so wide-spread that some kind of refutation of it, however brief, seems to have become an indispensable opening gambit for any study of Hispanic self-writing. We find the gesture in Randolph Pope's *La autobiografía española hasta Torres Villarroel* (1974), Adolfo Prieto's *La literatura autobiográfica argentina* (1966), Margarita Levisi's *Autobiografías del siglo de oro* (1985), and Sylvia Molloy's study (1985) on autobiography in Spanish America, to mention just a few examples. Hoping that the best way to legitimize Spanish autobiography as an object of analysis would be to analyze the texts, not their possibilities (or impossibilities) of existence, my first inclination, on undertaking this project, was to avoid the gesture altogether, to let my book, my bibliography and appendixes speak for themselves, as it were. What I wanted to avoid at all costs was a fall into the zealotry of the eager Hispanist, claiming that Spain had more or better autobiographers than other countries. This is simply not the case. My only claim is that there is a considerable number of texts that deserve our critical attention. And if I have been unable to avoid addressing the prejudice, it is because I think that its history is telling.

Spaniards themselves are in part to blame for the dissemination of this commonplace. "Spain lacks what are commonly titled memoirs" is the decision handed down by Antonio Alcalá Galiano.[1] Jacinto Benavente y Martínez proclaims, "In our literature there is a scarcity of works of this genre."[2] César González Ruano announces, "It is a genre which is hardly abundant among us."[3] Juan Goytisolo reasons, "Spaniards prove to be singularly reluctant to the idea of exposing . . . [their lives] in writing."[4] What is ironic about these statements is that they were made by autobiographers, Spanish autobiographers. An even greater irony: I have been able to gather a fairly large corpus of texts simply by following the leads offered by autobiographers themselves—at times those very same autobiographers who deny the existence of the genre in their country. Alcalá Galiano, in his *Recuerdos de un anciano,* sent me looking for the *Memorias* of Francisco Espoz y Mina. Benavente y Martínez mentions at least four Spanish precursors in his *Recuerdos y olvidos.* González Ruano's *Mi medio siglo se confiesa a medias* referred me to the autobiographical writings of Luis Ruiz Contreras, Pío Baroja, Alberto Insúa, and Azorín. Perhaps when these autobiographers deny the existence of the genre in Spain, they are really just indulging in a form of Rousseau's anxiety of influence: "The enterprise I am about to undertake has no precedent."[5] It would seem that when it comes to writing autobiography, everyone always takes the road not taken: *se hace camino al andar.*

Many have been quick to accept statements like these. Even worse, once the absence of texts is uncritically accepted, writers have tried their hand at offering explanations of this lack based on essentializing definitions of Spanishness. The most famous case in point is the philosopher José Ortega y Gasset who argued that "memoirs are a symptom of complacency in life. . . . The scarcity of Memoirs [in Spain] ought not to surprise us if we realize that the Spaniard considers life to be like a universal toothache!"[6] This is curious and specious reasoning, no doubt, which mysteriously attributes silence to the victim of a toothache.

It may be the case that the number of *published* Spanish texts is proportionately smaller than that of texts from some other nations. It is certainly true that in Spain the genre has not received much critical attention. Nonetheless, it seems to me that there are several lines of inquiry that might help us interpret this situation historically, without our falling back on simplistic notions of the un-autobiographical Spanish character. In other words, I believe that Spain's apparent poor showing in the genre is an issue that ought to be explored in terms of political and literary history, rather than in terms of any essentializing national psychology. In particular, the character or quality of autobiographical writing in Spain as well as the conditions of its transmission and reception would need to be studied.

It seems reasonable to assume that relative social and political stability would provide an atmosphere hospitable to benign, complacent old-timers, who might produce tranquil, stately, or even frivolous recollections. Inhabitants of a society that does not undergo momentous upheavals or shifts of hegemony might be afforded the luxury of living and writing normal(ized) lives, lives that take place within, and are narrated from, a relatively unproblematic or unproblematized paradigm. We would do well to remember then, that in the case of Spain, it is precisely the nineteenth century—Europe's epoch of great public men and their memoirs—that serves as the scene of a violent and prolonged battle between modernity and tradition, between revolution, reform, and reaction. Antonio Flores, a humorous and astute observer of nineteenth-century Spanish society would remark, "We have lived through half of the nineteenth century in a society of alternating persecuters and victims of persecution, taking turns emigrating to foreign lands, so that the world would not ignore our fraternal dissensions."[7] The French invasion of 1808, the liberal reforms of Cádiz in 1812, the return of absolutism in 1814 and subsequent persecution of liberals and *afrancesados,* the liberal triennium of 1820–23, the return, again, of absolutism in 1823, the fall, again, of absolutism in 1833, the Carlist wars waged throughout the century, the Glorious Revolution of 1868 and the First Republic, the Bourbon Restoration of 1874—this abbreviated catalog of major political crises should make one thing perfectly clear: if we consider an average life span to be approximately fifty years, there is not a single potential nineteenth-century Spanish autobiographer who would not have had to live through one, if not several, profound political shifts. If the autobiographer himself or herself were not exiled or persecuted at one point or another, chances are good that his or her parents or children were. Not exactly the stuff of complacent reminiscence. My point is this: perhaps many Spanish autobiographical texts have gone unnoticed at least in part because they fail to conform to a certain canon of well-wrought, apparently disinterested, complacent life narratives. Often written for the most worldly of reasons— to solicit a pension, to refute accusations of impropriety or treason, or simply to make money—these memoirs do not always make for the greatest read. In fact, as will become clear in chapter 1, for many nineteenth-century Spanish memoirists, artistry and rhetoric are purportedly antithetical to historical truth. In other words, it is in the memoirist's interest to produce a text that is aesthetically unpleasant, or at least to claim to do so.

Rather than venture essentialist hypotheses to explain an apparent scarcity of Spanish life narratives, I believe it would be helpful to historicize not only the quality or character of life (Was there constant political unrest? Was a great deal at stake in the writing of an autobiography?) and the conventions of autobiographical discourse (Was "art" seen as antithetical to "truth"?), but also the conditions of the texts' reception and transmission. The cultivation, preservation, and transmission of life narratives depend to a large extent on a devoted community of readers. After all, the origins of Christian biography are to be found in the Acts of the Martyrs, texts often "compiled from the official reports of [the martyrs'] trials" (de Ferrari 1952, p. 7). These texts and other narratives of opposition were, in effect, smuggled by eyewitnesses from the arena of martyrdom and preserved and transmitted, often at great risk, by the community of the faithful. Life stories are unusually effective pedagogical tools, which many communities (religions and nations, especially) have frequently used to promote or invent a sense of filiation or belonging. Might it not be the case that the political turmoil that has characterized modern Spanish history, with its recurrent bloody battles between two Spains, not only has affected the character of autobiographical writing in Spain, but also has never allowed that moment of tranquility and consolidation from which to constitute a canon of national texts? Indeed, the recent flood of autobiographical writing that has appeared since Franco's death, much of it produced by previously silenced, republican *vencidos,* is clear proof that, Ortega y Gasset's toothache notwithstanding, under the right conditions, the genre can and will flourish in Spain. And not only has the transition to democracy stimulated the production of new auto-biographical writing, it has also given rise to the publication or republication of the autobiographical writings of figures that had been neglected or erased by the previous regime. The name and prospectus of one prominent recent series of books is telling in this regard: *"Broken Memory: Exiles and Heterodoxies:* This significant title announces a collection of books whose goal is to reestablish the cultural continuity of Spain and its peoples, a continuity broken by the Civil War and the different misfortunes that perpetuated it."[8]

This example of Spain's recent transition to democracy does not mark the first time that profound political and social changes have fomented a considerable proliferation of autobiographical activity. The turmoil unleashed by the French invasion of 1808 also gave rise to an impressive number of autobiographical narratives, written by the agents, enemies, or victims of that awakening to modernity heralded by Napoleon's troops. As early as 1836, the great Spanish satirist, Mariano José de Larra, in a declaration Hispanists have been slow to heed, would refer to "that uncontainable flood of memoirs" being written by self-ordained witnesses or protagonists of the great transformation inaugurated in 1808 and prolonged throughout the topsy-turvy century.[9] To recover and reread some of the primary texts of that series is one of the main objectives of this book.

A group of political and military memoirs written in the aftermath of 1808 is the principal focus of chapter 1.[10] Chapter 2 is an in-depth look at one of nineteenth-century Europe's most stirring autobiographies, the *Life* (1845) of the Spanish exile and dissident Joseph Blanco White (1775–1841), a text that, precisely because of the vicissitudes of literary history and canon formation, remained all but unknown both in and out of Spain until the 1970s. Chapter 3 looks at the autobiographical writings of three relatively better-known authors. Ramón de Mesonero Romanos (1803–82) was an urban planner, publishing entrepreneur, author of countless *cuadros de costumbres* or *études de moeurs* and exemplary bourgeois; his auto-biography, titled *Memorias de un setentón* was first published serially in 1880. Spain's most popular nineteenth-century playwright and poet, José Zorrilla (1817–93) is best known for his nationaliza-tion—some would say emasculation—of Romantic formulas and rhetoric, and for his 1844 version of *Don Juan Tenorio;* his memoirs, written on his return from a self-imposed exile to Mexico and published serially in 1879, are called *Recuerdos del tiempo viejo.* Armando Palacio Valdés (1853–1938) was a turn-of-the-century author from the northern rural region of Asturias, who, though judged to be a mediocre novelist by many of today's critics, achieved a considerable international readership during his lifetime; he is the author of the autobiographical text *La novela de un novelista,* first published in 1921.

Hispanists, who are, after all, professional preservers and transmitters of texts, have also contributed to the dissemination of the old cliché about unautobiographical Spain. Not only have they been slow to hunt down forgotten works, but also they have not known exactly what to do with those few autobiographies that were more or less readily available. The uncertain status of autobiography has made it an uncomfortable genre to work with; historians have viewed it with suspicion and critics with apprehension. Typically, in the past, Hispanists might cull facts from a famous author's autobiography, for example, Zorrilla's, in order to clarify a certain passage of a book or a turn in the author's career. Beyond that, though, they had little use for these texts. Until not too long ago this was the situation of the genre as a whole, not only in the case of Hispanism. But recent developments in literary theory have provided us with a way of reading these works with renewed vigor and interest.

In particular, two (much-maligned) tendencies in literary studies since structuralism have, to my mind, made this book possible. First, the categories of the beautiful and the masterpiece have been sufficiently problematized and historicized so as to allow me, a student of literature, to work with texts that are neither. It is as if Hispanism could not even see these texts as long as literary studies were governed by criteria of aesthetic beauty. Second, and most importantly, the poststructuralist tendency to deny historical or autobiographical writing any privileged status as metadiscourse has invited us to view these works as *texts*—verbal constructs that deploy identifiable and analyzable narrative strategies. As long as literary studies accepted a clear-cut distinction between fact and fiction, between history and literature, these texts would remain largely irrelevant if not invisible to most Hispanists. But once we question this distinction and no longer grant an autobiography any special authority as a definitive metacommentary, it simply takes its place alongside the rest of the author's production. Like a novel or a poem, it, too, is an interpretation that needs to be interpreted. While scholars of other national literatures have made great progress in this enterprise, there is clearly much work to be done in Hispanism. I hope this book will be a first step in that direction. I also hope that my consideration of these relatively unknown Spanish texts in the context of current theoretical discussions on European autobiography will contribute to the ongoing critical debate on the genre.

At this point, a brief explanation of my title, *Apology to Apostrophe*, is in order. I use these two terms in a rather broad sense, to evoke a tension that is often at the center of autobiographical discourse. Apology, simply defined, is a verbal self-defense before one's contemporaries. But the implications of undertaking such a self-defense are often so varied and profound, that for the purposes of this study, I wish to link the notion of apology with an entire set of attitudes. Apology, as I use the term, inevitably signals an intense engagement with the here and now. The apologist implicitly declares that his or her actions on this earth are worthy of commentary and defense and, moreover, that the opinions that his or her contemporaries (and future generations) hold are important enough to warrant a sustained act of self-justification. Ultimately, I would argue, the stance of the apologist can be linked with a historicist understanding of identity and of one's place in the world. The apologist tacitly acknowledges, "I am, at least in part, a product of circumstance; and my reputation, a product of discourse, deserves to be cultivated, corrected or defended, through textual intervention." Apostrophe, on the other hand, defined as the rhetorical invocation of an absent (and often transcendental) listener, pretends to be a trope of detachment, of unworldliness. In a dense and provocative essay, María Zambrano even suggests that the plaintive sobbing of Job, addressed to an absent and apparently indifferent God—an apostrophe, of sorts—is the origin of confessional discourse (1942, pp. 1ff). And the ultimate Christian apostrophe, "Forgive them Father, for they know not what they do," belies a vision of the here and now as something ultimately inconsequential. The fact that the paradigmatic utterers of apostrophe tend to be self-proclaimed *victims* of historical circumstance—martyrs, or later on, the ever-suffering Romantic Poet or Patriot—who remain true to some absolute, transcendental principle is, I think, proof that the trope is essentially antihistorical or antihistoricist.

When I refer to the movement from apology to apostrophe, I do not mean to trace some sort of sweeping evolution of the genre. Rather, I wish to suggest that a movement or tension between apology and apostrophe, between worldliness and transcendence, historicism and essentialism, often lies at the heart of individual instances of autobiographical discourse. The tension, I would argue, is not peculiar to Spain, though it is of particular interest in the case of that nation, where there has been an extraordinarily strong tradition, throughout the centuries, of opposing Being to historical existence, Personal Identity to worldly experience, and National Identity to participation in the modern.

Approaching the Genre

Autobiography is a genre much given to emblems and synecdoches: a single event is said to capture the essence of an entire life, or an entire life, as in the riddle of the sphinx, is collapsed into one day: *Desde el amanecer (Since Dawn)* is the title of Rosa Chacel's book of childhood memories (1972); *Mi atardecer entre dos mundos (My Dusk between Two Worlds)* the name the Condesa de Campo Alange (1983) gave to her account of her later years. In a similar way, there is often an uncanny parallelism between the models adopted by individuals to fashion their lives, and those used by critics who would like to write the history of autobiography. Phylogeny recapitulates ontogeny.

Most people who try to narrate the history of autobiography—to write autobiography's biography, as it were—share a number of prejudices. One such prejudice is what William Howarth has called the evolutionary bias, which holds that "recent lives are necessarily more complex and their stories more challenging" (Howarth 1974, p. 363). Studies that claim to trace the evolution of the genre from simple to complex in the end have to rely heavily on selection and exclusion. Another related prejudice maintains that the history of autobiography is a history of liberation; as the genre evolves, writers move closer and closer to being able to describe faithfully who they are, without the use of simple, imposed models. In fact, there are descriptions of the modern autobiographer that read very much like naive, optimistic descriptions of the self-made man: "There are no rules or formal requirements binding the prospective autobiographer—no restraints, no necessary models, no obligatory observances imposed on the individual talent who would translate a life into writing" (Olney 1980a, p. 3). In *The Value of the Individual: Self and Circumstance in Autobiography*, K. J. Weintraub (1978) even emplots the history of autobiography precisely as a kind of long struggle against, and liberation from, models: "the knights of individuality have had to struggle against [what Weintraub calls] 'model' conceptions of personality" (Greenblatt 1979, p. 255). As Stephen Greenblatt notes in his review of Weintraub's book, this emplotment tells autobiography's story along the lines of a "historical romance of fall and redemption": "*The Value of the Individual* . . . locates in Augustine an original sublime vision that celebrates the purposes of the Creator in the intimate details of the life of one of his creatures. This vision is essentially lost in a Middle Ages dominated by external 'models' . . . and is slowly recuperated in the Renaissance . . . There gradually develops a "healthy" individuality whose supreme avatar is Goethe" (Greenblatt 1979, pp. 276–77). This account of the genre's history does indeed read like the history of an individual, though a special kind of individual: the epic hero, who is born whole, whose essence is beyond question, and whose battle is waged primarily against what G. Lukács called the "divinities of impediment" (p. 88) that would prevent that essence from realizing itself or from being recognized (Lukács 1983). This kind of essentialist thinking is behind a good deal of writing on autobiography.

There is another approach, though, that holds that the history of autobiography cannot be separated from the history of our social, religious, and legal institutions. Greenblatt writes, "The telling of the story of one's life—the conception of one's life as a story—is a response to public inquiry: to the demands of the senate, sitting

in judgment" (Greenblatt 1980, p. 72). Roberto González Echevarría (1980, 1987) and Antonio Gómez-Moriana (1980, 1983) have
drawn attention to the importance that certain bureaucratic and
legalistic discursive models have had on the picaresque, and, ultimately, on the history of first-person writing. This approach will
undoubtedly upset those other readers who see the "autobiographical impulse" as an ahistorical, natural desire in all human beings: "It
is my notion that, though it treats often of specific places and times
and individuals . . . autobiography is more universal than it is local,
more timeless than historic and more poetic in its significance than
merely personal. . . . The most fruitful approach to the subject of
autobiography . . . is to consider it not as a formal nor as a historical
matter . . . but rather to see it in relation to the vital impulse to
order" (Olney 1972, p. viii). For readers like these, the suggestion
that there is a link between bureaucratic, juridical forms and autobiographical writing represents a violent intrusion of that which is
conventional and contingent into the interior realm of essence and
identity; the noisy machine of rhetoric, of the law, of the third
person, invades the peaceful garden of the "I" conversing with
itself. The author of this last quotation, James Olney, even shows a
certain intolerance toward genre critics like Phillipe Lejeune or
Elizabeth Bruss who "tend toward a quasi-legalistic language of
contracts, rights, obligations, promises and pacts" (Olney 1980,
pp. 15–17). Paul de Man has also noted in another context how
both "writers of autobiography as well as writers on autobiography
are obsessed by the need to move from cognition to resolution and
action, from speculative to political and legal authority" (de Man
1984, p. 71). What is interesting is that, even in the work of Olney,
in virtually all criticism on autobiography for that matter, legal
terms always seem to crop up, albeit as more-or-less dead metaphors: pact, contract, denounce, accuse, witness, testimony, signa-
ture, ratify, judge, verdict, and so on.

My book subscribes to the view that sees identity—be it generic
or individual identity—as something that is invented, forged, precisely through tension and dialogue with those historical and social
circumstances, those models, those third persons. Dead metaphors
have life stories, too; their etymologies are their autobiographies.
And the fact that our vocabulary for speaking about the self and its

representations often has an institutional ring to it—consider the word "subject"—should give us pause. As John Meyer has written, "Individualism is a highly institutional historical construction: it is not centrally the product of human persons organizing their experience for themselves, but of various bodies of professional officials—religious ideologues, their secular counterparts (e.g. psychologists, teachers, lawyers, and administrators)—and . . . other institutions of the modern state" (Meyer 1986, p. 208). The emergence of the individual as an important historical category coincides with the emergence of a complex network of codes, practices and institutions that try to define or subject the individual. A similar stance is assumed by Michel Foucault in *Truth and Juridical Forms* (1984). This brilliant and little-known book is, among other things, part of Foucault's sustained critique of Marxism and psychoanalysis. In particular, Foucault is interested here in criticizing something that both these "master codes" have in common: the idea that the subject is at first some kind of pure origin, which is later veiled, distorted, or repressed by social, political, or economic conditions: "My goal is to show in these lectures how political and economic conditions of existence are not, in fact, veils or obstacles for the subject, but rather the very things through which subjects get formed" (Foucault 1984, p. 32). Perhaps the most radical gesture of this book is its very title, *Truth and Juridical Forms,* because many of us, like the autobiographers I study, still live with a desire to separate truth from convention, identity from the technicalities of legal proceedings, or from all forms for that matter. But as Foucault has relentlessly argued, not only do truth and the subject have a history; they have a history inextricably bound to the fallen world of institutions, of politics and the law.

If we subscribe to this view, we begin to see that institutions are not necessarily antithetical to the individual: not only does the Inquisition silence, it also provokes discourse; it not only represses individuals, it also plays an important role in the historical articulation of what individuals are or should be. In early modern Spain, the relationship seems especially striking. Indeed it could be argued that Spain's entire canon of early modern autobiographical writing is more or less inscribed within religious, legal, and bureaucratic institutions. Soldiers, prisoners, nuns, repentant *pícaros,* unruly *conquistadores;* these are the people most likely to write in the first person. Alonso de Contreras's autobiographical text is an "expansion of his *memorial de servicio."*[11] Diego de Simancas's *Memoirs* give evidence of a "juridical mentality."[12] Domingo de Toral y Valdés's text is an "official document" of sorts.[13] Santa Teresa's *Vida* is, in part, a document solicited by her confessors and, ultimately, by the Inquisition. Adrienne Schizzano Mandel has argued that, in the case of Sor María de San Jerónimo, "the judicial structure of the Inquisition organizes for her a concrete space within which the 'I' can be inscribed as the main character."[14] Mateo Alemán spent almost two months "listening to and transcribing galley slaves' autobiographical depositions" before writing his first-person *Guzmán de Alfarache.*[15] Ginés de Pasamonte, "with strictly legal criteria inserts in his *Life* a *memorial de agravios."*[16] Cervantes, in the encounter he invents between Ginés and don Quijote also seems to suggest that the tribunal of the Inquisition is "the appropriate communicative situation for conventional autobiographical discourse."[17]

Margarita Levisi, in her *Autobiografías del siglo de oro* (1985) writes that the three main models available to the golden-age autobiographer are the *"memorial de servicio,"* the *"confesión,"* and the *"picaresca."* The juridical, institutional foundation of the *memorial* is beyond doubt. Confession, particularly as it came to be practiced in Counter-Reformation Spain, functions according to a kind of "internal juridification of religious law" (Foucault 1983, p. 291). And as for the picaresque, several recent studies have convincingly argued that it, too, has an important discursive model in the legal world: the *carta de relación* addressed to the Santo Oficio.[18] Indeed, these three models seem to be at hand well into the eighteenth century; a *memorial* may have been the first draft of what later became Diego de Torres Villarroel's *Vida.* He ends his text with a series of *memoriales,* and mentions *frailes* and *ahorcados* (friars and hanged men)—that is to say confession (or perhaps hagiography) and the picaresque—as the only models of (auto)biography available to him.

The constant presence of institutional addressees—even the brutal Inquisition—in the history of a genre traditionally linked with individual freedom seems contradictory; I would argue that the contradiction is only apparent. Foucault's writings on the history of sexuality address a very similar paradox: "They describe . . . how the

Victorians managed to win for themselves the reputation of the most sexually, and indeed physically, repressive society in history precisely by bringing the body ever more fully into discourse" (Gallagher and Laqueur 1987, p. vii). This coincidence of repression and discourse seems contradictory because we have been taught to associate repression with silence, and freedom with language. What Foucault proposes is that in many cases repression is based on discourse, on the articulation of the acceptable descriptive and vital categories.

I do not want to insinuate that an autobiography is little more than a document in a police file. It is important to recognize, however, that religious, social, and legal institutions have elaborated an extremely powerful discourse on the "subject," which autobiography, as a genre, has had to deal with in one way or another. An autobiographer may uncritically or unconsciously adopt the categories of that discourse, though this is relatively rare. Much more common is the autobiographer who sees himself or herself as writing against that objectifying, institutional discourse; both of our hypothetical autobiographers, in any event, are working under its spell. There is no natural, timeless way of speaking about the self. And yet, as we will see, the history of autobiography can be thought of as a long series of attempts, throughout the centuries, to discover, or to tap into just such a timeless and natural perspective.

Approaching the Self

In his review of Weintraub's book, Greenblatt likens the distinction between modeled and free individuals to the distinction described by Norbert Elias between *Kultur* and *Zivilisation* in German usage: "Against the courtly, aristocratic French ideal of 'civilisation', based on external codes of conduct that distinguish the elite from the vulgar, there is set a bourgeois German ideal of Kultur, based upon inner qualities of refinement, moral responsibility and self-cultivation" (Greenblatt 1979, p. 277). Greenblatt brings up this opposition in order to point out its insufficiencies: "The pretension of Kultur to a wholly voluntary, internal self control conceals the bourgeois interiorization of the normative. The models Weintraub deplores still function, but less visibly. What originates as the naked expression of power—the sign of one group's domination of another—is translated into the expression of supposedly free choice, motivated by 'health' or 'regard for others' or 'self-respect' " (1979, p. 278). This book aspires to respond to Greenblatt's call for a study of autobiography that might subject these boundaries to critical analysis, that might eschew once and for all the idea of a completely free, model-less identity. There is no natural, timeless way of speaking about the self; nor is there a natural, timeless way of being. Because the "bourgeois interiorization of the normative" is part of what Leo Bersani has called modernity's "universal secularization of religious techniques of spiritual surveillance" (Bersani 1977, p. 2), one of my strategies has been to look for continuity, a persistence of models, between certain religious autobiographies—mainly Augustine's and Teresa's—right through the nineteenth century. I am well aware that this reading for sameness might lead me to neglect some fundamental differences among the texts I study. And yet I think that my stance—what happens if we read these texts looking for continuity?—has allowed me to uncover certain characteristics that might otherwise have been overlooked. To my mind, one of the most striking things that the secular texts often have in common with the religious texts is precisely an essentializing view of identity, of selfhood, a stubborn notion that holds that the true self is somehow independent of the circumstances in which it exists— independent of contemporary social and political institutions, of biographical experience, and, in a related way, of *writing*. The nature and the discursive strategies of these declarations of independence are what I wish to explore in this book.

For a genre so intimately linked with experience, autobiography is often antiexperiential. This paradox can be seen throughout the history of the genre. Augustine's treatment of experience is problematic if not contradictory. At times he seems to deny the importance of learning or experience and to claim that faith is the only thing necessary for salvation; at other times it seems as if faith is the end product of his *bildung,* his educational process. Ultimately, though, his conversion is portrayed as a result of "faith, not time or learning": "The way to God is not by ship or chariot or on foot. . . . All I had to do was to will to go there, and I would not only go but would immediately arrive" (Spengemann 1980, p. 14). Teresa's stance toward this-world experience is also rather complex. Even though her ultimate goal is a mystical union or immediacy between self and God that erases all third persons, that obliterates the entire realm of *lo de acá* (things down here) with its doubting confessors and ecclesiastical hierarchies, she is not at liberty to speak with total disdain about certain attributes of the world: "I consider my confessors to be substitutes for God."[19] Nevertheless, her itinerary toward this immediacy is brought about precisely by unliving wor(l)dly experiences, abandoning books, conversation, rhetoric, discourse—indeed, all things of this world: "virtually to die to all worldly things."[20]

This movement upstream, against the currents of experience toward identity or truth is not peculiar to a few eccentric ascetics: it is a conventional itinerary for Western epistemology. Eduardo Subirats has explained how Descartes's "path to perfection" is strikingly similar. To arrive at true knowledge the biographical experience of an individual subject must be set aside. The subject of Cartesian knowledge undertakes an eminently antihistorical task—that is, to make a tabula rasa of itself, cleansing the mind of any inherited axioms or prejudices, in order to recover the pure, neutral and natural gaze of reason.[21] Curiously enough, this arrival to identity "by subtraction," this "distrust toward the empirical reality of the world, of its customs, of everyday life, of practical values," remains largely intact in the autobiographies I study.[22] It becomes especially evident during those moments in which the autobiographer sees certain experiences, situations, or institutions as obstacles or threats to the natural development and the free expression of what he or she is "called to be."

For a genre founded on the pronoun "I," a shifter, which inevitably points to the conditions of its enunciation, autobiography is often extremely critical of its contemporary moment. Augustine is a harsh judge of his contemporary world and the alternatives, or, rather, distractions, it has to offer: empty eloquence, empty scholarship, empty unrealities. Teresa at times seems even more categorical in her condemnation: "*Lo de acá es asqueroso* (things down here are revolting)." Her disdain for her contemporary world becomes especially striking through her emphatic use of deictics in negative expressions: "*esta farsa de esta vida* (this farce that is this life)"; "*esta cárcel de esta vida* (this prison that is this life)." *Esta, acá,* even *yo* and their worldly attributes are all reminders of an imprisonment: an imprisonment within a fallen, contemporary world.

This disdain toward the present is not a characteristic peculiar to religious autobiography; for a so-called modern genre, secular autobiography is often very antimodern in its most fundamental stances. Worldly experience and, in particular, the experience of the phenomena of modernity is often seen as a curse, a condemnation, a sentence. This could be just another manifestation of the anticontemporary prejudice we find in Augustine or Teresa, only now, "contemporary" equals "modern." Rousseau's *Confessions* has been described as "the story of a soul struggling with the concrete circumstances it was condemned to experience" (Weintraub 1978, p. 301). Zorrilla complains in identical fashion: "God has condemned me to live amidst misery, pettiness, and meanness."[23] In fact, by reading Spanish autobiographies from the nineteenth and twentieth centuries, one could compile almost the entire inventory of conventional complaints about the modern world: the evils of industry, the aimless hustle and bustle of modern life, the disappearance of class or national distinctions, the supremacy of money, the excesses of ambition, and so on. Ultimately, however, whether in Augustine, Teresa, or the nineteenth-century authors I study, the primary feature of what I call an anticontemporary or antimodern stance is the following: the autobiographer's contemporary moment is invariably characterized by a loss of self-evident truth and identity and by a proliferation of partial, equivocal, and often slanderous discourse. Ironically, it is this proliferation that both provokes autobiographical writing and at the same time endangers the correct reception of the autobiographical text.

As part of this antimodern stance, certain modern institutions are systematically portrayed as threats to authenticity. In particular, there is great suspicion toward political, legal, and educational institutions; those very same bodies so central to the formation of modern "subjectivity." As we will see, politics, the law, and the schoolhouse have a very important feature in common: they are represented as the spaces of unending language, convention, rhetoric, and discourse, as opposed to the supposedly quiet, tranquil space of presence and identity, the self at home with itself.

There is a paradoxical gesture we find repeated in texts as varied as Teresa's *Vida,* Manuel de Godoy's *Memorias,* and José Zorrilla's *Recuerdos del tiempo viejo.* The gesture goes like this: the autobiographer puts forth, imagines, or invents an ideal, happy situation, which would make autobiographical writing unthinkable, or superfluous. It is as if the autobiographer were saying, "I would rather not be writing this, but . . ." Many autobiographers from the nineteenth century, like Teresa, claim to be writing out of duty or obedience, "the fulfillment of a duty";[24] "a solemn and sacred assignment."[25] There is little delight at being looked at, at least on the surface. Mesonero Romanos frequently begins anecdotes with expressions like "I return, not without repugnance, to the narration. . . ."[26] Joseph Blanco White's editor writes in his introduction to the *Life:* "the happiest . . . times of his mind have often no record here" (BW, I, p. vi). Zorrilla, who is forced to peddle his *Recuerdos* to a newspaper because he is penniless, complains about this necessity to "descend to prose" and to "die while still working, a situation to which my old sins apparently condemn me."[27] José de Palafox y Melzi tells his reader, "If my political and military life had always been happy, I would refrain from this kind of work."[28]

These lost utopian situations can vary a great deal; the ideal world could be childhood, the home, the nation, the rural countryside, or favorable public opinion, but they all have one thing in common: within their confines, writing and representation seem remarkably absent. Writing, and particularly autobiographical writing, become only possible, or necessary, after the abandonment of that utopian space.

These two facets—the experience or institution that jeopardizes identity, and the coincidence of writing and unhappiness—are neatly joined in what is almost a set piece of the genre, the schoolhouse scene. There are many autobiographers who describe the abandonment of the childhood home in order to study as a definitive rupture in their lives. The tranquility of the home, that realm of simple presences, is left behind, and the autobiographer is thrown into the cruel, arbitrary, and deceptive world of socialization, appearances, and representation. *"La letra con sangre entra* (Literacy is inculcated by the schoolmaster's bloodied rod)"; so goes the Spanish proverb, and, in fact, it would be very easy to put together a long list of autobiographers whose first contacts with violence, with injustice, take place in the schoolhouse. And among these acts of classroom violence, the imposition of the alphabet occupies a prominent place. This imposition can be seen as a figure of the imposition of an arbitrary, conventional, impersonal system through which the student must learn to observe, or (mis)represent, the world.

Nearly all the autobiographers I study portray themselves as bad students—that is, as students who were somehow able to remain impermeable to the unfortunate lessons imparted in the classroom.

The politicians and patriots I analyze in chapter 1, for example, more or less all repeat at least the spirit of the affirmation made by Palafox y Melzi:

> I hope . . . that my readers . . . will be understanding and will overlook the lack of elegance of my style and the natural character of my expressions. I hardly benefitted from my teachers' wise lessons; my natural impatience since childhood has kept me from learning the rules of rhetoric.[29]

Francisco Espoz y Mina not only writes but also acts in a natural way: "As a man more of nature than of art, I am in the habit of saying things ingenuously, and my actions also follow the impulse of this natural character."[30] Incidentally, throughout the *Memorias,* Espoz y Mina plays up his rural, rustic upbringing, which he aligns with sincerity and truth in opposition to the sophistication and rhetoric of others; duplicitous city folk, we presume.[31] Others, like Fernando Fernández de Córdoba, also constantly emphasize the artlessness of their accounts with self-disparaging expressions like "these sloppy *Memoirs.*"[32]

This imperviousness to the bad influence of school is not only literal. It is not limited to actual lessons on rhetoric; in a more figurative way, these political autobiographers often see the public life—in which they were slandered or frustrated—as a kind of school; as García de León y Pizarro would have it, *"la escuela del mundo* (the school of the world)" (GLP I, p. 29). And once again, what is taught in this school is negative, and should be avoided at all costs: "I learned to loathe the things of this world."[33] The goal of these autobiographers is to remain tried and true, to themselves and to the nation, despite their passage through the not-so-hallowed halls of the school of the world. We might imagine that Juana de la Vega (the Condesa de Espoz y Mina) had this goal in mind when she tells us how she admired the good habits of her husband: "[His good habits] made him resemble more and more those great men of antiquity. . . . The severity of his habits was noteworthy amidst the lures of that voluptuous capital."[34]

Joseph Blanco White, the subject of chapter 2, also assumes a thoroughly problematic stance before education and experience. He might very well have used the title of an essay on John Stuart Mill's *Autobiography* as a subtitle to his own life: "An Admirable Education and the Recovery from It" (Griggs 1908, p. 5). Blanco White writes out of a sense of the "importance of rending facts which bear on the character of institutions I deem most pernicious" (BW, I, p. 69), and among these institutions, the Catholic church, the one responsible for his early education, occupies a special place. And yet he admits that this institution played an important role in his intellectual development: "I concluded that Christianity could not be true. This inference was not properly my own. The Church of Rome had most assiduously prepared me to draw it" (BW, I, 69). In any event, his lifelong struggle against orthodoxy runs parallel to the antiexperiential, mystical itinerary: he sets out to criticize and disarm institutions that found their authority on "the direction of consciences, moral trusts—all that is practised in obedience to the opinions of others" (BW, I, p. 33). His is a process of purification; he attempts to "cleanse the inner sanctuary" (BW, III, p. 389), to silence the noisy chorus of equivocal voices that different orthodoxies have "implanted" in him, in order to attend to the unique, immediate "voice . . . within us"—"the internal voice is the voice of God" (BW, II, p. 148; III, p. 442).

The three autobiographers studied in detail in chapter 3—Mesonero Romanos, Zorrilla, and Palacio Valdés—all share a considerable disgust for certain institutions of their times. Mesonero Romanos, in an attempt to erect himself as the representative of the new Spaniard, obsessively reiterates his independence, his truancy

from the school of the world, that is, politics, "the incipient political and bureaucratic machinery of the State."[35] He also claims to
worry little about the demands of art: he pretends to have written a
sloppy and prosaic autobiography, "paying no attention to rhetorical
artifice."[36] Curiously, Zorrilla unfavorably compares his own supposedly disorderly and worthless recollections to what he calls Mesonero Romanos's tidy, well-organized memoirs.[37] More importantly,
Zorrilla plots his life almost as if he were telling the story of the trials
and tribulations of poetry in the prosaic and politicized world of the
nineteenth century. He abandons law school, which would have
secured him a comfortable position in government, in order to
remain true to himself—and to his nation—as a poet. In Zorrilla,
school is clearly linked with the law, and law with the fallen world of
politics, the antithesis of poetry; for this reason, the realization of
his essence as a national poet depends on his being a bad student.

For Palacio Valdés, the rural countryside of Asturias, the place of
his childhood, represents a kind of paradise. He leaves that countryside behind in order to study law in Madrid and from that moment
forward is unable to see things as they are: "Which is in truth the
real world, the one I used to see in my childhood, or this other one I
now contemplate through the veil woven of perfidy, treason, lowness and vileness that the years have placed before my eyes?"[38]
Again, this expulsion from immediacy, presence, identity, and happiness is related to school and the law; it is almost as if, on leaving
Asturias, Palacio Valdés were to hear Wordsworth's "turning key"
forever locking him out of unselfconsciousness: "There was never a
fifth-year student more eager to graduate. This grand achievement
was, I thought, the key to Paradise. And in fact, it was the key,
though not to open the gate, but rather to close it."[39] The acquisition of letters, of the law, is what locks one out of paradise. Experience—especially adulthood, or public life—is a threat to identity.
Paul de Man has observed that "autobiography veils a defacement of
the mind of which it is itself the cause" (1984, p. 81); in other
words, it seems that the genre often longs for a situation that would
eliminate its very conditions of existence: letters/writing/graphy
and life/experience/bio. We arrive to identity by subtraction. Autobiography. Autobio. Auto . . .

1

Addressee
Unknown

L'essence de mon être, est-elle dans leurs regards?
The essence of my being, can it be found in their gaze?
—*J. J. Rousseau, "Histoire du précédent écrit"*

To Whom It May Concern

Who writes? How is the scene of writing represented in the text? To whom is the text addressed? What kind of reader is inscribed in the text? Perhaps more than any other literary genre, autobiography forces us to deal with these questions concerning both the historical conditions and the literary stagings of textual production and reception. I would like to begin this chapter with a series of reflections on some peculiarities of the communicative circuit of a good deal of autobiographical writing. In particular, I am interested in a trope that governs the addressee situation of a remarkable number of texts: from Augustine through Teresa right on to Torres Villarroel and the nineteenth-century Spanish politicians whose autobiographies are studied in the second half of this chapter. The trope in question is apostrophe. Quintilian defines apostrophe as "a diversion of our words to address some person other than the judge" (in Culler 1981, p. 135). Even though autobiography is very frequently a form of apology, or a self-defense submitted to the court of public opinion, autobiographers often feign indifference to the verdict of that tribunal; they may even call into question that court's jurisdiction through their use of apostrophe. Ultimately, apostrophe pretends to highlight the inability of the autobiographer's contemporaries to adequately see, judge, or appreciate his or her true self; the trope endeavors to point out a primary incommensurability between one's true identity and others' (mis)perceptions, between the self and others, or even between (private) identity and (public) speech. In other words, true to its etymological sense of "turning away from," apostrophe represents a suspension of apology or of normal communication between present, contemporary interlocutors, and the invocation of an absent, but higher authority.

Sins, Signs, Stories

"[L]et us each note and write our actions and impulses of the soul as though we were to report them to each other. . . . Now then, let the written account stand for the eyes of our fellow ascetics" (St. Athanasius 1980, p. 73). St. Anthony's recommendation to his monastic companions invites them to internalize and reproduce the gaze of others: a third-century formulation of the superego. The advice is an early example of the constant connection in Christian culture between writing or speaking about the self and surveying or policing the self. Of course this self-surveillance takes place within a community. How else would one know what to look for? The way a self looks at itself, or, in other words, the individual's reconstruction of the community's gaze, presupposes a body of shared beliefs and taboos, an "instructed conscience," which might seem natural or God given to a believer—"the voice of conscience is the voice of God"—but which from the outside looks like a fallible, culturally specific construct, implanted by identifiable techniques. When the ascetic reproduces the gaze of his or her fellow ascetics in a text, who is doing the writing? And for whom does he or she write?

It seems that the saint's advice produces a kind of communicative short circuit: a fusion between writer, text, and addressee. The eyes of one's fellow ascetics produce the text (in that they tell one what to look for), are the text ("let the written account stand for the eyes . . .") and read the text ("as though we were to report . . ."). Communication, it would seem, has become superfluous. But then again, perhaps that is the desired effect: silence, the blank page. For when it comes to self-observation, sin or transgression is what is eminently reportable. If, for Christians, universal history itself be-

comes possible because of sin, because of a transgression of divine
law, personal history will also be linked to deviance or transgression.
This connection between sin and story is a central issue for autobiographers throughout the history of the genre.

When Augustine narrates his life in the *Confessions,* for example,
his self-narrative virtually ends at the moment of his conversion.
The remaining books are dedicated to prayer, meditation, and exegesis. The sinful life can be represented in narrative, in time: life in
God has no possible narration. It is sin that opens up a space for
narration: the soul that has once been estranged from God can be
narrated, but "an eternal union with God, prized above all things by
the theologian, would deprive the man of his life and the artist of his
art" (Spengemann 1980, p. 26). Teresa will link self-writing with
transgression in the same way: "While alive it is clear that one
should not speak about one's good things."[1] Her mystical itinerary
toward union with God is, in fact, an undoing of her "vile life," an
unwriting of her worldly autobiography, an autothanatography.

Not only is story or narration linked to transgression; at a more
basic level, language, the need to communicate, or signification
itself often appear to be the product of the Fall. Both Augustine and
Teresa practice what might be called the mortification of the word: if
the body is mortified in order to raise up its signified—the soul—
here the "word"—human language, all things of this world—will
be mortified in order to raise up its signified, God. "Sin has been
defined often . . . as the inversion of the natural relationship between
the soul and the body through passion" (Derrida 1976, p. 34); in
terms of the sign, to sin means to privilege the signifier over the
signified, to rejoice in the letter that killeth. Signs, like the body,
exist exclusively to be put into the service of the greater glory of
God. "God alone is to be enjoyed—frui—, all other things are to be
used—uti. The distinction seems somewhat out of place until we
recall that all things are signs and that God is the terminal point on a
referential chain" (Freccero 1975, p. 38). God, then, is the *transcen-*
dent signifié, that one and only real Presence that exists outside the
degraded, human chain of signs, the play of representation.

It seems appropriate, then, that Augustine's sinful youth is characterized by his double indulgence in the pleasures of signifiers; he
gives himself up to the flesh, in fornication, and to the letter, in

rhetoric. (Prior to his conversion, Augustine was an ambitious and accomplished orator.) As Eugene Vance has argued, Augustine portrays himself as a victim of the "twin vices of lasciviousness and eloquence": "With puberty and lust, his faculty of speech becomes similarly perverted—from this point forward sexual desire dominates his narrative as an arch metaphor for the abuses of language. Persuasion now becomes the primary goal. . . . At 16 he begins to frequent brothels. His figurative sin now becomes literal. . . . Having chosen the creation over its creator, Augustine is enslaved to signifiers" (Vance 1973a, pp. 20, 19). His conversion can take place only after a double death: death to the flesh, celibacy, and death to the letter, his withdrawal from the "marketplace of words." "Augustine's move toward God is opposed to his decreasing eloquence" (Vance 1973a, p. 18). In fact, the communion achieved in book 8 of the *Confessions*—in a garden—signifies the absence of degraded representations, it is an immediate communion with full, prelapsarian Presence.

Teresa's repudiation of signs takes place at several different levels. First, her decision to enter the convent is represented as a rejection of idle conversation and dangerous books—"[the books] of chivalry and [other] . . . works teeming with vanity and lasciviousness" as Luis de León would say.[2] Second, with regard to her own literary style, Teresa constantly and astutely represents herself as someone who is neither learned nor skilled at language—*"no tengo letras"*— thus highlighting the authenticity of her account. Third, her mystical experience, which, by the way, also takes place in a (rhetorical) garden, involves the elimination of those very gaps that make language possible or necessary: the space between signifier and signified, between speaker and addressee (see Fernández 1990).

One of the most telling ironies of Teresa's *Vida* is the fact that the section devoted to the description of her mystical union, that most unrhetorical of experiences, is perhaps the most densely rhetorical passage of the text. The saint makes use of the sustained analogy of the garden and the four waters to describe the four levels of her prayer, her trajectory toward communion with God. According to this analogy, as she approaches the fourth, most perfect level of her prayer, what steadily decreases is the amount of work: if the first, least perfect level corresponds to a garden whose keeper must cart water from a far-off stream, the last level corresponds to the garden being effortlessly showered with rainwater. What is important to note here is that this elimination of work stands for a suspension of the mind's cognitive faculties, of discourse, of language, of the need to communicate or to interpret. Repudiating the signifier raises up the signified, and Teresa's itinerary toward full meaning in the center—"that dwelling in the center and middle"—involves struggling upstream, against the centrifugal, concentric waves of a dispersive "discourse."[3] As she approaches the center, "the discourse of the understanding is suspended," "words stay off to one side," "noise" is abandoned: "By noise I mean having the mind wander, seeking words, . . . turning rhetoric upside down."[4] In the context of Teresa's mystical concentration, the word *discurso* takes on pejorative connotations; it is associated with a fluttering butterfly, with noise, with its etymological sense of "running to and fro." In other words, the verb *discurrir* (to discourse) is opposed to the verb *recoger* (to withdraw or recollect) in Teresa's system. And the centripetal distance covered by Teresa's *recogimiento* is precisely the distance of discourse, the distance between signifier and signified, between speaker and addressee. Normal experience is degraded, secondary; her experience of Christ is not comparable to the experience of contemplating a painting: "It is nonsense to think that one thing has any resemblance to the other . . . any more or less than a living person has to his or her portrait."[5] The noise of human language is contrasted with the silence of God's language, the pure signified that is immediately, formlessly injected: "The Lord places whatever He wants the soul to understand deep inside the soul, and there He represents it without image or form of word."[6]

The strength of this historical link between self-writing and transgression, or between perfection and silence, is so great, that most autobiographers will be forced to address it in one way or another. Writing, especially writing about oneself, inevitably implies a distance, a space that the language attempts to bridge. One of the most frequent strategies of autobiographers, throughout the centuries, is to displace the gap that writing pretends to bridge from the model of transgression—"I" separated from God or from the community by sin—to the model of misunderstanding—a false "I" misrepresented, misunderstood, separated from the true "I." I write in the first person not because I have done anything wrong, but rather because I am misunderstood, misrepresented by my contemporaries. This need to dissociate autobiographical writing from transgression helps explain the frequency with which autobiographers tend to represent themselves as misfits; people who were born into the wrong environment, or the wrong historical moment. Faced with this irreducible incommensurability between the autobiographer and his or her only available audience, between the self and other, it would seem that there is just one way out: apostrophe.

The Locked Gate

When Rousseau completed *Rousseau juge de Jean Jacques,* he pondered what to do with the manuscript. He recalled how the manuscript of his *Confessions* had caused him only suffering and persecution and decided to confide this new text to his only understanding reader: God. "No longer able to trust any man—they would all betray me—I resolved to confide exclusively in Providence and entrust her and only her with the handling of that package which I wanted to leave in good hands."[7] He copied over the manuscript, composed a note to Providence, and set off with his package to Notre Dame. He planned to leave the manuscript on an altar:

> I wanted to go in one of the side doors, through which I was counting on penetrating into the choir. Surprised at finding it closed, I decided to pass through the other side door that opens up on to the nave. Upon entering, my eyes were struck by an iron gate that I had never noticed before . . . the doors of this gate were closed . . . and . . . it was impossible for me to get in.[8]

With the entrance to God tightly locked, he has no choice but to turn to his contemporaries: "I am left no alternative but to try to communicate with the very people designated by my persecuters."[9]

The episode is a perfect emblem of the autobiographical communicative circuit which I am trying to describe. Jean Starobinski has written, "Autobiographical discourse takes form by creating, almost simultaneously, two addressees, one summoned directly, the other assumed obliquely as witness" (1980, p. 77). This addressee problem is a very real one for many autobiographers, beginning with Augustine; he addresses God, but somehow has to justify informing an omniscient being: "Where do I call You to come to, since I am in You? Or where else are You that You can come to me? Where shall I go, beyond the borders of heaven and earth, that God may come to me, since He has said 'Heaven and earth do I fill'?" (1943, pp. 3–4). Significantly, in this short passage, "God" changes from second to third person; from "You" to "He." Throughout the *Confessions* Augustine prays, gives homage to his Creator, and he also narrates, describes the history of his salvation. The two types of discourse are at times hard to distinguish, as witnessed in this comment by a modern translator of the work: "In passages of straight prayer, I have used Thou, but when he addresses God in narrative or discussion, I have used You. . . . [However,] the borderline between prayer and discussion (or narrative) is not always clear" (Augustine 1943, p. xxi).

Augustine addresses God, but he also addresses other men and women, with the hope that his text might convert them, the third persons or *tiers exclus*—the Manichaeans, for example—that might read his text. In another passage, he offers what I read as a microversion of the communicative scheme of the entire *Confessions:*

> I pitied them because they did not know our sacraments and our healing, but they were insanely set against the medicine that would have cured their insanity. I wished that they might be somewhere close at hand—without my knowing that they were there—and could see my face and hear my words. . . . Would that they could have heard me—without my knowing that they heard me, lest they might think it was on their account I was speaking (Augustine 1943, p. 188).

The quotation wonderfully illustrates the rules for the effective use of apostrophe in autobiography: it might even be considered a kind of primer or user's manual for the trope. If the apostrophic invocation is to be genuine and effective, the speaker must seem detached, oblivious to those "close at hand," lest they think he or she apostrophizes "on their account." Here, and throughout the *Confessions,* Augustine appears to write from a blissful union with God; nonetheless, his text is ultimately pedagogical. The "we" is the redeemed community, united with truth: the "they," though apparently excluded from that community by sin, is the real addressee of the text. On whose "account" does one write? Autobiography in this, as in so many instances, becomes a kind of spectacle; it stages Augustine's joyful communion with eternal truth, which contemporary outsiders may or may not understand.

At first sight, Teresa's *Vida* has the same structure as Augustine's *Confessions:* a union/death/conversion occupies the center of the text and marks the passage into a new life. In Teresa's case, the conversion scene would be the entire central treatise on the four levels of her prayer; the description of her trajectory toward union. After closing that treatise, Teresa declares: "It is another new book from now on, I mean, another new life."[10] Nevertheless, Teresa does not write—she cannot write—with the apodictic authority of Augustine: the validity of her conversion, of her unions with God, has been called into question. Luis de León pointed out in the sixteenth century how women's credulity makes them especially susceptible to Satanic illusions.[11] Michel Foucault has more recently made a similar point: "For Christians, the possibility that Satan can get inside your soul and give you thoughts you cannot recognize as Satanic but that you might interpret as coming from God leads to an uncertainty about what is going on inside your soul. You are unable to know what the real root of your desire is, at least without hermeneutic work" (Foucault 1983, p. 244). Teresa's text, unlike Augustine's, is not in the form of a prayer addressed to God: it is rather, a text about her prayer, addressed to God's "interpretive community," the Catholic church. The second person of the text is a certain *vuestra merced* (Your Mercy)—her confessor, and, ultimately, the Inquisition—who will establish the identity of an undetermined third person: Is it God, or the devil; does "he" belong to us or to them? The *Vida* is a text of submission, a text submitted to the hermeneutic work of its authoritarian readers, who exercise the material power of producing truth, the final and definitive reading of Teresa's experience.

Teresa, of course, is acutely aware of this situation, and her text constantly plays on the tension between two communicative schemes, between two addressees. At times she portrays herself in union with God, conversing with God; during these moments her earthly reader can do little but overhear the experience from afar.

"The one supposed to make her confession becomes the confessor" in the words of Américo Castro (1972, 79), and indeed Teresa does assume great authority during these moments; at times she even takes the liberty of addressing her confessor as *hijo mío* (my son). At other times though, Teresa describes herself as a powerless, vile woman, who submits herself to the authority of her earthly readers; her readers, at these moments, are seen as being united with God. The oscillation between these two attitudes is, however, not at all arbitrary. When constructing her defense of the divine source of her mystical experience—of the union between her and God, first and second person in prayer—Teresa repeatedly offers a version of that experience that makes the third person superfluous and excluded; again, the *tiers exclu*. She suffers greatly when she is urged to translate an experience of communion that is essentially ineffable into a language susceptible to multiple and equivocal interpretations: "This business of giving notice to a third person—as I have said—is what I always regret the most, especially when I did not know how they would take it"; "it is wondrous how you have no need of third parties!"[12] In a very daring exclamation, Teresa will offer herself up in an apostrophic spectacle and align herself with God, while she associates doubting *letrados*—a word she often uses to describe her confessors—with demons:

> I lack everything, my Lord; but if you do not forsake me, I will not abandon You. Let all the learned men rise up against me, let all of creation persecute me, let the demons torment me. . . .[13]

But this type of bold affirmation or apostrophe is almost always immediately followed by a request for forgiveness, and a recognition of the real authority, the unquestionable jurisdiction, of her *letrado* reader. The second addressee situation, of submission to a human reader, is quickly assumed: "May Your Mercy tear apart what I have just said—should you will to do so—and take it for a letter to yourself, and forgive me, for I have been too bold."[14]

The communicative scheme of religious autobiography might be articulated in four elements: (1) an old, unredeemed self; (2) a new, converted and writing self; (3) a community of human readers; and (4) God, an ultimate, ideal reader. The space of autobiography is constituted by the distance—the play—between these four pieces.

The conversion narrative presupposes the union of (2) and (4), which look back on (1) for the benefit of (3). A text like Teresa's apparently follows the same setup, although the real situation of the text is that (3)—her confessors, the Inquisition—brandish the material power of (4), and are going to question the separation of (1) and (2).

Objectivity might be defined as the view an omniscient God would have of a given human occurrence, the view of an ideal reader, free from the prejudices, the passions, and power struggles of historical existence. Barthes defines objectivity as a "lack of traces of the speaker"; "the story seems to recount itself" (Barthes 1967, p. 68). This notion would seem to explain the radical censure of the enunciation and its circumstances undertaken by positivist historiography. The speaker is to disappear: "The enunciator attempts to efface himself from his own discourse and . . . consequently there is a systematic lack of any sign that might remit the reader back to the transmitter of the historical message" (Barthes 1967, p. 68). Obviously, this notion creates problems for autobiographers aspiring to some form of objectivity, because autobiography is founded on the pronoun "I," a shifter, which constantly and inevitably belies its own enunciation. Everyone is chained to his or her "I," a wandering pronoun; "*yo y mis circunstancias.*" De Man has succinctly summed up this aspect of the autobiographer's plight: "The interest of autobiography is not that it reveals reliable self-knowledge—it does not—but that it demonstrates in a striking way the impossibility of closure and totalization . . . of all textual systems made up of tropological substitutions" (de Man 1984, p. 71). Cervantes's image of the unrepentant, shackled Ginés de Pasamonte, who cannot finish his autobiography because he has not finished living, is a humorous emblem of this problem central to the genre.

The epistemological problem inherent in autobiography—how to narrate from the inside—leads many autobiographers to strategies like that of the conversion narrative. "Being inside is like being in Plato's cave," once again, in chains (Kermode 1979, p. 39). Conversion is a death of sorts, which breaks the fetters and raises the convert out of life, to a higher plane from which to narrate, and thus allows closure. But even autobiographers who do not use the conversion structure often try to align themselves—the "I" that writes, that is—with some noncontingent, transhistorical perspective; what Richard Rorty has called a "transcendental standpoint outside our present set of representations from which we can inspect the relations between those representations and their objects" (Rorty 1979, p. 293). Rousseau tries to entrust his text to Providence: only God and Rousseau know how to look at, how to read Jean-Jacques. The grille is always closed, though, and the appeal to that perspective—apostrophe—inevitably is articulated through language, and ultimately addressed, however indirectly, to men and women, to social institutions, to human structures of power. Autobiography enacts a struggle: it takes part in the contending claims to possess the key—the power of the keys—to that locked gate of Presence. The genre reenacts on a personal level the epistemological problem faced by human knowledge in general: "What was it in Western philosophy that insured that the things to be known and knowledge itself were in a relation of continuity? What assured knowledge the power to know well the things of this world and not to be indefinitely caught in error, illusion, arbitrariness? Who but God guaranteed this in Western philosophy?"[15] God, or some substitute object of conversion or apostrophe, becomes the outside, the observer free from the contingencies—the passions, interests and desires, the commerce and base politics—of historical beings. "The West will be dominated by that great myth that says that truth never belongs to political power, that political power is blind, that true knowledge is possessed by those in touch with the gods. . . ."[16] Autobiography, through apostrophe, often functions as an elaborate staging of the appeal to that outside, absolute authority. Let us now turn to a group of Spanish texts from the eighteenth and nineteenth centuries that illustrate various aspects of this great myth: a power without truth—*leurs regards* (their gazes), misrepresentation, slander—is opposed to a truth without power (the autobiographical account), through a manipulation of the addressee situation.

Diego de Torres Villarroel at the Threshold

In *Inquisiciones,* Jorge Luis Borges lists Diego de Torres Villarroel (1693–1770) as a practitioner of what he calls *la nadería de la personalidad* (the nothingness of personality). According to Borges, Torres recognized that conventional personal identity is a fiction, an a posteriori construct, built of selected fragments and strategic omissions. "There is no such wholeness of the I" is Borges's dictum.[17] Indeed, the multifaceted character of Torres Villarroel's life—which he himself proudly and incessantly put on display—does seem to resist any simple, unified plotting. Writer of horoscopes, mathematician, popular hero, university professor, dance instructor, would-be ascete, bon vivant, professional writer: he was all these things and more.

This multiplicity of *métiers,* along with certain declarations made by Torres Villarroel himself, have led many to consider his *Vida* a late picaresque novel: the text has even been anthologized as such. Nevertheless, as Luis Fernández-Cifuentes has convincingly shown, unlike the syntagmatic organizing principle of the *pícaro,* who moves from *amo* to *amo,* role to role, Torres Villarroel, and his long, contradictory curriculum vitae is best characterized by a constant tension between paradigms.[18] That is to say, his *Vida* is not so much a chronological succession of masters as it is the repeated staging of a stubborn, unresolved conflict centered on the very problem of mastery, authority. Within Torres Villarroel a battle is waged between antagonistic visions of life: submission to others versus autonomy; self-renunciation versus self-promotion; an ancien régime notion that bases personal worth and authority on birth and lineage versus a more modern vision that values experience and enterprise. As Fernández-Cifuentes puts it, "We are dealing with a conflict between an *I* generally identified with secular happiness and that OTHER external advocate of miserable life and continuous death."[19] In this section, I would like to explore some of the repercussions of this conflict of paradigms on the autobiographical form of Torres Villarroel's *Vida.* More specifically, I would like to look at how this tension conditions the rather complex relationship Torres establishes with three of his possible audiences: God, political power, and a burgeoning reading public.

When Torres Villarroel, at the threshold of modernity, describes being born "amid scraps of paper and rolls of parchment" he offers an emblem of the fate awaiting future men of letters.[20] Not only will they become, figuratively, literary characters, men *made* of letters, born in a printing shop, but they will also be born into a world littered with paper and the printed word. For Torres Villarroel, to publish something is to litter—the sections of his *Vida,* called *trozos* (chunks), are projectiles destined for the street: "I am jotting down the misfortunes of the sixth [chunk of my *Vida*] and if God wills that I finish it, I shall throw it out on the street with the other ones."[21] Torres Villarroel himself lives on the border between oral and print cultures: writing is almost always paired with speaking, reading with listening. The very first words of his prologue conflate writing and orality: "You will say (it is as if I could hear you) as soon as you take this paper in your hand . . ."[22] When he encourages his reader to respond to his text, he invariably invites spoken as well as written comments.[23]

This bewildering proliferation of words, and this conflation of writing and speaking are almost always associated with questions of public opinion or reputation: "[I wished] to refute, with my truths, the accusations, the bastard novels, the mysterious stories that were being told about me in the kitchens, streets and taverns, selected from 500 sheets of curses and satires that run about the world on all fours."[24] Torres Villarroel, from the opening of his text, assumes the posture of the maligned victim, who writes in order to refute slander. At the same time, however, he realizes that the posture of the victim is what justifies his writing, and his writing, in turn, allows him to make money. After all, Torres Villarroel is arguably Spain's first professional writer in the age of print.

This pairing of writing and orality is not simply a reflection of a historical reality; it also forms part of one of Torres Villarroel's most persistent tasks—the deconstruction of the hierarchy between writing and speaking. Torres Villarroel recognizes that the book's authority can often be attributed precisely to its invisible enunciation, to its apparent independence from a historical speaker, a historical context, a human body. "The absence of the speaker leaves us facing the written word, dislocated from the expressive complex that was the speaker's body."[25] A witness to—and agent of—the explosion of printed matter that took place in the eighteenth century, Torres Villarroel is determined to put the printed word in its place. And he does this by means of what Bakhtin (1981, 1983) has taught us to call a carnivalistic gesture: he incessantly calls attention to the body of the author. For Torres Villarroel, the body becomes a kind of figure of the necessary entrapment of the writer in a contingent locus of enunciation: "I advise everyone . . . to examine carefully and methodically the reputations of famous and applauded men, especially of those from the two castes of erudites and saints; more often than not, underneath an inordinate reputation for wisdom and experience, you will find a stubborn idiot, a hollow talker, a mystifying eccentric, an impertinent fellow, . . . a scoundrel, an *idle glutton* filled with *greed* and *lust*."[26] The alleged highness or outsideness of the book—outside of history, of a body—is constantly called into question. At one point Torres Villarroel even refers to his books as *"cuerpos* (bodies)" (TV, p. 72). At other times he sounds like a typical figure of the Enlightenment, as he ridicules scholasticism and untested claims of so-called authorities: "Fat and skinny, small and big, all books are jewels that amuse and are instruments of *human commerce.*"[27] In a line of reasoning quite similar to that of Groucho Marx, who declared, with impeccable logic, that he would never join a club that would accept him as a member, it is precisely Torres Villarroel's achievement of the status of author that, in his eyes, discredits the authority of books.

The longest and most persistent example of this kind of undermining of authority, or of the authority of books, is to be found in the episode of Torres Villarroel's prolonged illness. Again, the book is criticized by being attributed a body, but now in a different way. Torres Villarroel donates his body to science—he gives his doctors carte blanche to use any means necessary to restore his health. The doctors' learning, faced with a real body, is utterly insufficient: "The doctors studied in the chapters of their books justifications for their blunders. . . . They were well aware that my nature and my pain were making a mockery of their recipes, aphorisms, and speeches and yet, despite all these failures [*desengaños*], not once did I hear them confess their ignorance."[28]

The episode of Torres Villarroel's illness is central for another reason, though: it reproduces, on a reduced scale, the situation of the entire *Vida.* The ailment significantly begins with a confession that relentlessly juxtaposes and conflates matters of the body with matters of the soul:

On April 14, 1744, I confessed generally and particularly the vices, virtual and actual sins of my humors to the professors of Salamanca. The confessional was one of the lecture halls of Law in the University's courtyard, and there I let go of my crimes, and subjected to their absolution all my venialities, relapses and grave sins. I made a punctilious accusation of my past life and present state . . . and I was so satisfied by the diligence with which I had made this confession of the body, that my soul became jealous, and wished that it too had the same powers of examination, clarity and expression for the confession of its ailments. [29]

In fact, the expression Torres Villarroel uses to describe this medical confession—"*la historia de mis males* (the history of my illnesses)" (TV, p. 212)—echoes the kinds of expressions he often uses to describe his entire *Vida,* particularly when he assumes the submissive, life-hating stance of the baroque *desengañado:* "I reveal, amidst rare instances of happiness, the persecutions . . . , the wretchedness to which my haughtiness condemned me, the abyss to which my habits exposed me and the rest of the errors which justifiably gave my life its renown of a bad life." [30]

The episode of the illness is referred to as an *accidente.* Accidents and incidents seem to be the breeding ground for autobiography: difference, adventure, and sickness intrude on and cut into routine; they upset tranquility. "The event is first and foremost an accident, a misfortune, a crisis" (Certeau 1987, p. 205). Tranquility is the unautobiographical, the unnarratable: its verbal tense is the imperfect. Narrativity, with its preterite and with what William Labov (1972) has called "temporal juncture," cuts into the repetitiveness, the perfection of the imperfect. This kind of interruption signaled by a shift from imperfect to preterite occurs frequently throughout the autobiography: "I *used to be* [*hallábame*] an easygoing chap, taking it all very lightly, without remorses or scruples about my health, nor suffering from the slightest alteration of the spirit, because *I would not even remember* [*ni yo me acordaba*] that there were justice, thieves, prisons, doctors, fevers, critics, evil-tongued people, nor other ghosts and bogeymen who have us continuously threatened. . . . This peacefulness *lasted* [*duróme*] until the month of August. . . ." [31] Those very situations that Torres Villarroel associates with autobiography, that provoke autobiography—injustice, sickness, criticism—are forgotten during moments of *sosiego.* The word "confession" belongs to the religious, medical, and juridical domains, and Torres Villarroel constantly plays on this ambiguity: his illness is caused by delinquent materials; his symptoms are sins, crimes, or vices.

Torres Villarroel seems to have clearly understood that conventional autobiography is inevitably linked with rupture and transgression: in fact, the kernel of each of the first five *trozos* of his *Vida* is a crossing of borders—*accidente, incidente, lance, aventura*—an incision on sameness. Even Torres's *ascendencia* (genealogy) begins with an exit, a *salida* or exclusion: "Francisco and Roque de Torres left the city of Soria, I know not if they were cast out due to poverty or some act of youthful mischief."[32] Whether we look as his picaresque years of study, his adventures in Portugal or Madrid, the episode of his illness or the run-in with the Inquisition, it seems clear that the matrix of autobiographical discourse in Torres Villarroel is friction with authority.[33]

Nonetheless, this constant association of adventure or experience with transgression is not without profound ambivalence; for even though Torres Villarroel uses words such as "sin," "crime," and "sickness" to describe his escapades, he clearly derives great pleasure from living and recounting his adventures. This ambivalence is at the core of his autobiographical project: he consistently evokes an autobiographical model that allows only for the confession of wrongdoings and that equates adventure with sin, but at the same time he joyfully declares that his adventures have made him what he is—a personality, a singular and autonomous man. Perhaps the clearest example of this ambivalence is the episode of Torres Villarroel's allegedly expiatory pilgrimage to Santiago de Compostela. As a distilled version of Christian life, the *peregrinatio* is supposed to be a journey of suffering and mortification, in which the pain of the road is to be completely subordinated to the bliss of the destination. And yet, in Torres Villarroel's case, the pilgrimage becomes not only an eventful and joyful leisure trip, but also the scene of the happiest days of his life.[34]

We can begin to discern a certain pattern of carnivalesque subversion. Orality, or embodied language, calls into question the alleged authority of the written word. The corpus of Torres Villarroel's works, by rubbing elbows with other revered books on the library shelves of the ancien régime irrevocably discredits those volumes' claims to authority (see Fernández-Cifuentes 1987). Torres Villarroel's slight, scarred, and ailing body is capable of discrediting the accumulated knowledge of Spain's medical community; faced with a single, humble, but real, body, that knowledge is shown to be thoroughly inadequate. And finally, the fact that Torres Villarroel's adventurous life and "ailing soul" make him happy seems to invalidate, albeit implicitly, the authority of the nation's life-hating doctors of the soul. In other words, if the contemporary medical gaze is shown to be incommensurable to that mysterious illness that afflicts Torres Villarroel, the religious-juridical gaze, apparently the sole discourse available for speaking about the self, also turns out to be entirely inappropriate, incapable of accounting for the irrepressible sickness of the soul that, I would argue, is nothing less than selfhood.

The final *trozo*, however, composed mainly of *memoriales*, apparently represents an ultimate gesture of submission, of integration. In one of these *memoriales*, Torres Villarroel petitions the right to retire from the university: "Having the right to retire after twenty years of residence, he could not achieve that rest, because that University did not wish to count the years 732, 33 and 34 on his behalf, which he spent in Portugal as ordered by His Majesty D. Felipe V, who, making use of his Royal clemency, had him restored to the kingdom, the nation and all the honors of his chair and the University: . . . [and so,] he asked to be granted an exemption for those three years and for his other absences caused by illness and misfortune."[35] Exile, illness, and misfortune; those are the three topoi where Torres Villarroel seems most apt to live and to cultivate his autobiography. And yet here he closes his autobiography by requesting an *indulto*, an erasure of those escapades; he asks that those years of anomalous episode be reinstated into his twenty years of uninterrupted service. "I confessed . . . all the faults I committed, brought forth by the trifles of my nature, my misfortune, idleness and illness. . . . [and] I implored His Highness to absolve me of the comings and goings . . . granting me in my retirement . . . quietude and rest."[36]

By ending his text on this apparent scene of submission, Torres Villarroel frames his life of transgressions—of *idas y venidas* (comings and goings)—with an image of inclusion, integration. The text from the very beginning is clearly addressed to two readers, or two kinds of readers: the *vuestra excelencia* of the dedicatory pages, and the *tú* of the prologue. The contrast could hardly be more extreme: "I beseech Your Excellence to be so kind as to receive the life I live and the Life I write, for Your Excellence has exercised an enviable mastery and a necessary slavery over one and the other"; and if you "(*tú*) think I'm lying, come over here next to me, and I'll leave you in such a state that your own mother won't recognize you."[37] The text has the structure of an exhibition of contained violence, a kind of literary boxing match. Exclusion, transgression, contradiction, and struggle take place inside the text, though roped off, framed, by the dedication and the *sexto trozo.* Run-ins with justice, doctors, and critics are what make Torres Villarroel what he is, just as they make possible his text, but they are buffered by these initial and ultimate gestures of submission and self-renunciation. Torres Villarroel's *Vida* is indeed a scandal, though we might ask to what degree is scandal a kind of social institution here. Torres Villarroel wishes to manipulate the *tú* of his text, he even attempts to instigate misrepresentations in the public opinion at the same time he responds to them: he recognizes that he owes to his slanderous enemies "a good deal of . . . [that fame] which makes my life today happy and successful."[38] He questions the hierarchy between books and conversation in order to show that both belong to "human commerce." But he inscribes that public opinion, that questioning, and that commerce, within another hierarchy that, when push comes to shove, he leaves untouched: "I owe everything to His Highness and to the respect with which I have looked upon his substitutes on this earth."[39]

When his *Vida natural y católica* is condemned by the Inquisition, Torres Villarroel subjects himself fully to the judgment of the tribunal, quickly edits the text, and produces a new edition

> because nothing mattered more to me than to correct my errors, loathe my follies and obey completely their determinations and decrees. The pious ministers examined my simpleness, my Christian intentions and the goals of my Catholic desire, and 15 days later

they gave the book back to me, which I printed for the second time, along with the *memorial* I had submitted and a new prologue . . . and if you want it, you can buy it, for there are still come copies left in Juan de Moya's bookstore, in front of San Felipe el Real. . . . Now I anxiously hope my productions will undergo, and be improved by, their admonitions.[40]

Torres Villarroel clearly recognizes that the run-in with the Inquisition might turn out to be a commercial success. He plays to his two audiences, or rather, he plays them off each other. Public opinion is still more or less independent from political power: Torres Villarroel's task then, or rather, his achievement, is to remain in the attention of his new reading public, through adventure, scandal, and self-promotion, while avoiding the wrath of the life-hating powers that be.

Who Is the Public and Where Can It Be Found?

Guy Mercadier has contended that the ultimate goal of Torres Villarroel's *Vida* was "to present a self-defense to a Judge, perhaps one more frightful than the King, the omnipresent and multiform Judge, delegated by society, not to mention that which awaits Christians in the afterlife."[41] Although in Torres Villarroel's case we might wonder to what extent this self-defense before society is a literary pose, a way to justify endless writing and profit, Mercadier's comment does pinpoint a problem central to modernity: the substitution of one judge for another. Torres Villarroel perceived with extraordinary clarity the limited, but ever-increasing authority of the public. In fact, it could be argued that not only did he manage to cash in on his run-ins with authorities, but he also learned to take advantage of his *visibility* as celebrity and publishing sensation to hold in check the arbitrary exercise of irrational power among certain branches of the ancien régime.

The *Vida* offers numerous examples of this kind of astute use of visibility and spectacle. For instance, when Torres Villarroel seeks a professorship, the reluctant University of Salamanca, recognizing the astrologer's immense popularity among both students and the *vulgo,* and hoping to thwart his candidacy, decides to carry out the competition in a closed, secret exam. Torres Villarroel cleverly protests, arguing with his characteristic *soberbia cautelosa* (cautious haughtiness) that, in the first place, the university did not have judges competent in his field and, in the second place, that his primary objective was really not to become a professor, but simply to speak in public.[42] Or when he and a friend are unjustly exiled, he resorts to a tactic we might consider a forerunner of the open letter; that twentieth-century genre, practiced by celebrities who would expose the arbitrary and brutal exercise of power to—they hope—the indignant gaze of a large, potentially powerful public. Torres Villarroel sends some three hundred *memoriales* to different personages of Seville, informs them of his situation, and solicits their intervention in the name of justice.[43] Later on in the *Vida,* he refers to *las voces de la publicidad* (the voices of publicity or of the public) as "the judge and witness who is less passionate and more truthful than all those who strut about the world."[44]

This kind of repudiation of irrational decisions made in dark chambers—and the resulting appeal to visibility—are closely related to a phenomenon that Foucault, among others, has described at length: a shift in the concept of power typical of the Enlightenment, *el siglo de las luces*:

> When the Revolution examines the possibilities for a new form of justice, it asks what is to be its mainspring. The answer is public opinion. The Revolution's problem, once again was not one of insuring that people be punished, but that they could not even act improperly on account of their being submerged in a field of total visibility where the opinion of one's fellow man, their observing gaze and their discourse would prevent one from doing evil or detrimental deeds. . . . The reign of "opinion" invoked so frequently during this period is a mode of functioning where power is to be exercised on the sole basis of things known and people seen by a kind of immediate observing gaze that is at once collective and anonymous (Foucault 1978, pp. 10, 11).

The shift represents a fundamental secularization of political authority; the ultimate gaze no longer belongs to God or his chosen substitutes on earth, but rather, to the People. "In place of the omniscient God peering into the depths of the human conscience was a new eye. It was the eye of humanity, reformed, idealized, perfected" (Amato 1982, p. 57).

Although in Torres Villarroel's case we can only begin to sense the potential power of a nascent public, the concept of public opinion does assume an essential role in the articulation of nineteenth- (and twentieth-) century Spanish autobiographical discourse. An idealized, natural Public Opinion, supposedly free from the pressures of the market and the power struggles of historical existence, comes to replace God as the primary addressee of autobiographical apostrophe. An exhaustive, narrative account of the history of public opinion in Spain is beyond both my talents and my present needs. I do wish, however, to briefly sketch three distinct attitudes toward public opinion and their repercussions on autobiographical writing: Feijoo y Montenegro's total disdain, the reverence of certain early nineteenth-century Spanish liberals, and the profound ambivalence of the brilliant journalist, Mariano José de Larra.

In a very brief but illuminating article, Nigel Glendinning (1984) illustrates the radical change which the concept of public opinion underwent in Spain between the eighteenth and the nineteenth centuries. To do this, he juxtaposes Feijoo y Montenegro's essay from the 1720s on the *voz del pueblo* (vox populi) with Pérez de Camino's poem from 1820, "La opinión." Feijoo y Montenegro's article, the very first in his vast *Teatro crítico universal* is indeed the cornerstone of his monumental project of enlightenment through *desengaño:*

> That misunderstood maxim which holds that God manifests Himself in the voice of the people authorized the masses to tyrannize good judgment, and made them into a tribunal authority, capable of oppressing literary nobility. An infinite number of errors springs from this fundamental mistake; because once the conclusion is reached that popularity is the measure of truth, all the mistakes made by the masses are venerated as if they were inspired by Heaven. This consideration incites me to combat this error in the first place, because I realize that I can overcome many enemies in one, or at least that it will be easier to eradicate other errors by first taking away the authority which, for less cautious men, the vox populi provides.[45]

Feijoo y Montenegro argues that the existence of large numbers of ignorant people does not make them any less ignorant, and he goes on to ridicule certain errors or atrocities that are commonly accepted and practiced by other (mainly non-Catholic) cultures: cannibalism, pantheism, widow suicide, and so on. His conclusion is categorical: "The vox populi is totally devoid of authority, for we so frequently witness it siding with error."[46]

Just a century later though, in the aftermath of the French invasion, as Glendinning (1984) has written, public opinion would be invoked with respect and even reverence; it had become a powerful political category, capable of guiding the nation toward progress. "In 1820, . . . the beneficial force of public opinion had become admirable. The opinion could dethrone tyrants, restore the liberal and democratic regime ('the empire of the law'), and express itself freely."[47]

"Express itself freely"—it has been noted that the "accurate reconstruction of public opinion becomes impossible at the very time when public opinion emerges as the dominant factor in politics" (Lukacs 1985, p. 79). This paradoxical situation comes about because the birth of the reign of public opinion coincides, more or less, with the establishment of the reign of the printing press, and the astonishing proliferation of political pamphlets and newspapers. This coincidence, and the resulting confusion, are particularly striking in the case of Spain in 1808. The heroic, spontaneous resistance of the *pueblo* to the French invasion marks the birth of public opinion in Spain as a political force to be reckoned with. At the same time, in the explosion of printed matter that followed the invasion and resistance, the usual pejorative terms like *bajo pueblo, plebeyo,* and *villano* give way to expressions like *pueblo noble* and *pueblo heroico.* María Cruz Seoane Couceiro describes the situation very well: "before 'national sovereignty' is defined as such in the Courts of Cádiz, . . . the People act as the sovereign, picking up and assuming . . . the sovereignty that their monarchs had left in the gutter. And the innumerable writings which try to educate, indoctrinate, and warn are addressed to that new sovereign. A novel and already fundamental factor has made its appearance, 'public opinion,' and the nascent nineteenth-century press devotes its efforts to shaping, guiding and channeling that opinion. . . ."[48] Marx perceptively summed up the situation: "In Cádiz, ideas without action; everywhere else, action without ideas" (in Vilar 1986, p. 82). The relatively spontaneous, undirected popular resistance immediately became something that needed to be interpreted, inscribed within an agenda, an ideology.

While this unity in the face of a common enemy temporarily suppressed some very profound differences—differences that would explode with the French withdrawal—politicians from all camps were eager to speak in the name of the public and to ascribe the resistance to an unequivocal *voluntad popular* (popular will). Liberals were quick to attribute the resistance to an irrepressible will for democracy among the *pueblo;* traditionalists saw in the uprising a defense of tradition and monarchy, a violent rejection of that political modernity heralded by the French troops. A good deal of nineteenth- (and twentieth-) century Spanish history can be read in terms of this conflict between different factions that claim to be the sole legitimate interpreters of that public opinion that led the Spanish people to defend their sovereignty from the French invaders.

The precise relationship between this public opinion expressed in actions and the press is extremely slippery. The extraordinary variety of verbs used at this time and throughout the nineteenth century to characterize the link between the subject "press" and the predicate "public opinion" demonstrates the problematic nature of their relationship: to enlighten, to educate, to warn, to express, to reflect, to direct, to form, to strengthen, to foster, to sustain, to guide, to corrupt, to tyrannize, to indoctrinate. The catalog of verbs runs the gamut from "reflection" (the press simply mirrors public opinion already formed) through "fostering" (the press merely strengthens or sustains public opinion) to violent "deformation" (the press corrupts, deceives, or counterfeits public opinion). Nevertheless, when convenient, Public Opinion might be evoked by all sides as a natural category, the unmediated conscience of the social body, which is uninfluenced by the petty mechanisms of political rhetoric or the press—the Nation's conscience.

Liberals, of course, were more supportive of a free press. Quintana, for instance, one of Spain's greatest liberal patriots, wrote a glowing "Ode to the Invention of the Printing Press" in which he deifies Gutenberg. In Quintana's ode, the press becomes the sacred organ that proclaims a single truth throughout the world: "El hombre es libre (Man is free)." This kind of defense of the press, as Susan Kirkpatrick has noted, can be seen as an application of the liberal economic principle of the free market, to the world of ideas, "the free market in which the people's interests seem to guarantee the success of the best product."[49] According to this view, with a free press, ideas and historical versions compete in an open market, and the best ones win out. As Espoz y Mina clearly recognized, a struggle against tyranny is a struggle against a monopoly of information: "It [was necessary to] denounce the tough monopoly that, as in all things, in matters of writing the tyrannical faction had exercised . . . for so many years."[50] Even when forced to recognize the possible misuses of the press, Quintana does not abandon a metaphor drawn from commerce: he compares irresponsible users of the free press to pirates and responsible users to those essential commercial navigators who, crossing the seas, distribute food and life around the world.[51] Of course, as history has shown us, it is not always so easy to distinguish piracy from commerce. One nation's pirates are another nation's life givers.

Throughout the 1830s, Mariano José de Larra returned constantly, almost obsessively, to the question of the public and public opinion. This constant preoccupation is not completely surprising because what is ultimately at stake in these debates on the existence of a public is nothing less than the constitution of a national identity, a national will. Larra's thoroughly ambivalent attitude toward the phenomenon is in many ways characteristic of early nineteenth-century Spain and similar to the attitude of many political autobiographers of the moment.

An author of hundreds of *costumbrista* sketches and articles, Larra frequently begins his essays with introspective reflections on the difficulty of writing for daily newspapers. In particular, he often complains in his opening remarks of the frustration involved in writing for an undefined public. In one of his finest articles, "¿Quién es el público y dónde se le encuentra? (Who Is the Public and Where Is It to Be Found?)" this introspective concern becomes not a preface, but rather the focus of the entire text. Larra begins by asking a question, "Where is that public which is supposed to be so understanding, so enlightened, so impartial, so fair, so respectable, the eternal giver of fame that so many people have told me about; where is that public whose verdict is unchallengeable and constant, led by an invariable good taste . . . ?"[52] In a rather pessimistic response, which calls into question the very fabric of the nation by suggesting that affiliations of social class might outweigh those of nationality, Larra concludes, "That word *public,* which is on everyone's lips, always supporting the speaker's opinions [is the] . . . wild card for all parties, for all points of view." He goes on to lament, "There is no such invariable public, no such impartial judge, as some people like to pretend; . . . each social class has its own public . . . [which] is capricious, and almost always as unfair and partial as the majority of men that constitute it."[53]

At other moments, though, Larra adopts a positive attitude toward the notion of public opinion that is almost identical to the classical liberal stance; he invests public opinion with considerable authority: "The light of truth finally dissipates, sooner or later, the fog in which the advocates of ignorance want to conceal it; and the power of opinion, which we could call, morally speaking, the *ultima ratio populorum,* is eventually more forceful and irresistible than that momentary one which has been called the *ultima ratio regum.*"[54] Curiously enough, this optimistic stance is the one adopted by Larra when he writes a review of a political autobiography: Manuel de Godoy's memoirs. In this two-part article, after arguing that the vast proliferation of printed historical versions can endanger the recognition and transmission of the truth, Larra unconvincingly pretends to assume the position of the impartial columnist, who, rather than offering an opinion, simply calls attention to Godoy's memoirs as a new product out there in the market, a new historical version. It is not his role to make pronouncements; the free market of opinions will work things out:

> It is not for us to decide on such an important issue; the reading of the prince's Memoirs and the other facts that public opinion has available are the proceedings of that great confrontation between the favorite and society. Public opinion . . . [that supreme tribunal] must pass judgment.[55]

Public Opinion vs. public opinion

The pleasure that Torres Villarroel seems to derive from occupying the public's attention will all but disappear from many Spanish political autobiographies of the first part of the nineteenth century. Juan de Escoiquiz, Antonio Alcalá Galiano, Francisco Espoz y Mina and his wife Juana de la Vega, Fernando Fernández de Córdoba, José García de León y Pizarro, Pedro Agustín Girón, Manuel de Godoy, and José de Palafox y Melzi: each of these authors produced texts in which, to a greater or lesser degree, the writer's pleasure seems sacrificed to duty. The same might be said to hold true for the reader; these texts are not especially pleasing to read. Most of them are extremely long and tedious. Nonetheless, we might do well to ask: To what degree is this absence of pleasure not a mere accident, but rather an essential characteristic of these texts?

The autobiographers I wish to consider here establish a dichotomy, which reproduces the ambivalence we saw in Larra and, at the same time, parallels that distinction we saw in Augustine and Teresa between a fallen, worldly interlocutor (apology) and a timeless, transcendent interlocutor (apostrophe). For these authors, public opinion is divided in two: there is the degraded, partial opinion manifested in contemporary political publications, and there is real authentic Public Opinion—otherwise known as Posterity, History, or the Nation—which exists outside temporality, outside the play of textuality. For these autobiographers, as Francisco Sánchez Blanco has written, "It is no longer an issue of a rectification before God or conscience, but rather before a public opinion which now manifests itself in patriotic societies, posters, broadsheets, the press and books."[56] This opinion constitutes the worldly reader; the reader engaged, that is, when autobiography takes the form of apology. "[But the idea of Public Opinion]," adds Sánchez Blanco, "transcends the limits of the court or the city and takes on the dimensions of the Nation or History."[57] This opinion constitutes the ideal, transcendent reader; the reader available, alas, only through the offices of that handiest of tropes, apostrophe.

This distinction is not completely unfamiliar to students of Romantic poetry. The Romantic Poet, writing at that crucial moment in which literature became fully subject to the fickle laws of the market, established a similar dichotomy between the People and the public precisely in order to claim for his work a certain independence from the market. According to Wordsworth, for example, the People have an admirable and innate sense of taste that is "neither transitory nor of local origin"; the public, on the other hand, is made up of the "clamour of that small though loud portion of the community, ever governed by factitious influence, which, under the name of the Public, passes itself upon the unthinking for the People" (in Ross 1988, p. 41). As Raymond Williams puts it in his essay on the Romantic Artist, "whatever the reactions of actual readers [the public], there was . . . available a final appeal to the 'embodied spirit of the People': that is to say, to an Idea, an Ideal Reader, a standard that might be set above the clamour of the writer's actual relations with society. The embodied spirit, naturally enough, was a very welcome alternative to the market" (Williams 1983, p. 34).

An almost identical tension between these two kinds of opinion has been a constant in modern political history as well. Foucault writes:

> It is the illusion shared by practically all of the 18th century reformers, who invested public opinion with considerable power. Public opinion had to be correct since it was the immediate conscience of the entire social body: these reformers really believed that people would become virtuous owing to their being observed. Public opinion represented a spontaneous reactualization of the social contract. They failed to realize the real conditions of public opinion: the "media" i.e., a materiality caught in the mechanisms of economy and power in the forms of the press, publishing, and then films and television (Foucault 1978, p. 17).

Miguel Artola has described how Spain's postinvasion political figures frequently try to impose this new political criterion, public opinion, "of which they declared themselves the sole, legitimate interpreters."[58] Many autobiographers, in a similar way, will portray themselves as bearers—performers, *intérpretes*—of this Public Opinion, who have been caught up in the snares of public opinion—those unjust, partial mechanisms of economy and power. They are invariably subject to calumny, slander, or unjust accusations; they relentlessly portray themselves as victims of "that multitude of pam-

48   *Apology to Apostrophe*

phlets, lampoons, memoirs, biographies, and gazette articles."[59]
Espoz y Mina's lament is rather typical: "There are Spaniards, and
non-Spaniards who have occupied themselves publishing partial
facts about my political and military life, disfiguring them at will
according to whatever passion dominates them."[60]

This debased public opinion is evoked in these autobiographies,
as the authors seem to address another, nonmaterial, transcendent
reader. To publish memoirs is an *"encargo solemne y sagrado* (a solemn
and sacred assignment)" (AG, I, p. 252), a *"deber sagrado* (sacred
duty)" (PM, p. 45). These texts are ultimately addressed to the
"Tribunal de la Historia," as Godoy puts it (MG, I, p. 59). Even texts
ostensibly addressed to descendants—like García de León y Pizarro's, Palafox y Melzi's, or Girón's—are ultimately directed to the
gaze of Posterity, of History.

But each of these writers seems careful not to infringe on the field
of History.[61] They prudently try to distinguish their texts from
History because, they would like to argue, History is not written;
History is not a text. In fact, History takes on many forms for these
autobiographers; publisher, for example: "History has already published all that is official for this mission,"[62] or voice: "History, whose
concern it is, shall not be silent about this strange event."[63] Ultimately, however, History is portrayed as an ideal reader, a judge, a
privileged interpreter, free from the contingencies—the passions
and the interests, the mechanisms of economy and power—of human hermeneutics. As Godoy puts it: "But History . . . shall be the
judge—I would tell myself—this queen of opinion does not collect
the rubbish that the waves of passions piled up on the shoreline
while the storm roared: no, History is never the organ of wrath, or
the battle cry of partialities and factions: she observes, she sees, she
compares, she weighs and pronounces her verdicts without being
subjected to the factions."[64] Or Pedro Agustín Girón: "Few people
judge him [the Statesman] with impartiality: some cry out because
they are afraid, others because they were expecting something and
did not receive it, and amidst the biases of the majority, the voice of
reason, in such cases weak and dull, is hardly audible, as it enumer-
ates successes or recalls the benefits in order to pass them on, in more
serene days, to History."[65] History has taken the place of God as the
ultimate judge, the ultimate reader, not of texts, but rather of men

and women, of events: "the secularization of the capitalist world in the 19th century elided the judgment of God into the judgment of History" (Berger 1980, p. 46). These authors at times even feign indifference to libel and contemporary historiographical struggles, and suggest that History's ultimate verdict will be independent from what gets written and read. But here we return to Augustine's dilemma—Why bother writing, then? Why address a text to an impartial, omniscient viewer? And as in the case of Augustine, the answer is to be found in the relationship established by the auto-biographer between two audiences: the appeal to an ideal reader serves to verify the account given by the autobiographer to his or her real reader; the real reader is invited, through the apostrophic spectacle of autobiography, to have his or her perception coincide with the perception of God, or History. Apostrophe, in other words, is enlisted into the service of apology.

Certain textual moments bring to the fore the double addressee situation; the autobiographer is seen playing to two audiences: "I am sorry to bother the reader insisting on certain things . . . but the true narration of the facts forces me to do so."[66] The aesthetic pleasure of the real reader is suspended as the autobiographer performs his or her duties to the ideal reader. The autobiographer characteristically leads an agitated and hectic life, and this adventurous existence, which allows not a single moment of tranquility, is often reflected in the autobiography's supposed lack of design; Fernández de Córdoba more than once refers to his text as "*estas desaliñadas memorias* (these sloppy memoirs)" (FdC, I, p. 11, et al.). Francisco Espoz y Mina opposes nature to art and artifice: "As a man more of nature than of art, I am in the habit of saying things ingenuously, and my actions follow the impulse of this natural character."[67] One of the conventional distinctions between art and life is that art chooses and life does not, and these texts often cover up the process of selection, the artistry of their life story. The monumental length of most of these texts attests to this fact: the autobiographer has attempted to tell the whole truth, even though the demands that telling places on the reader might be excessive. Godoy writes, "It is not my intention to fatigue my readers," but "historical truth, like judicial truth, is made up of the complete set of facts that form it and illustrate it."[68]

If these texts juggle two audiences, they also juggle two stories, or two histories: the personal and the National. The feeling of being caught up in a larger process, a bigger story, is ever present in these texts. The writer must then justify centering a narrative on his or her insignificant self. A gesture of humility is indispensable at the start; self-effacing or self-disparaging comments are frequent.[69] Personal history is often characterized as *pequeñeces* or *menudencias* (pettiness or trifles): "Let us put all these trifles aside . . . and return to the seriousness of political issues."[70]

And yet these same humble, self-effacing authors ultimately justify their texts by forging a link between personal and national history: "I am going to recount the events of my life, which are linked to many of the most important ones of my Nation."[71] Humbly recognizing their own smallness, these individuals project themselves into collective history.

There is a structure common to most of these texts: an almost sacred, relatively tranquil domestic life is sacrificed for a more sacred, hazardous national life. But in between these two possible lives, the autobiographer encounters an obstacle: the base world of partiality, nepotism, intrigue, and personal ambition—in a word, politics. It is in this base world that the autobiographer is slandered, misrepresented, shown to be but another *ambiciosillo.* He or she will, in turn, attribute this slander to ambition, greed, baseness: "Only the feebleness characteristic of little men can induce them to bring forth their publications, passions and petty interests, envy, arrogance, vanity and maybe, just maybe, unjust resentment, for not having found me as docile as they would have liked."[72]

In the autobiographer's account, National History interrupts, or cuts into personal history: these memoirs often depict a kind of Annunciation scene, in which the author is suddenly called to a higher duty:

> I was living in the bosom of the most profound peace and perfect tranquility, when the revolts and convulsions of the Nation, in the beginning of the year 1808, came to rob me of this happiness which I enjoyed.
>
> I was torn from this sweet tranquility . . . by the unexpected announcement that the King had elected me to be the Tutor of the Prince of Asturias don Fernando . . . Talking a few days before . . .

with some relatives of mine . . . I had told them that we should really thank God for the calm and pleasant life which we enjoyed in Madrid, and that I, as far as it concerned me, would not trade that life for whatever could be offered to me in Palace, except for such a job that would allow me to be useful to the Nation, which I would place before all my conveniences.[73]

This portrayal of an entrance into national life as a response to a vocation, a calling, might be a defensive strategy. The sudden and unexpected Napoleonic invasion catapulted many Spaniards into key political positions; many men, in a matter of days or months, went from relative obscurity to being Spanish history's principal protagonists. The fear of being considered an *aventurero* (one who took advantage of a national crisis for personal gain) might be behind these portrayals. Godoy writes, "Those who have wanted to detract from me and belittle me by any means have spoken about me as an *aventurero*."[74] Alcalá Galiano describes the wealth of his ancestors for a curious reason: "I give these particularities concerning my family background because many take me for a political adventurer of the kind that rise with revolutions, when it has been the other way around, since the revolution has taken a terrible toll on me."[75] Others display their poverty as proof of their noble intentions: Espoz y Mina includes pages and pages of accounting sheets in his *Memorias* to document his honesty.

The autobiographer manipulates the contrast between personal and national histories: the individual may appear "like an object of reduced scale, good and handy for measuring the dimensions of the surfaces."[76] Although a writer might project his or her history on to national history, he or she can also use autobiography to discredit others who have set themselves up as bearers of the Nation's standard. The insider's view of the world of palace or bureau intrigue gives the autobiographer the ability to discover real motives, to calculate real stature. Girón and García de León y Pizarro are the most notable practitioners of this measuring; both of them set out to demonstrate "*la pequeñez de los grandes hombres* (the smallness of great men)" (PAG, II, p. 34; GLP, I, p. 257).[77] The strategy is invariably the same: personal ambition rather than patriotism is shown to be the driving force for these little big men. It is for this reason, we might imagine, that Juan de Escoiquiz portrays himself as soliciting but one favor from the queen before agreeing to offer her advice: "— My Lady—I told her—my only request is that Your Majesty give me your word that you will never grant any income, honor or employment to me or any relative of mine."[78] The autobiographer will try to ward off the same kind of reduction he or she might carry out on others.

The figure of Francisco Espoz y Mina is particularly interesting in this respect. He himself wrote an autobiography in which he presents the details of his public life, "referred with the simplicity of a man of nature. . . ."[79] And his wife also wrote a book of memoirs, in which she presents "these details which give evidence of what Espoz y Mina was, who is only known as a warrior and patriot, but not as the particular individual, blessed with so many special traits to live at home."[80] Although gifted in both the domestic and the patriotic spheres, Mina and his wife must recognize the hierarchy: first *Patria,* then *domos.* In fact, Mina's apparent inactivity during his years as an exile in England would provoke criticism suggesting that he was enjoying the good life in London and losing sight of the Nation's priorities. He responds: "And even when at first sight it might seem to bear no connection with what I am currently narrating, what follows, which is the account of the means by which I have been able to subsist with my family during my emigration, will in fact be seen to have such a connection, for it not only obliterates calumnious insinuations . . . but also proves that even my particular position away from my homeland does not have the attractions that could allegedly keep me from wanting to return to it."[81] General Espoz y Mina will consistently contrast individual and public interests, to show how he privileged the collective: "I, without harming [the sacred religion of my parents] also had to fulfill the dogmas of another religion, the patriotic one."[82] When Espoz y Mina's family is taken hostage, he tells the captors to do as they willed, "for I was incapable of failing in the duties of a good and patriotic Spaniard for any consideration in the world."[83] His wife, although praising his domestic prowess, also constantly makes reference to Espoz y Mina's powers of abnegation. The condesa portrays herself as marrying both a husband and a cause, *la Patria. Patriotismo* and *"adhesión a mi esposo* (adherence to my husband)" are one and the same (CEM, p. 77).

Faced, when her husband is at war, with the "necessary separation to which the Nation's welfare condemned me,"[84] the condesa's domestic fate is identical to the historical fate of her Nation: "Day by day our situation worsened, and mine in proportion to that of the Nation."[85]

Apostrophe

In a very provocative essay, Francisco Sánchez Blanco suggests that Spain's nineteenth-century autobiographers abandoned the appeal to some sort of transcendent perspective:

> The discovery of interiority in this century has some special characteristics. The subject comes to ignore the theological categories and to lose sight of the horizon of transcendence, once he observes himself immersed in the unstoppable course of historical changes. Individual identity can no longer be found in the continuity of character, of opinions, of social rank, but rather in the experience itself of internal wars, of the transformations of institutions and of the innovations that take place in the cities. The interior world is the reflection of the turmoil that follows the collapse of the foundations of the Old Regime.[86]

We are now ready to take issue with this statement. Has not History or the Nation, to a great extent, replaced those theological categories of transcendence characteristic of spiritual autobiographies? Faced with a noble, indeed, a sacred task, the advancement of the Nation, these autobiographers see those internal wars, those transformations and innovations much the same way Augustine or Teresa viewed the debased reality of unredeemed, worldly life. This repudiation of politics is especially clear in García de León y Pizarro and in Girón: both authors are extremely careful to emphasize their *independencia:* "independence . . . from the incipient political and bureaucratic machinery of the State."[87] General Espoz y Mina refuses to compromise his patriotism for any worldly thing: "por ninguna consideración del mundo" (FEM, I, p. 60). *Mundo,* in this text and others, seems to take on those negative characteristics it bears in ascetic literature and throughout the baroque. García de León y

Pizarro even uses language reminiscent of that tradition in his autobiography, when he addresses his readers: "You shall see how worthless the world is."[88] Palafox y Melzi considers his autobiography to
be a legacy left to his children; a valuable lesson for them on "*los
desengaños*" of "*el mundo*" (PM, p. 88).

One of the outstanding characteristics of this *mundo* is the prolific
production of discourse: it is this *mundo,* this *mundillo* (petty world)
that generates language and more language, paper and more paper.
Girón describes a short vacation from his government post as a
retreat from paper: "Without papers, without news, . . . it seemed
to me I was in Heaven."[89] And among these *papeles* are the partial
accounts to which the autobiographer is forced to respond; Girón
returns to work, "and when I was least expecting it, I suddenly
found myself in the middle of the court, and hence a target again of
all my enemies' gossip and slander."[90] In what seems to be one of the
most frequent postures of the genre, Torres Villarroel justifies his
text by evoking "the accusations, the bastard novels and the mysterious stories" that were being disseminated about him by his enemies.[91] Gómez Arias, a contemporary of Torres Villarroel who also
wrote a *Vida,* refers to "the army of doctors big and small, [who]
have hurled abuse and horrors against my name, have spit out toads,
have vomited snakes, have belched up poisonous bugs, and shame-
less slander [against me]."[92] These early nineteenth-century autobiographers might be somewhat less hyperbolic, but not much.
They, too, will be victimized by "the horde of copyists and makers of
dictionaries and biographies . . . who proliferate these errors."[93]
They will be misrepresented in "fables . . . , lies and the rubbish of
passions";[94] "insults and threats . . . [which their enemies] vomit
against [them]."[95] The proliferation of the word that Torres Villarroel so skillfully and happily manipulated has become nightmarish:
as Larra would say in his review of Godoy's *Memoirs,* the vulgariza-
tion of the press makes possible "falsity on a daily basis and accessi-
ble to all."[96]

These autobiographers dutifully, and at times painfully respond
to that maelstrom of malicious discourse: the "multitude of pamphlets and Memoirs, alleged materials for History, . . . [which] in
fact [are] nothing but sewage flowing into a river and mixing with

the water, though not without first polluting it and hindering its course."[97]

The space of this noise is the debased, contemporary political arena, the tempestuous public arena, where true patriotism is often frustrated by ambition and greed, *aventurerismo:* "My enemies . . . multiplied the confusion and gossip within palace so as to indispose me in a thousand ways," writes Godoy.[98] Juan de Escoiquiz is dismissed from public life "pained by the futility of my efforts in favor of the Nation, but extremely happy to see myself out of Babylon and restored to my old freedom and idleness."[99] Babylon, or, alternately, the noisy space of Babel; places of confusion and captivity, of commerce and prostitution; the prison of this life, Teresa's *"esta cárcel de esta vida,"* Augustine's "market of words"—in short, the space of unredeemed human textuality.

Rousseau's gesture of offering his text to Providence, Augustine's words addressed to God, Teresa's frequent discourse with a loving, *understanding* Divinity—each of these cases represents an attempt to liberate the speaker from this captivity, the captivity of a contingent enunciation, in which there can be no last word. The attempts are variations on apostrophe. Apostrophe is essentially, as we have already seen, a juridical trope: "a diversion of our words to address some person other than the judge" (Quintilian, in Culler 1981, p. 145). In apostrophe, voice "calls in order . . . to dramatize its calling, to summon images of its power so as to establish its identity as . . . prophetic voice" (Culler 1981, p. 142). "Dramatize"— apostrophe, like a great deal of autobiography, is a kind of spectacle, and more often than not, a spectacle of undeserved suffering, of martyrdom. "Prophetic voice"—apostrophe is an attempt to "jump out" of the debased communication circuit of human textuality in order to appeal to the authority of a noncontingent, timeless absolute. Teresa, as we have seen, in her boldest moments, apostrophizes God, the ultimate judge: "I lack everything, my Lord; but if you do not forsake me, I will not abandon You. Let all the learned men rise against me, let all of creation persecute me, let the demons torment me. . . ."[100] Godoy apostrophizes the Nation or the *Patria* in the same way: "Adored Patria of mine, I loved you, I served you, with my life, with my heart, with my soul; . . . and yet, this same man, slandered by many . . . does not find your justice!"[101] To these *calumnias,* the autobiographer responds with, alas, yet another text, but with one that attempts to differentiate itself from the others; a text that, in the end, is but barely a text. Apostrophe legitimizes prophecy; fair judgment is displaced into the future: "History, when it removes the rubbish scattered by passions, *shall tell* better and *shall tell* more. . . ."[102] "History and the public *shall judge* everyone."[103] "Spain *shall finally see* in my misfortune, uncommon in history, the innocent victim of the errors inflicted upon me by her enemies and mine."[104] To the contingency, the captivity and partiality of *leurs regards* (their gazes), the autobiographer tries to oppose the impartial and totalizing gaze of History.

2

A Life of Reading,

the Readings of a *Life:*

Joseph Blanco White

Literary history is the great Morgue where everyone
seeks his dead, those whom he loves or to whom he is related.
—Heinrich Heine, *"The Romantic School"*

An Archive of Silence

"Spanish literature of the romantic period can boast no Byron, Shelley, Wordsworth, or Keats, no Goethe, Schiller, or Heine, no Leopardi, not even a Hugo or a Vigny" (Tarr 1940, p. 35). These words, which appeared in the PMLA some fifty years ago, point to a sore spot among some Hispanists: the apparent absence or scarcity of great figures in the landscape of modern Spanish literary history. The words also seem to reflect a popular mentality that imagines that great figures, rather than being invented by certain readers and their institutions, are dealt out by the heavens to the different nations that participate in a kind of literary card game. By almost anyone's standards, throughout the eighteenth and nineteenth centuries, the deck was stacked against Spain; in fact, a person whose knowledge of Spanish letters depended on conventional, sweeping histories of European literature might very well wonder: What happened to Spanish letters between, say, Calderón and Pérez Galdós? Quite a dry spell.

Given the starkness of this landscape, together with the alleged scarcity of Spanish autobiographers, one would think that a writer of the stature of Joseph Blanco White (Seville, 1775–Liverpool, 1841) would long ago have been canonized. His *Life* is, in my opinion, one of the most searching autobiographies of nineteenth-century Eu-

rope. And even a cursory look at any of his writings shows a profound, learned, and often strikingly original mind at work. A quick
look at his life shows a man in contact with some of the greatest
minds of the nineteenth century: Andrés Bello, Manuel José Quintana, Thomas Carlyle, John Stuart Mill, and John Henry Newman.
Coleridge even called a sonnet written by Blanco White the finest
of the English language. He was probably overstating his case,
though, and I do not wish to overstate mine. First, I do not think
that Blanco White was a Wordsworth, and second, I realize that
there are several objective historical circumstances that may very
well have hindered Blanco White's entrance into the Spanish canon.
He lived half his life in England and wrote a good deal of his work in
English, and many of his writings in Spanish appeared in ephemeral
journals destined for Latin America. And yet, even when we add up
these objective facts, we still cannot account for the neglect of
Blanco White in Spain. As usual, we have to look elsewhere to
understand the mechanisms of canonization and exclusion. Blanco
White provides an extraordinary case for a study of these mechanisms because of the nature of his life and because of the availability
of certain documents written by some very powerful men who attempted—quite successfully—to write him out of serious consideration, out of the canon.

During his life, Blanco White entered and abandoned several
positions, institutions or faiths: a Catholic priest in Spain, he emi-
grated to England during the French invasion and became an Anglican. Later, he abandoned Anglicanism to become a Unitarian. He
wrote a three-volume autobiography that painstakingly documents
his reasons for abandoning these movements and that exposes their
insufficiencies. Blanco White emplots his entire life as an unending
struggle against orthodoxy; his *bildung* is portrayed as a laborious
"undoing" of his religious and intellectual "formation"; his "education [has] implanted" (BW, I, p. 382) in him a noisy chorus of
equivocal voices, and his self-discovery consists of thinning out
those extraneous voices, in order to attend to the one authentic,
internal voice of conscience, which, he believes, is the voice of God.
This peculiar trajectory makes Blanco White's text extremely problematic for those who still believe in the truth of the institutions
Blanco White left behind, for here is a man who claims to have fully

experienced Catholicism and Anglicanism, for example, and to have found their truths insufficient.

The posthumous publication of Blanco White's *Life* in 1845 provoked a number of essays and reviews, several of which were written from within one of the various truths Blanco White had embraced and abandoned. These texts constitute a battlefield of interpretations, of rereadings and rewritings of Blanco White's life and *Life*. The Unitarian J. H. Thom, who edited and published the *Life,* wrote in order to defend the publication; the Anglican and future Prime Minister W. E. Gladstone reviewed the *Life* in the *Quarterly Review;* the theologian Baden Powell wrote "The *Life* of the Reverend Joseph Blanco White" in the *Westminster Review* (Powell 1845); J. B. Mozley, a defender of the Oxford movement Blanco White had renounced, published "Blanco White" in the *Christian Remembrancer* (Mozley 1874); the *Eclectic Review* printed an anonymous essay (Anonymous 1845) as did the *Dublin Review* (Anonymous 1846). We add to the dossier the letters written by Anglican Archbishop Whately on two subjects: Blanco White's rejection of Anglicanism and the publication of the *Life.*

Blanco White writes:

> We are Englishmen, and they are Frenchmen—a set of rascally beggars.
> We are Frenchmen and they are Englishmen—Sacre.
> We are Spaniards and they are Americans. . . .
> "Is it not curious that words so very different in meaning as Englishman, Frenchman, Spaniard, . . . , etc. have the same effect on the passions and feelings of mankind?"
> "You are mistaken—you attribute the effects in question to the wrong word. It is the WE that produces them" (BW, II, p. 29).

Spain figures among the different faiths, the different "we's" Blanco White held and abandoned. (Not only did Blanco White leave Spain definitively during the French invasion, he was also accused of committing the unthinkable, treacherous act of supporting the independence of Spain's colonies in Latin America.) Blanco White's case makes clear how many of the same strategies used in religious polemics are also taken up in debates on loyalty and patriotism. It is the "we" that produces them. *Pro Deo et Patria:* as we saw in chapter

I, History, the *Patria,* and God all share the same pair of eyes; on this point there is general agreement. The question is: To whom do those eyes belong? Who has access to their vision? Blanco White's relation to Spain is treated in some other texts—other readings—that should be added to our dossier: the chapter that the great Spanish philologist Menéndez Pelayo devotes to Blanco White in his *Historia de los heterodoxos,* Vicente Lloréns's reading of Blanco White in several of his works, and Juan Goytisolo's forceful, one-hundred-page-long "Presentación crítica," published at the head of the *Obra inglesa de Blanco White.*

Blanco White's *Life* is remarkable both as a text and as an event. That is to say, the issues he addresses in the *Life*—the relationship between institutions and selfhood, or between orthodoxy and truth, for example—are themselves worthy of analysis. At the same time, the history of the text—its embattled and almost aborted publication, its reception and dismissal as the work of a proud, lustful wretch or a diseased mind, its rescue by Vicente Lloréns, Juan Goytisolo, and, ultimately, Spain's fledgling democracy—engages in a fascinating counterpoint with those very issues addressed within the text. In the pages that follow, I will attempt to transcribe this counterpoint. I will begin with some reflections on the relationships between autobiography and reading; after an analysis of Blanco White's *Life,* I will concentrate on several texts from our dossier.

A Life of Reading, a Reading of a *Life*

An autobiography is as much a reading of a life as it is a writing of a *Life.* In fact, the genre has had a long and interesting relationship with the problems and processes of reading. Augustine, Teresa, and Rousseau—three of the great canonical autobiographers—are all fervent repudiaters of the sign; each mortifies signifiers, as degraded, treacherous representations of an absent, unrepresentable wholeness or presence. And yet, in addition to being prolific authors, these three autobiographers are also among the West's most prominent readers.

In book 8 of the *Confessions,* Augustine's conversion takes place in the midst of a sort of frenzy of narratives, texts, and readings. First,

Simpliciano tells Augustine the story of Victorino, who was converted by reading scripture. Then, Ponticiano, after seeing a copy of Paul's Epistles on Augustine's gaming table, relates how he was converted when he came across a copy of St. Anthony's *Life*—a text that tells how Anthony was converted by reading from the Gospels. And finally, Augustine, hearing the words *"tolle lege, tolle lege"* and interpreting those words according to the narratives he has just heard, picks up Paul's Epistles, and reads the verse that brings about his conversion. He passes the text to his friend Alypius, who reads on and is likewise converted.

Teresa is also a great reader: standard iconography portrays her with a book in her hands; she is the *santa lectora,* the reader saint. Her "path to perfection" is marked by several textual milestones—a number of books that God places providentially in her hands, among them, Augustine's *Confessions:* "At this point I was given Saint Augustine's *Confessions,* which seemed to have been ordered by the Lord"; "I learned a lot from having read the story of Job in Saint Gregory's *Moralia;* it seems that the Lord had arranged this."[1]

And for Rousseau, the modern seeker of pretextual or atextual presence, reading ironically marks a kind of birth, or perhaps, death: "I do not know how I learned to read: I only remember my first readings and their effect on me; I date the unbroken consciousness of my own existence back to these first encounters with books."[2]

But the autobiographer does not merely portray a life of reading—he or she also performs a reading of a life, an interpretation or fashioning of an amorphous past. This reading is frequently a response to other, real or imagined, readings: the autobiography takes part in a conflict of interpretations. The conversion narrative, and the apostrophic autobiography we saw in chapter 1 utilize strategies that attempt to legitimate the particular reading of a life carried out in the text. Conversion and apostrophe attempt to distinguish the autobiographical account from other erroneous contemporary accounts (or, for that matter, from the author's preconversion account), by pretending to free the autobiographer from the contingencies of his or her contemporary moment, and the limited, fallible world- and self-view that that moment offers. Conversion and apostrophe pretend to allow unmediated readings—readings free from the pressures of media, of rhetoric, imposed models, or political expediency. This pretense of immediacy is why it is ironic when autobiographers who claim to be following no model—"The enterprise I am about to undertake has no precedent"—also show themselves to be avid readers, and often of biographies and auto-biographies.[3] This claim to immediacy is also why Augustine's conversion scene is so striking; it vividly depicts the community into which he is converted—a community of friends and texts, readers and readings—at the very moment he pretends to sever all worldly ties. (Incidentally, the persistence of that community, and the inclusion of Augustine's text within its canon, is evidenced when, over a thousand years later, Augustine's text providentially finds its way—*tolle lege*—into the hands of Teresa.) In any event, conversion and apostrophe are claims to transparency, a claim that holds that the convert's signs refer not to other signs but, rather, to reality, and in an unproblematical way. Conversion acts primarily on the eye, the organ of reading: "The eye that was in bondage to the phenomenal world (had as its constitutive principle the autonomy of that world) has been cleansed and purged and is now capable of seeing *what is there*" (Fish 1980, pp. 271–72).

Of course this claim is often disputed and rejected: the auto-biographer's words take on an opacity; the opacity of a signifier with a latent meaning, of a passion, of a diseased body. No text—no life, for that matter—is invulnerable to this diagnostic interpretation. "Augustine is depicted as the victim of a diseased psyche, finding in his devotion to mother Church, compensation for a passion mor-bidly fixed upon the memory of Monica, his mother" (Cochrane 1940, pp. 379–80). Although today it would be anachronistic to attribute Teresa's mystical raptures to the devil, we do have our modern demons: Teresa's texts have often been subjected to "clinical analyses of those who attribute Teresa's raptures and ecstasy to hysteria and sensuality."[4] And Jean-Jacques Rousseau, "a man filled with the love of humanity, desiring to teach men how to live with their true and uncorrupted selves" (Weintraub 1975, p. 832) also receives this clinical treatment:

> . . . in Rousseau's case the misreading is almost always accompanied
> by an overtone of intellectual and moral superiority, as if the com-

mentators, in the most favorable of cases, had to apologize or to offer a cure for something that went astray in their author. Some inherent weakness made Rousseau fall back into confusion, bad faith or withdrawal. At the same time, one can witness a regaining of self-assurance in the one who utters the judgement, as if the knowledge of Rousseau's weakness somehow reflected favorably on his own strength. He knows exactly what ails Rousseau and can therefore observe, judge and assist him from a position of unchallenged authority, like an ethnocentric anthropologist observing a native, or a doctor observing a patient. The critical attitude is diagnostic and looks on Rousseau as if he were the one asking for assistance rather than offering his counsel. The critic knows something about Rousseau that Rousseau did not wish to know (de Man 1983, p. 112).

These references to the doctor-patient relationship are curious; once again, as we saw in Torres Villarroel, the body comes to stand as a kind of emblem of the writer's entrapment in a contingent, limited locus of enunciation. Ironically, these clinical readings may manipulate some of the same strategies used by autobiographers, in order to legitimate their perspectives or readings of a text/life. Many interpreters, with a blind faith in their own objectivity, in the unshifting, impartial, bodiless perspective of their enunciation, offer definitive readings of those flawed self-interpretations embodied in an autobiography.

Even Phillipe Lejeune, who has tried to shift the emphasis of autobiography criticism from a search for the ultimate meaning of a text toward an analysis of the way a text functions, seems to fall back into a kind of search for latent truth. Although in chapter 1 of *Le pacte autobiographique* (1975) he sees the autobiographical text as being defined by its relationship with its reader, in chapter 2 he goes on to discard systematically all previous readings of Rousseau as insufficient: "This text is not read," "a deliberate refusal to listen," "refuse to read it," "the uninformed reader," "the arbitrary choice of [this reader]."[5] Only Lejeune's reading, it seems, allows "the spanking episode to recover its founding position."[6] He does this, he claims, without really reading: "Up to this point I have tried to say nothing which Rousseau does not say himself. If I have not adopted his language, I have at least adopted his concerns and his point of view."[7] This "without really reading," this access to *what is there,* the recovery of an original point of view, is a claim to a fusion of horizons, a claim to objectivity, transparency. The same claim that is made for conversion. Lejeune's interpretation, it would seem, has little or nothing to do with the phenomena of his moment—the trends and friends at Seuil and *Poetique,* for example—it is a simple encounter with meaning. The authority of this interpretation pretends to be completely unrelated to the authority of any reading community. Nevertheless, as Frank Kermode has written, "the discovery of latent senses may appear to be a spontaneous and individual achievement, but it is privileged and constrained by the community of the ear" (Kermode 1979, p. 5). It would seem, then, that, rather than mentioning and discarding previous interpretations as insufficient, a study of these privileges and constraints might be in order, an analysis that, to use Lejeune's words, might "make the enunciation the site of its research." That study could account for this "evolution of systems of reading contracts," an objectification of objectivities, we might call it.[8]

Recording the Internal Work of Selfhood

As Blanco White's *Life* moves forward, the autobiographical form slowly disintegrates. The text begins with two conventional, retrospective autobiographical narratives, "Narrative of His Life in Spain" and "Sketch of His Mind in England," continues with journal entries and letters, and concludes biographically: J. H. Thom, Blanco White's editor, seems almost to remove the pen from Blanco White's dead hand, in order to describe the death scene, that one change the autobiographer could not record. The distance—both temporal and mental—that separates the narrated events from the moment of their narration steadily diminishes as the book goes along. At the start, Blanco White narrates his birth in 1775 and his life in Spain from the vantage point of exile in England in 1830; toward the end, reflexivity has become so great that there is virtually no space between what is narrated and the moment of narration: "But the most harassing symptom is that of an unconquerable drowsiness, which seizes me minute after minute in the very act of exerting myself to check it. I would be fortunate if I could lie down on the sofa and make up for the wake of the night: but the moment I lose myself in sleep a panting seizes me, and gives me the sense of choking. (It has come upon me just as I wrote that last Word of the last Sentence.)" (BW, III, p. 14). Although the inclusion of letters and journal entries was a normal practice in a certain genre of Victorian lives, I would like to argue that this virtual simultaneity of living and writing takes on a special significance in the case of Blanco White.

John Henry Newman, an acquaintance of Blanco White from their days at Oxford, followed a path opposite to that of Blanco White: from Protestantism, he converted to Catholicism. In his autobiography, *Apologia pro vita sua,* Newman spends some 225 pages narrating the wanderings of his preconversion life, but life after conversion, as in Augustine's case, has no narration: "From the time I became a Catholic, of course I have no further history of my religious opinions to narrate. . . . I have had no anxiety of heart whatever. I have been in perfect peace and contentment" (Newman 1956, p. 227). Once again, conversion provides little new to narrate and a peaceful and tranquil outside—an unshifting locus of enuncia-tion—from which to narrate the unredeemed past. Of course his "outsideness" with respect to his narratable Anglican life coincides with his "insideness" with respect to the Catholic community; the very same community that will take pains to preserve and canonize his *Apologia.*

This unshifting perspective is precisely what is not to be found in Blanco White's *Life:* his is a life of permanent transition: "I fear that my Memoirs will be understood but by few. I have written them at different periods, and as my mind has been constantly in a state of transition, the colouring of the language must necessarily want consistency. But even this circumstance may help such as have the power of *reading* in other men's souls, to penetrate more deeply into the internal work, the long process that has been going on within me for many, many years" (BW, II, p. 346). In fact, this very shifting becomes a criterion of sincerity, of truth: Blanco White's aim seems not so much to portray an ultimate and definitive reading of his life, but rather to record the history of his different readings throughout time. The process is the thing:

After commenting upon his own [text, Blanco White] then comments upon his own comments. The very act of reflection is itself
reflected on, and the tone of the former stage of review is too
orthodox for a latter. The autobiography becomes itself a kind of
animal and seems to move; and the very narrative turns narrator.
The extended trunk we were sitting on begins to creep. We think we
are stationary, at last, when a little note at the end of the page
transcends the text and converts the ground we are on into an
inferior and moving stratum (Mozley 1874, p. 72).

These little notes at the end of the page are perhaps the most
prominent device Blanco White uses in order to convey a sense of
constant mutability. The footnotes are primarily the space in which
the autobiographer rereads himself: "All this has been read again in
December, 1840. . . ." (BW, I, p. 70n). "Deprived of the use of
my legs these three years, and now cruelly tormented by a most
severe rheumatism, I have nonetheless made an effort to read the
preceding manuscript" (BW, I, p. 235n). "I thank God that I have
been enabled to read these memoirs for the last time" (BW, III,
p. 159n).

Blanco White was constantly rereading himself: there are notes
dating from 1832, 1834, 1835, 1836, 1838, 1839, 1840, and
1841. At times they simply bring the main narrative up to date:
"He is one of my friends whom death has carried off since I began to
write these memoirs {1841}" (BW, I, p. 217n). At other times the
notes cancel out, as if placing *sous rature,* what is affirmed in the main
narrative: "I am sorry to be under the necessity of withdrawing my
thanks from one whom I have reason to believe one of the false
friends of my youth {1840}" (BW, I, p. 71n).[9] The note makes
evident a later and greater awareness, though without erasing the
previous state. This technique can be clearly seen in a series of notes
added to the *Life* that concern Blanco White's mastery of English:
"It is needless to advert to the evident marks of difficulty in the
employment of the English language which are visible in these
[texts]. I will not correct or alter anything, lest I should deprive
them of any internal marks of genuineness" (BW, I, p. 245n). From
this point forward, Blanco White will annotate awkward turns of
phrase: "I meant to say" (BW, I, p. 245n); "This is very ill expressed"

(BW, I, p. 261n). Again, rather than effacing these signs of imperfection, or ignorance, Blanco White leaves them in the text, and adds to them his present greater, though not definitive, awareness. This palimpsestic performance constitutes what I would call the deep strategy of the entire text, and particularly of the two retrospective narratives that open the *Life*.

The "Narrative of His Life in Spain (1775–1809)" is basically an Anglican reading of Blanco White's years in Spain and of Spain's Catholicism. He wrote this narrative in 1830 when still a firm believer in the truth and authority of the English church. In fact, the narrative was originally addressed in letters to the soon-to-be Anglican archbishop of Dublin, Richard Whately. The footnotes, however, relentlessly undermine this apparently steady vantage point: "I am copying the original Manuscript which I wrote at Oxford, in my residence at Liverpool about ten months after the resolution which produced my separation from the Archbishop of Dublin [and the Anglican Church]. I feel everyday more convinced that as long as I submitted to the yoke (lightly though I bore it) of a Church creed, I was not in a fair condition to take a correct view of the complicated and much obscured subject of Religion [1835]" (BW, I, p. 105n). The difference, or outsideness, of Anglicanism with respect to Catholicism and of England with respect to Spain is undone by these notes. The idea that moving from one religion to another, or from one nation to another, can provide a privileged or a definitive vantage point is discarded. "Why should one be surprised to find such charges brought against Christianity, in a country such as Spain, when even in England the mind is often staggered by the multitude of evils which every form of orthodox Christianity is daily and hourly producing among us? Is not my heart aching at this moment from the inflictions of the orthodox Spirit?" (BW, I, p. 115n).

In the second narrative "A Sketch of His Mind in England," written between 1834 and 1836, the perspective of these last two notes—from outside Anglicanism—has become the perspective of the main narrative: "though I embraced the theological system of the Church of England with perfect sincerity, it happened, in the course of time, that many of its views appeared to me quite untenable" (BW, I, p. 240). This narrative is quite literally a reading:

Blanco White reads and extracts journal entries from the first years
of his life in England, the time of his entrance into the Anglican
church. He quotes himself, incorrect English and all, in order to
demonstrate the sincerity with which he had embraced the Church
of England: "Examining, as I do now (March 18, 1835) this authentic record of my own thoughts . . . and finding myself in regard to
this document exactly as if I were reading the words of a stranger, I
feel delighted and grateful that I possess a proof so perfectly satisfactory of my earnestness and sincerity" (BW, I, p. 359). The journal
may be earnest and sincere, but Blanco White does not leave it at
that: he goes on to comment on the limitations of this earlier vantage point as well: "Reading these resolutions [found in a journal
entry from 1822] at the distance of more than 14 years [a footnote
tells the reader that Blanco is writing in Liverpool, April 22, 1836],
I can discover within them some traces of that pervading spirit of asceticism which my education implanted" (BW, I, p. 382). Even this
perspective of the main narrative—which, significantly, is dated in
the last two examples—is supplemented by footnotes from another
time, another level of awareness: "I am struck with the absurdity of
the expression which I used, from habit, only two years ago" (BW, I,
p. 273n).

The transition from retrospective narrative to dated entries seems
to be dictated not so much by the genre, as by the workings of
Blanco White's life and mind: within these narratives and their
notes, the multiplicity of readings, of moments of reading, renders
the word "now" meaningless, unless accompanied by its circumstances: now, March 18, 1835; now, April 22, 1836; now, March,
1836. The dated journal entry seems by far the most appropriate
means of recording Blanco White's life. The pronoun "I" belongs to
the same class of words as does the adverb "now"; it is a shifter.
Blanco White's autobiography is not so much the result, but rather
the "records of [his] self-examination," the documentation of his
constant shifting, "the internal work, the long process" (BW, I,
p. 346). The note, "I request that the time when I expressed these
sentiments be remembered" (BW, I, p. 214–15), could be appended
to almost any sentence in this three-volume *Life*. The written pronoun "I" ought to be dated.

A Rejection of Mediums

Generations of readers have been confounded by Augustine's decision to end his *Confessions* with three nonbiographical books, which consider the problems of memory and offer an interpretation of Genesis's first verses. We might read this gesture as the staking of a claim, which will be repeated throughout the history of autobiography: the genre reserves the right, the space, to conduct theoretical discussions on the possibilities of knowing, reading, and interpreting. In Augustine's case, it is as though conversion not only affords him the right—and the ability—to interpret his former life correctly, but also entitles him to perform an authoritative exegesis on the "source of narrativity," the beginning of the book of Creation.[10] Conversion makes of him a consummate reader.

Blanco White writes:

> Autobiographies are instructive . . . provided that the reader knows how to study mankind, for even when the account is written under the influence of vanity or some other passion, it will afford opportunities of studying the workings of the heart and mind in a state of transient or settled moral disease. . . . It is true that both the writer and the reader must see the working of the individual human soul through a medium containing sources of visual distortion and obscuration: for the narrator must have seen himself and all his actions through the more or less coloured glass which every man's prejudices interpose between everything and his intellectual vision: but as the prejudices and passions of the reader can scarcely ever be identical with those of the writer, there is the greatest possibility that the delusions of the latter will generally be apparent to the former, merely from the circumstance that he is placed in a different position (BW, III, pp. 366–67).

This comment appears in a letter written to Thom and included in the *Life;* it refers to another autobiography, though once again, Blanco White's words capture his own predicament in an uncanny way. As we have seen, the *Life* is an accumulation of writings and readings: the "delusions" of the earlier Blanco/writer become apparent to the later White/reader as "he is placed in a different position."

But the comment also establishes a certain equivalence between readers and writers: both work with, and through mediums, prejudices and passions. One of Blanco White's lifelong tasks is the questioning of mediums, those colored glasses placed between every man and every thing: "What has to pass through the distorting human mind, with all its feelings and passions, cannot be taken for granted as that pure effluence from the Divine Mind that persons think it to be. As a philosopher, a rejection of mediums is his system" (Mozley 1874, p. 138).

This rejection takes on many forms: Blanco White comes to reject the doctrine of the incarnation as a form of idolatry: the idea of God inhabiting a human body is completely unacceptable to him; he "want[s] a truth bodiless" (Mozley 1874, p. 138). He throws aside the notion of revelation, because of the fallibility, the "fallenness" of human mediums, human language:

> How is it possible that Words convey to men any notion to which there is nothing analogous in their own minds? . . . If Revelation is the only source of our knowledge of Him, we can know nothing of his character when he begins to address any man in human language. The invisible or falsely visible speaker (for in whatever shape he might show himself, the image employed would be already a gross misrepresentation), the floating Voice, might come from some wicked agent unknown to us. . . . If the language which conveys inspired thoughts is human, infallibility is at an end (BW, II, pp. 366–67).

Communication or communion with God cannot be textual; textuality, in fact, is a sign of man's inability to communicate/ commune with God, a sign of his fallenness. And for Blanco White, not only is the text of the Bible—the writing—a medium, so is the so-called sense, the meanings handed down through time, the readings: "All those creeds and statements, the whole body of teaching, the product of the Church's collected intelligence, the *simply* expositional and interpretative form of the original truth, as it came from the Apostle's mouths—all this is thrown aside because it is a medium" (Mozley 1874, p. 138). Perfect transmission and reception are impossible, and the authority supposedly inherited by modern Churches is illusory: "No teacher can secure his pupil from error, can impart his mind perfectly to others. Our reception of the thoughts of a higher mind must be proportioned to our capacity, our preconceptions, our moral progress. The very circumstance that men are taught by words, makes a mixture of error necessary. . . . How little did Christ's disciples understand him, whilst he was with them; and were the apostles able to protect their converts from error?" (BW, III, pp. 25–26).

For Blanco White, full conversion, the ultimate removal of scales—of prejudices and passions, of mediums—from the eyes, never takes place. The human mind is incapable of purely and *simply* perceiving "what is there," that "pure effluence from the Divine Mind." "Conversion," says Blanco White, is a "strange word" (BW, III, p. 100). "Truth has never manifested itself to me in such a broad stream of light as seems to be poured upon some men" (BW, I, p. 213). Understanding—whether of the self or of the scriptures—can only be provisional.

Blanco White primarily takes issue with the way in which different orthodoxies use the word "simply": the "simply expositional and interpretative form of the original truth": "[An acquaintance said,] 'if you would deliver yourself up *simply* to the Scriptures, etc.' 'So I have (answered I), to the best of my power: but by simply, you mean according to your own sense. Certainly. That is, if I deliver myself up to you, we shall agree' " (BW, II, p. 13). Truth and orthodoxy do not coincide: giving oneself up "simply" to "meaning" often means giving oneself up simply to an orthodoxy: "Is it the material book—the figure of the letters—the sound of the words which are to perform this beneficial office for man? People are shocked at the supposition. Then it must be the sense, i.e. one sense out of a multitude which the words of the book may bear. Which? Here we split. Numerous answers are heard, all in angry and uncharitable accents" (BW, II, p. 19).

"The discovery of latent senses may appear to be a spontaneous, individual [simple] achievement: but it is privileged and constrained by the community" (Kermode 1979, p. 5). Augustine's conversion narrative is followed by an authoritative interpretation of Scripture; Blanco White's anticonversion narratives are followed by meditations on the impossibility of full, unmediated understanding.

In the end, the medium against which Blanco White most earnestly rebels is the institution, the complacent, immobile community of readers—be they readers of texts, or of selves. He eventually comes to see membership in any of these communities as a threat to truth and identity, because they are founded on "obedience to the opinions of others" (BW, I, p. 33), extraneous voices. Blanco White's first conversion, into Anglicanism, provided him with a community—a community that both encouraged and disseminated his anti-Catholic writings and the Anglican version of his "self" put forth in the "Narrative of His Life in Spain." Yet when he moved forward, out of Anglicanism, and came to reinterpret both his Catholic and his Anglican lives, he was left without a community, left without a "we."

What then, does "Blanco White" mean? "Here we split. Numerous answers are heard all in angry and uncharitable accents." The *Life* is openly a response to these numerous and uncharitable answers: Blanco White writes in order to "refute the calumnies and misrepresentations" (BW, I, p. 1), the "unfair surmises" (BW, I, p. 147) and the "false impressions" (BW, I, p. 234) propagated by his enemies. But the book, conceived of as an answer, becomes a question; the diagnosis, a symptom: the *Life* is interpreted, from several orthodoxies, which claim to have the ability to uncover the real meaning of "Blanco White." "Confusion" or "withdrawal"— these readers know something about the writer that the writer did not wish to know or did not wish to make known.

Truth, it would seem, is simply syntagmatic; the paradigm, the axis of selection, belongs to fiction, or ideology. Omissions, the spaces in blank, or blind spots, the things the writer does not wish to know—these are the places, or the nonplaces of autobiography that will be used to discredit the text, to undo it. Let us turn to some prominent instances of this undoing, to some episodes in the history of the black legend of Blanco White.

Gladstone's Autopsy

"This is a book which rivets the attention and makes the heart bleed." These are the first words of Gladstone's review of Blanco's

Life, which he published in the *Quarterly Review* for June 1845. In this essay, Gladstone chooses to "regard Mr. Blanco White in several characters; first as a witness to facts, and next as the expositor, and still more as the victim, of opinions" (WEG, p. 7). He states that, "with regard to the first of these capacities, [Blanco White] had abundant talent, remarkable honesty and singleness of purpose" (WEG, p. 7). Especially valuable, for Gladstone, are the accounts Blanco White has provided of the "state of things in Spain" (WEG, p. 8). That is to say, of the depravity of Catholicism.

It is in his analysis of the second character—Blanco White as an expositor and victim of opinions—that Gladstone is most severe. "Blanco's arguments are constant to nothing but mutability" (WEG, p. 17). "We are alike baffled by the weakness, the incongruity, and the perpetual defluxion of his doctrines" (WEG, p. 13). "The contradictions with which his work abounds are indescribable. He indeed wonders at his own intellectual consistency, probably because he had forgotten many of the opinions he had renounced, and because of the remarkable positiveness with which he in most cases adopted for the moment every successive modification of his views" (WEG, p. 14). "Little then," Gladstone concludes, "[have we] to fear from the posthumous influence of Mr. Blanco White, through the medium of his arguments, if they be carefully and calmly sifted" (WEG, p. 62).

He goes on to search out the root of Blanco White's wrongheadedness, though, and finds it to lie not so much in the lack of a system or logic as in a lack of faith: "We have stated that these volumes do not contain any regular system of unbelief; but their author has presented to us very distinctly the particular stumbling-block which first, and also latterly overthrew his faith, and which appears to have been the disposition to demand an amount, or rather a kind of evidence in favour of a revealed religion different from that which the nature of the subject matter and the analogies of our human state, entitle us to expect" (WEG, pp. 21–22).

Even more, this lack of faith comes to be described as a sickness: "We can scarcely measure the miserable intensity of his disease" (WEG, pp. 13–14). "Let us, then, advert to the delusion to which Mr. Blanco White became a prey" (WEG, p. 22). "With the lapse of time, the malady proceeds" (WEG, p. 37). "He became rabid in his infatuation" (WEG, p. 38); "and all this," to conclude, "under the dismal delusion that he has been a discoverer of truth" (WEG, p. 58). Gladstone even suggests a physiological source for Blanco White's malady; "We know not whether it be irrational to indulge the hope that bodily disease may have been in a greater or less degree the source of Mr. Blanco White's morbid speculations, and that the severity of its pressure may, at least at times, have placed his free agency in abeyance" (WEG, p. 49).

Blanco White, in his *Life,* though, claims always to have moved only from strong conviction; he did believe on entering the Church of England: "I feel delighted and grateful that I possess a proof so perfectly satisfactory of my earnestness and sincerity [upon embracing Anglicanism]" (BW, I, p. 359). So Gladstone's task is to show how he knows something Blanco White does not know; Blanco White may have thought he believed, but he really did not; this is what Gladstone must demonstrate. What is more, he even pinpoints the source of this self-delusion in Blanco White's life: "We are disposed to look for the solution to this dilemma chiefly in the fact that the mind of Mr. Blanco White had in his early years suffered a wrench from which it never recovered; that the natural relation between his speculative and his practical life was then violently and fundamentally disturbed" (WEG, p. 44). Gladstone is referring to the fact that Blanco White lost his belief in Christianity when he was a Catholic priest, yet he continued to carry out his duties as a priest for ten years. It is during this time of prolonged role-playing, according to Gladstone's argument, that Blanco White lost the ability to know what sincerity, or sincere belief, was:

> The moral consequences of maintaining a Christian profession for ten years upon the basis of Atheism—the Breviary on the table, and Anti-Christian writers of France in the closet—may have been fatal to the solidity and consistency of his inward life thereafter. . . . And surely it is not too much to say . . . that after so long a period of contrast the most violent and unnatural—after the habits of mind belonging to such a position have been contracted, and hardened, as in so considerable a tract of time they must needs have been hardened—after the purposes and the general conduct of life have been so long and so entirely dissociated from inward conviction—it has become too late to reestablish their natural relations to one other.

We cannot with impunity tamper with the fearful and wonderful composition of our spiritual being. Sincerity of intention, after this, can only subsist in a qualified and imperfect sense (WEG, pp. 48–49).

Not only has Gladstone recognized Blanco White's disease and its symptoms, he has also done forensic work on the posthumous *Life*, and uncovered the very source of Blanco White's illness. "Blanco White," and his text then become a specimen, for they present "a remarkable number of curious phenomena" (WEG, p. 17). His *Life* becomes a "warning he left behind him, written by the dispensation of Providence for our learning" (WEG, p. 58). His "example [is] useful for our warning" (WEG, p. 62) for "it may well fortify our hold on Divine Truth, when we observe the desolating and exhausting power with which unbelief lays waste the mind of its victim, and the utter shipwreck that it made of happiness along with faith" (WEG, p. 63).

Gladstone thus closes his essay on Blanco White by arriving at the conclusion we expected: Blanco White claims to have experienced the insufficiency of Gladstone's truth, Anglicanism; Gladstone has "proven" the insufficiency of Blanco White's experience: "For this much we conceive is clearly proved, with regard to his life in this country, by the work before us, if it were previously in doubt; the faith of the English Church he never left, for he had never held it" (WEG, p. 63). Gladstone's astute argument is, in many respects, incontrovertible, and, ultimately, uncannily disturbing; it maintains not that Blanco White was dishonest or hypocritical (something ascertainable), but rather that he had lost the ability to know himself, the very ability to be sincere.

Whately's Warnings

Blanco White's "Narrative of His Life in Spain" was originally written in letters addressed to Richard Whately, who was later to become the Anglican archbishop of Dublin. The reason Blanco White gives for writing his memoirs in this fashion is curious:

Without some additional motive, some stimulus which may be repeatedly applied, I cannot expect to complete a narrative, scarcely any part of which I cannot hope to write without pain. One such stimulus, however, has offered itself to me—namely, to address the narrative to you making it a point to send a portion every week. The power of that stimulus lied in this. Of the many friends for whose kindness in a foreign land I am indebted to Providence, you alone seemed to have an instinctive knowledge of my character. The rest had to study me; you *read* me, without preparation (BW, I, p. 2).

Why would Blanco White address such a long autobiographical narrative to someone who already has an "instinctive knowledge of [his] character," to someone who has already "read [him]"? The technique is not that far from Augustine's: addressing the narrative to someone who "can see into his innermost marrow" is a way of authenticating what he says. The main part of this narrative was written while Blanco White was still an Anglican; Whately is a friendly interlocutor—a fellow reader—amidst a sea of enemies. Ironically, however, on Blanco's death, Whately tried to prevent the publication of the *Life*. Why?

Blanco White frequently speaks of his homelessness: "To the last day of my life I could not consider myself completely at home" (BW, I, p. 249). "My wretched Birth-day: 65 years old—without a place of rest to die in" (BW, III, p. 192). This homelessness is both literal and figurative: the home, as in the parable of the Prodigal Son, is a figure of submission to the law, the paternal law, orthodoxy. In Blanco White's case, his departure from Anglicanism coincides literally with his abandonment of a home: he came to reject Anglicanism when he was living in the Anglican Archbishop Whately's house. He left the house feeling that as long as he lived there his religious freedom would be hindered.

Blanco White's decision to leave the house of Anglicanism made Whately extremely uneasy: the letters provoked by Blanco White's departure are interesting and relevant to the history of the *Life*. The archbishop was concerned about the effects Blanco's subsequent publications might have on him. He wrote to Blanco White:

A man (suppose) has been living with me for years on terms of the closest brotherly intimacy and supposed confidence. He publishes a work, we will suppose, proclaiming his separation from the

Church, and disapprobation of its doctrines, without in any way discussing the question with me, or allowing me to see his work before publication; but of course the public are led to believe, if he does not expressly declare the contrary, that he did consult with his most confidential friend, and that I concur, or nearly concur, in his opinions and may be expected . . . to secede from the Church also. But if, again, he does declare that he had never communicated with me at all on the subject, either orally or in writing, then it must appear that the person who knows me the most intimately has the most contemptuous opinion either of my understanding or my sincerity, or both: such an impression could not but be injurious to the character of one at least, and most likely both of us (RW, p. 263).

As Whately sees it, no matter what Blanco White says in his declaration of secession from Anglicanism, Whately's reputation could be damaged. His letters to Blanco White from this period show a cunning man, determined to prevent Blanco White from publishing anything at all. The letters are filled with hypothetical instances, like the "suppose" of the last quotation, which are veiled, or not-so-veiled references to Blanco White's situation: He writes about a "common friend" of a "morbid constitution" (is it Blanco White?) who has "bid adieu to humility" (RW, p. 268). "For *if* a work of yours appeared" "the result of your publishing under such circumstances *would* be . . . most unspeakably unpleasant to both of us" (RW, pp. 258, 257).

Whately urges Blanco White not to publish anything without his approval. He is constantly warning Blanco White in these letters, putting him on his guard. He obviously knows that Blanco White was an obsessive journal writer, and he is worried about this:

Making private memoranda of our thoughts from time to time, so far from necessarily proving a help to the accuracy of the memory may, if especial care be not taken to guard against the danger, tend even to mislead the memory: because it may occasion our forgetting more completely whatever we do not enter in the book. . . . Hence, there is the danger of our remembrance becoming not like a book partially defaced and torn, in which we perceive what deficiencies are to be accounted for, but more like a transcript from a decayed

MS, which the ancient copyists, by trade used to make: writing straight on all they could make out and omitting the rest without any mark of omission, for fear of spoiling the look of their copy (RW, p. 283).

But warning Blanco White of possible omissions is perhaps the gentlest of Whately's tactics; the harshest is his apparent attempt to make Blanco White doubt his own sanity: "I cannot but remark to you, my dear friend, before I close this letter, how much I am alarmed and distressed . . . by finding you so often appearing of late to misunderstand the meaning of my letters, where I have every reason to think I had expressed myself with complete perspicuity. . . . Shortly afterwards, you mistook the sense of . . . a very simple sentence in another letter . . . convert[ing] a coherent and intelligent passage into a tissue of absurdity" (RW, p. 262). Whately represents his own fears in the voice of a supposed "future reviewer" and then censures Blanco White for supposing "(as you seem to do, though I had no idea of conveying that meaning) that the 'future reviewer' I was impersonating was to be myself" (RW, p. 286):

"Why should he publish [writes the would-be reviewer, Whately] when he cannot be sure that he knows his own mind? Whether he was under a delusion and self deceived for several years . . . or only for some months past . . . on either side of the alternative, he stultifies his own work and proclaims himself unqualified to come forward as an instructor of the public. . . . For what has happened may happen again, or may be taking place now. We have every reason to expect that next year, or next month, he will publish a book declaring that he not only is, but has been all along unconsciously, a Deist or an Atheist, a Quaker, a Swedenborgian or a Papist? . . . He can neither give nor have any security that he is not equally self-deceived now. He says indeed, that he is conscious of no delusion. To be sure not. Who ever was?" (RW, 284–85)

These same two elements—omissions and delusions—will reappear many years later when Whately tries to prevent J. H. Thom from publishing Blanco White's *Life*. Thom asks Whately for any pertinent correspondence that might be included in Blanco White's memoirs. Whately responds that he has in his possession some very important papers, "such that any life of him published without them must be, not merely imperfect, but erroneous, conveying false notions to the reader . . . and Mr. Thom, I added, could not be ignorant that in such a case a man may appear perfectly sane to those ignorant of certain facts, while one knowing the facts would perceive that (supposing him to be honest) he must be insane" (JHT, p. 92). The papers are supposedly doctors' opinions that assert Blanco White's mental derangement. Their inclusion in the *Life*, which Whately would forbid for the sake of decorum, would invalidate the entire text; their exclusion would make the text erroneous and dangerous. Thus Whately tries to destroy the value of a whole life; "he takes a stab at a whole existence" (JHT, p. 102) and argues that "no weight should attach to Mr. White's adoption of any convictions on account of his insanity" (JHT, p. 86). Thom, however, went ahead with the publication, openly casting himself in the role of a compiler of the Acts of a Martyr: "I have a duty to perform, and I trust in God I should find strength if the gallows or the stake awaited me" (JHT, p. 119).

"We esteem these parts of his history as of the highest importance" (WEG, p. 63) writes Gladstone; indeed both Gladstone and Whately concentrate on very specific episodes in the *Life*. One part of the narrative explains the rest: delirium, withdrawal, or delusion, these interpretations, somewhat like the interpretation of dreams, consume the text, they render the text familiar, impotent in its indictments of Anglicanism and orthodoxy.

Curiously, both Gladstone and Whately center their attention on turning points: Gladstone focuses on Blanco White's entrance, or false entrance into the community of the Anglican church; Whately looks primarily at Blanco White's exit. In the same way, an anonymous Catholic review of the *Life*, published in June 1846 in the *Dublin Review* admits being primarily concerned with Blanco White's entrance into Catholicism. Other reviewers have shown that his conversion to Anglicanism was not authentic, and, "for a parallel reason, our interest is naturally fixed on his first [religion/ conversion]" (Anonymous 1846, p. 348). Menéndez Pelayo will find another point, another exit in the *Life*, which he reads as central—Blanco White's departure from Spain.

Fathers and Sons: Menéndez Pelayo

"Because travel occurs in time and space, it leads only to more
wandering, more time, and eventually to death. Peace and happiness can be found only at home. . . . Here and throughout part one
[of Augustine's text], travel stands for fruitless human ambition,
home for spiritual resignation to the eternal will of God" (Spengemann 1980, p. 20). If Blanco White was careful to show the connected and directed nature of his wanderings through mental wil-
derness, Menéndez Pelayo represents them as chaotic and pointless:
"Thus he spent his laborious and miserable days, like a pilotless ship
caught in a fierce storm, amidst constant apostasies and turnabouts,
each day doubting what had been asserted the day before, denying
even his own intellect, waking up every morning with new passions
that he took for convictions and that would tumble with the same
ease as their siblings from the day before. . . ."[11]

Just like Gladstone, Menéndez Pelayo attributes Blanco White's
restlessness to a lack of faith, a refusal to submission: "He hopelessly
demanded from knowledge something which knowledge could not
give him: serenity and peace of mind."[12] "First a Catholic, then an
encyclopedist, later a supporter of the Anglican Church, and in the
end a Unitarian, barely a Christian. . . . Such was Blanco's theological life, governed only by the idol of each moment and by the
unbridled love of independent thinking, which, rejecting any dogmatic solution, failed to find tranquility even in skepticism; instead, he galloped wildly, along winding paths, in search of unity."[13]

Thus Blanco White is cast clearly in the role of the rebellious son
who abandons home, the faith, his mother tongue, and his father-
land *en busca de la unidad* (in search of unity). Menéndez Pelayo even
briefly sketches the genealogy of Blanco's Irish and very Catholic
family (MP, p. 174). Tradition, inheritance, genealogy—these are
the guarantees of truth for Menéndez Pelayo, the truth that Blanco
White abandons, he says, simply because of pride and lust: "He lost
[serenity] forever when pride and lust made him abandon the benefi-
cent shadow of the sanctuary."[14]

Lujuria (lust)—here begins the rather complicated *leyenda negra*
of Blanco White that Menéndez Pelayo helped institute. At one
point in his *Life,* without ever having made any mention of a mis-

tress or a wife, Blanco White speaks of his son. He had also written in the magazine *Variedades* that he had lived immorally when he was a cleric. It was not until Vicente Lloréns, in the 1970s, studied Blanco White's family correspondence, that the facts of this mysterious son were brought to light. The mother of Blanco White's son was Magdalena Esquaya. The child was born in January 1809—in other words, when Blanco was already in Seville, in flight from the French. Blanco White did not even know of his son's existence until 1812, when Wellington liberated Madrid, and contact between Spain and England was reestablished.[15]

In Menéndez Pelayo's reading of Blanco White, though, this missing episode becomes the center of Blanco White's text, the pit into which Blanco White's *Life* falls, as does his life. In Menéndez Pelayo's account, Blanco White leaves Spain not for those complex reasons he alleges in his *Life,* but rather because "he had several children; he loved dearly those products of his sins and he wanted to give them a name and social prestige, at any cost."[16] Likewise, Blanco White's minute explanation of his entrance into the Anglican church is discarded; he did so, says Menéndez Pelayo, with "the hope of attaining honors and social admiration for himself and his children."[17] The missing episode is read into every single event of Blanco White's *Life:* "May [my reader] learn what to expect from Blanco's theologies and liberalisms: we are always sure to find skirts amidst all this business about heresies."[18] The words *unitario* and *conversión* are written within quotation marks in the subtitles to Menéndez Pelayo's chapter on Blanco White; by attributing all the autobiographer's doubts and transformations to *faldas* (skirts), he puts the entire *Life* within quotation marks and invites his reader's complicity in smirking with disdain—*"risum teneatis,"* he says—while reading Blanco White's autobiography.

Blanco White, the unrepentant Prodigal Son becomes, in this chapter, an incarnation of two larger rebellions, which profoundly disturb Menéndez Pelayo—the emancipation of Spain's colonies in America and the Protestant Reformation. He attacks Blanco White's defense of Anglicanism on these grounds: "And would it not be absurd to invoke arguments of unity, authority and dogmatic tradition in favor of the Anglican Church, that is to say, of a Church which was born yesterday, rebellious and schismatic, and to disdain the same unity and tradition applied to the Church of Rome, the most ancient and robust institution of the modern world, founded on the unshakeable rock of centuries? [That would be] . . . granting the rebellious daughter what was denied to the mother. . . ."[19] And just as he attributes Blanco White's religious independence to pride and lust, Menéndez Pelayo holds that the Church of England was "born virtually yesterday, from a lustful king's indecent concubinage, the aristocracy's greed and the servilism of an opulent and degraded clergy."[20] Juan Goytisolo has spoken of the tendency of Spain's *ortodoxos* to attribute all errors or crimes to a sin against the sixth commandment (JG, pp. 7–8). In a vainglorious crescendo, Menéndez Pelayo makes an impassioned exhortation to Protestants: "Confess," he writes, "that you are a handful of rebels, and dare not call yourselves the heirs of the primitive Church, which would have surely expelled you from its bosom."[21]

Menéndez Pelayo ends his essay on a note of complacent pity: "Let us not be angry with Blanco; it is enough to pity him. His life had not been touched by a single robust idea. . . . He was . . . the leper of all parties, and he walked toward his grave without even enjoying a faith in doubt."[22] Ironically, after having helped institute a black legend of Blanco White, he closes his essay by citing the sonnet "Mysterious Night" and by declaring that "only this poetic flower grows, like an evergreen, on Blanco's slandered grave. When the last echo of his debates and of his noisy life is finally extinguished, the Muse of Song will preserve his memory linked to these fourteen verses of melancholy harmony."[23]

A Captive Text and Its Rescue: Juan Goytisolo

At the roots of Christian biography lies a confrontation between the individual and the institution, or the state:

> The beginnings of Christian biography are clearly evident in the Acts of the Martyrs. The "Acts" were compiled from the official reports of [martyrs'] trials or from the testimonies of eyewitnesses, and were read to the congregations on the anniversaries of the martyrs. . . . In relating the life of a martyr, we usually find a more

or less detailed account of the persecution: . . . the hero of the story . . . is arrested and cast into prison; brought before the judge, he confesses his faith, and suffers horrible tortures; he dies and his tomb becomes the scene of miracles (de Ferrari 1952, p. vii).

During the first centuries of Christianity, the stories of the martyrs, the witnesses, were frequently retold, for they constituted a tradition of resistance to the harsh persecutions of Rome; they helped define a community. The public execution—the clearest and most horrifying spectacle of confrontation between the individual and the state—is an attempt to silence dissent. Ironically, though, through the use of official documents and eyewitness testimony—and the efforts of a group of readers—the spectacle produces a strong narrative of opposition. Curiously, as Christianity consolidates its hegemony throughout the West, its canonical life stories change: the courage and defiance of the martyr give way to the submission and self-effacement of the ascetic. Defiance and opposition; submission and obedience: the history of life writing seems tied to conditions of shifting insides and outsides.

Just before narrating his definitive departure from Spain in his autobiography, Blanco White describes a rescue mission he undertook during the French invasion. Charged with the preparation of a report on the proposed constitution of the Cortes, he "went about his task without delay,"

> but before I began I agreed with my colleague in forcing the Inquisition to let us have some of the prohibited books which at different times they had seized and thrown together to be destroyed by the worms in one of the halls of their odious Palace. . . . [T]here was a kind of triumph in this recovery of books that were completely lost to the world. They indeed belonged to nobody. . . . The Holy Tribunal authorized me to enter the place where the confiscated books were thrown together, and take out whatever I pleased. . . . I now forget what . . . works I was able to save from the worms . . . which had reduced a great number of volumes to fragments. The liberated captives were shared equally between my colleague and myself: and as the Inquisition ceased to exist soon after . . . my own portion are likely to be still in the hands of some of my Spanish friends (BW, I, pp. 153–54).

Books as captives—the image is not that strange if we recall that autos-da-fé existed for texts as well as for bodies. The episode, like many of the episodes in the *Life,* can be read as an emblem of Blanco White's entire text, and of a certain kind of autobiography. First, the historical link between autobiographical writing and captivity is a strong one; the captured Spaniard who endures the tortures of the enemy is liberated; his or her first-person testimony becomes extremely valuable. In fact, the captivity narrative is structurally similar to the conversion narrative; it describes the trials of the narrator in the belly of the beast, *esta cárcel de esta vida,* and his or her eventual liberation. Second, in Blanco White's anecdote, a moment of flux—the impending French invasion—is taken advantage of in order to rescue another history, the history silenced by the Inquisition. Within the individual, autobiographies seem to crystallize around borders: conversions, transgressions, *idas y venidas.* On another level, the genre itself seems to surge at those moments when hegemonies are about to shift. Official, normal history is invariably written in the third person; a new, revolutionary history will have to liberate captive voices, first-person accounts, in order to rewrite the past. Democratic Spain's recent attempt to rescue lost voices, lost texts—and Blanco White's among them—is a clear example of this phenomenon.

"In all works of interpretation there are insiders and outsiders, the former having, or professing to have, immediate access to the mystery. . . . A correct understanding of the New Testament may be had only by the faithful: the outsiders will see without perceiving, hear without understanding" (Kermode 1979, pp. xi, 10). Gladstone, Whately, and Menéndez Pelayo claim to show how Blanco White never really understood their truths, he remained an outsider to their mysteries, separated from them by sin or delusion, omission or oversight—a sick man in either case. Mozley even talks of mental sin, mental lust, the "mind's body": "And as the undisciplined bodily appetite rushes into grossness, so the undisciplined intellect abandons itself to a lie—the first issues in carnal sin, the latter in the sin of heresy" (Mozley 1874, p. 144).

Menéndez Pelayo leaves Blanco White to the worms, buried in a slandered grave, fertilizing a *flor poética.* Whately uses the same kind of image; he writes of the editor of Blanco White's *Life:* "And still more disgusting is the sordid and heartless avarice of those (so called) friends who are eager to turn a penny . . . by digging up the corpse of a friend, and selling it to be dissected and exhibited in a school of anatomy" (JHT, p. 94).

These presentations of Blanco White as a pathetic, pathological case study will not prevent Juan Goytisolo from speaking of him as one of the most brilliant, misunderstood, and misrepresented men that Spain has ever produced: "His ideas, his sensitivity, his language had to be incomprehensible for those who were clinging on to a tradition which he had long ago left behind."[24] In his long and forceful "Presentación crítica" to the *Obra inglesa de Blanco White,* Goytisolo speaks of Blanco White precisely as a martyr: "He preached in the desert." "He was the scapegoat of our feverish patriots." "He is beaten from all sides with hardly a soul to thank him for anything."[25] All this because he committed "the unforgiveable crime of thinking and writing on his own."[26] Goytisolo's essay on Blanco White at times is openly autobiographical: "While speaking of Blanco White I have not ceased speaking about myself."[27] In fact, this critical essay can be seen as a sort of pre-text or outline of Goytisolo's own autobiographical project: *Coto vedado* and *En los reinos de taifa.* In these autobiographical narratives, Blanco White occupies a prominent place as a precursor—or even a previous incarnation—of Goytisolo. Blanco White's experience with both Catholicism and Anglicanism becomes a prophecy of Goytisolo's own victimization at the hands of two, apparently different orthodoxies: fascism and communism. The novelist sees in Blanco White a brother in that new genealogy that he forges for himself in opposition to the cultural-familial mediocrity into which he had been born (see Fernández 1991b).

In the end, Goytisolo's task is to put forth a "we," a paradoxical "we" made up of loners, "a fraternity of outsiders, pariahs and marginals," from which to read and rescue Blanco White.[28] Goytisolo's reading of Blanco White is explicitly part of his "invention of a tradition," an alternative Spanish tradition, a genealogy of outcasts, independent thinkers, expatriates: Blanco White, Américo Castro, Luis Cernuda, Vicente Lloréns, and, of course, Juan Goytisolo. In this dialogue across a century, Goytisolo understands Blanco White's words, and perceives in them not a warning, or a pitiful specimen, but rather exemplary behavior and useful lessons; he hears and understands "the extinguished voice of Spain, a voice that in 1971 *we* recognize as *ours*—an unconditional, prophetic, and free voice which calls out from the hell where, to the shame of all, it remains buried."[29] Blanco White had been buried alive.

Moral

Ironically, Blanco White wrote his text "to refute the calumnies and misrepresentations of [his] enemies," but the text meant to erase, had been erased and buried. The text meant to put out the fire of calumny has instead become fuel for his enemies. Blanco White's transgression, which gives rise both to the *Life* and to those effacing interpretations, is his belief that truth exists, though the claim to truth made by human institutions is poorly founded: "My love of truth, however, and the importance of recording facts which bear on the character of institutions which I deem most pernicious, demand a brief yet explicit declaration" (BW, I, p. 65).

One text, several Blanco Whites—Whately and Gladstone come close to deeming him "fitter for Bedlam than for the pursuit of philosophical inquiries" (WEG, p. 44); Menéndez Pelayo condemns him to the fiery circle of lust; Goytisolo makes of him an exemplary man and Spaniard. They may all be representations, but they are not all equal: until very recently Blanco White's work was all but ignored; it was not even available to Spanish readers until the 1970s. As Goytisolo says, Spanish literary history is yet to be written.

Blanco White calls his "entire life a prayer" (BW, III, p. 278), and I would argue that his entire *Life* is an apostrophe, an appeal not only to the world, but also to a higher authority for Justice: "Could I speak freely . . . it would clearly appear that the world, and especially that country whose barbarous laws connected me with the Church *I must impeach before heaven,* have no ground of accusation against me" (BW, I, p. 131). He frequently apostrophizes God and His primary attribute: "Thou dwellest within me. . . . Thou hast placed thy oracle in my conscience" (BW, III, p. 276); "an internal monitor" (BW, III, p. 156); "thy still small voice" (BW, III, p. 271). Blanco White's text is a performance of the drama that ensues when that oracle, that voice, that truth, is said to reside within an "I" rather than a "we." And the history of the text, in fact, the history of Blanco White—his neglect, dismissal, and belated, partial recovery—is a powerful example of the inevitable outcome of such a drama. Literary history, like political history, is written by readers, not the Muses or the heavens. Spain's "lack of great figures," or "lack of autobiographers," rather than indicating a shortcoming in the literature might—to some degree at least—reflect a problem among Hispanists: our willingness simply to pass along inherited prejudices, silences, and texts. The gravelike silence to which Blanco White's apostrophic pleas for fairness and understanding had been condemned could teach us an important lesson: when it comes to writing history, there is no Justice—there is just us.

3

The Experience of Crisis,
the Crisis of Experience

For ruins, we must remember, are
by their very nature modern. —*Harry Levin,*
The Broken Column

Autobiography and Epitaphs

I closed the last chapter with a series of images that related Blanco White's *Life* with a cemetery, with tombs and tombstones. The connection is frequent in both autobiography and writing about autobiography. George Misch (1950), in his monumental attempt at chronicling the history of autobiographical writing, begins with first-person Egyptian tomb inscriptions. "My life, [does not] deserve any honors or epitaphs other than oblivion and silence" is what the anything-but-silent Torres Villarroel says in his *Vida.*[1] More recently, Paul de Man has centered a study of autobiography around Wordsworth's "Essays on Epitaphs."

One of de Man's central tasks in this essay is to question the idea that autobiography "belong[s] to a simpler mode of referentiality" than fiction: "But are we so certain that autobiography depends on reference, as a photograph depends on its subject or a (realistic) picture on its model? We assume that the life produces the autobiography as an act produces its consequences, but can we not suggest, with equal justice, that the autobiographical project may itself produce and determine the life?" (de Man 1984, p. 69). Here de Man is extending to the case of autobiography what has been called the deconstruction of the sign. Conventional thought would have us believe that the sign is secondary and posterior to its referent: the sign, after all, tries to re-present something that was already present, out there in the world. Deconstructing the sign means suggesting that representation produces a referent and at the same time creates a sense of distance from this miragelike presence, a sense of its own insufficiency. Eugenio Donato has written: "Representation cannot function without generating within itself the pseudo-presence of an 'object.' The 'object' however, is secondary and derived with respect to the play of representation. The error . . . is to identify this necessary but constructed object with an original 'Natural Object,' to place as cause what is an effect, as origin what is a product" (Donato 1979, p. 52). In other words, if, as we have seen, conventional thought tends to mortify the signifier, deconstructive thought mortifies the signified; it drags the signified down to the level of the signifier and denies the existence of any pure "what is there" outside the play, or even better, outside the work, of textuality, of signification.

According to this view, the so-called signified—in the case of autobiography, the life or personality or authentic identity—is itself always pointing toward something else, always caught up in signification, whether in the form of the knight errant who lives for or through his chivalric romances, the politician who lives for or through the history books to come, or the old-timer who looks back at a shapeless past and fashions a life out of words. There is no moment of absolute fullness or presence; any given moment in life—not only the moment in which one sits down to write an autobiography—is fraught with signification. It is only through the distorting lens of nostalgia or hope that the past or future comes to seem whole, identical to itself.

The original experience—autobiography's signified—becomes for de Man and Donato, a "product," a "construct," something that is "generated" through representation. This mechanical imagery is telling, because one possible definition of romantic irony is the recognition of the work, of the production or construction behind what was previously thought to be a natural object. In this sense, the kind of criticism outlined by de Man and Donato is a romantic enterprise, an ironic project, which seeks to question the conventional conceptions of origins and products. If origins are discovered and products are invented, deconstructive thought seeks systematically to replace the word "discovery" with the word "invention." It is this kind of thinking that has facilitated the literary and rhetorical study of autobiography: after poststructuralism, the genre comes to be seen as an arena not for value-neutral self-discovery, but rather for ideologically laden self-invention.

For a critic like de Man in any case, autobiography is different from other forms of representation in degree, not in kind. It is not more reliable, nor is it less problematic; rather, it reveals in a more striking way the irony of all representation. In his argument, auto-biography becomes the epitome of representation because of its problematic nature. Like an epitaph, or ruins, the sign—or autobi-ography—attempts to make present the very thing whose absence it marks. The essential problem for the writer of epitaphs—how to evoke that presence—is not a problem peculiar to those representa-tions that try to bridge death: it is *the* problem of representation in general. The so-called signified of an autobiography—we see this time and time again in the texts—is always just around the corner, never quite done justice. It will not stand still. We are accustomed to keeping the medium (language) separate from the object of repre-sentation (life). But if we subscribe to the poststructuralist view of autobiography, we realize that living autobiographers face a task no easier than that of a writer of epitaphs—that is, to express one me-dium, "being," in another medium, language (see Jay 1984, p. 21).

Autobiography, then, is considered to be exemplary—but exem-plary because of its essential insufficiency. And this insufficiency/ exemplarity makes for a special relationship between autobiography and modernity. For many, modernity or the modern consciousness is characterized by irony, and autobiography, a genre that inevitably and relentlessly highlights the limits of representation and the im-possibility of closure, is nothing if not an "immense irony" in the words of Eagleton (1981, p. 18). Spengemann even proposes that "the modernist movement away from representational discourse to-ward self-enacting, self-reflexive verbal structures seems to make the very idea of literary modernism . . . synonymous with that of autobiography" (1980, p. xiii).

In this chapter I would like to study some of the relations be-tween autobiography and modernity in Spain. In particular, I am interested in a certain resistance to modernity, certain antimodern

gestures or stances found in the autobiographical writings of the
costumbrista author Ramón Mesonero Romanos, the Romantic playwright and poet José Zorrilla, and the turn-of-the-century novelist
Armando Palacio Valdés. In contrast to what Eagleton and Spengemann suggest about the genre, there is, in my opinion, very little irony in these and most nineteenth-century autobiographical
texts in Spain. While Sánchez Blanco contends that for nineteenth-
century Spanish autobiographers "individual identity can only be
found . . . in the very experience of internal wars, of the transformations of institutions, and of the innovations that take place in cities," in the autobiographical texts I consider, those struggles and
transformations are portrayed as threats to identity, not its foundation.[2] I would argue that to find the primary forum for irony in
nineteenth-century Spanish letters we would have to turn to the
better, polyphonic novels of Pedro Antonio de Alarcón and Juan
Valera, Leopoldo Alas and Benito Pérez Galdós. The autobiographers, on the other hand, rather than give themselves up to irony, to
the loss of truth, to constant flux, tend to wax nostalgic for certain
places or moments—invented or remembered—that were supposedly prior to, or insulated from, the turbulence described by Sánchez Blanco. Mesonero Romanos's tranquil premodern life or natural, apolitical progress; Zorrilla's lost home, sweet home; Palacio
Valdés's utopian childhood in the countryside; these moments and
places of Presence are either implicitly or explicitly opposed to the
troubled present of the autobiographer: a present, alas, of the written word, of autobiography. Once again, it is as if the genre had a
death wish: the situations autobiography longs for would eliminate
the genre's very conditions of existence.

And yet, following the lead of de Man and Donato, we ought to
ask: Are these longed-for situations real, or are they rather the
necessary products of autobiographical discourse, the founding fictions of autobiographical writing?

Witnesses of Crisis

Change, conversion, crisis, loss—these are the engines of autobiography. In the texts we have seen thus far, autobiography has

been written from a position of deprivation or defacement: the autobiographer's real self has purportedly been disfigured by erroneous and malicious biographical accounts written by others. Blanco White's *Life* propels itself forward, in a constant process of self-supplementation, but it is also propelled by the proliferation of others' misrepresentations; at one point he complains: "The periodical press has become the established organ of private malice" (BW, I, p. 185). Once again, this proliferation of discourse is frequently associated with, or attributed to, modernity, industry, and production. Using an image that explicitly and humorously links the mechanization of the means of production with issues of personal identity, Mesonero Romanos writes:

> The most important product manufactured in the capital city, whether it be considered as raw material for later applications, or as a product already finished and of comfortable and immediate use, is the fabrication of reputations: a fabrication which is so vast, that it not only supplies the court and royal sites, but it also extends its commerce and generally stocks all the markets of the kingdom. This powerful industry, greatly exploited in Madrid, relies on the tribunal, the press and the public square as its rich mines of information and active workshops.[3]

Steam is the "motor of the nineteenth century" and this new force powers not only railroads and factories but also the printing press and representation.[4] If the railroad, that "machine in the garden," threatens idyllic regional identities, and the factory threatens the aura of handmade objects, the printing press endangers truth and authenticity by sheer proliferation, and by substituting representations—reputation—for the real thing, virtue.[5] As Richard Sennet has written: "[In the city] . . . one can make up one's own identity . . . , rather than submit to the identity the Higher Power has assigned one. The pursuit of reputation replaces the pursuit of virtue" (Sennet 1978, p. 119). This is particularly poignant in the case of the capital of Spain: not at all a productive or industrial capital, Madrid readily lends itself to portrayals as a prolific factory of nothing more than empty discourse, bureaucratic fictions.

Blanco White's unending autobiographical project is a response to movement, to difference: either the difference between truth and

others' fabrications, misrepresentations, or between his previous
self-representation and his present one. In the end, his *Life* is a
chronicle of internal movements, of constant crises. In fact, the
anonymous reaction to the *Life* that appeared in the *Dublin Review*
portrays Blanco White precisely as a survivor, or a witness: a survivor of and to himself. He experienced profound crises and lived to
tell about it: "[For here is a man who] lived to express such sentiments as the following . . ." (Anonymous 1846, p. 346).

In his book *All That Is Solid Melts into Air*, Marshall Berman
interprets Goethe's *Faust* as an externalization of the "romantic quest
for self-development" (1982, p. 62); Faust's internal intellectual
ambition, his endless thirst for knowledge is externalized when
modern society is contaminated with a similar unending thirst for
development—in this case, economic development. The move from
Blanco White to the texts we will consider in this chapter follows
the externalization described by Berman. If Blanco White inde-
fatigably chronicles his perpetual intellectual crisis, a certain kind of
autobiographer will endlessly respond to, or record the constant
crises out there in modernity. These are autobiographers whose texts
dialogue with, or are propelled by, the constant movement of the
modern world. Curiously, standard descriptions of Blanco White
usually include the same words that appear time and time again in
conventional descriptions of the nineteenth century. If Blanco is
described as "fickle," "mutable, impetuous and violent," "constant
to nothing but mutability,"[6] the nineteenth century is said to be
governed by a "constant principle of uneasiness, fickleness and agi-
tation"; it is an "agitated, agitating century."[7] Both are ideal objects
of description. If Blanco White lived to tell about the violent upheavals he experienced within himself, many autobiographers in the
nineteenth and twentieth centuries will live to tell of the permanent
catastrophe that is modernity. The stance of the survivor, of one
"whose past reaches back [as if across an abyss] to another epoch" is
frequently assumed.[8] Alcalá Galiano writes in the nineteenth century, "Today there are very few of us left who have actually been
eyewitnesses: very few and we resemble ruins on feet, but for whom
it is not wrong whenever we can, to speak, for we are not made of
stone."[9] Jacinto Benavente y Martínez, in the twentieth: "I have a
reason and a purpose for surviving and hoping to survive for much

longer. To tell my story, as Hamlet told Horatio, keeping him from suicide. Thus will I live . . . to tell my story."[10]

Progress or Farce?

Blanco White, while portraying his life as a perpetual crisis, maintains a firm belief in his progress toward truth. His life is marked by a series of ultimately insufficient mediations that, nevertheless, in his opinion do mark a path toward perfection, identity, self-knowledge: "I am, and . . . I have always been ready to follow Truth . . . ; but . . . Truth has never manifested itself to me in such a broad stream of light as seems to be poured upon some men; . . . Truth has appeared to my mental eye like a vivid, yet small and twinkling star in a storm. . . ." (BW, I, p. 213). His detractors, as we have seen, deny any such progress; Menéndez Pelayo and Gladstone curiously use the same type of navigational metaphor: in their opinions, though, Blanco White's life was a *"nave sin piloto* (pilotless ship)" (MP, p. 174), or an example of the "utter shipwreck of faithlessness" (WEG, p. 63).

In a similar manner, there are two opposed ways of looking at the constant movement of the modern world. In 1858, the novelist Pedro Antonio de Alarcón would write to his friend Castelar: "Take a look at Paris, Emilio, and meditate for a couple of hours; then tell me if the century is moving toward perfection or rushing headlong into madness!"[11] These are the two options offered time and time again by nineteenth-century writers who wish to interpret modernity; progress toward perfection or madness. There are optimistic writers who see crisis as a necessary condition for progress; these writers often describe with enthusiasm their experience of crisis. Other writers, however, assuming a more pessimistic stance, view modernity not as a movement toward fullness but rather as a directionless wandering or madness. These authors tend to testify to the crisis of experience brought about by modernity. For a great many inhabitants of the nineteenth century, the modern world poses a clear threat to pure, authentic experience.

"Everything there is in turmoil and confusion."[12] This description of Madrid was written in 1849 by the Barón de Parlaverdades, but we could find almost identical passages in any number of nineteenth-century Spanish writers that attempt to describe their society. Antonio Flores, Mesonero Romanos, Larra, or Pérez Galdós—all these authors see their century as an "epoch of confusion";[13] their society as a "true image of the first confusion of the elements";[14] their lives as "agitated and vertiginous."[15]

Most twentieth-century analysts of modernity have attributed this heightened sense of confusion to the dissolution of the old order, the collapse of a hierarchical worldview, which was brought about by political, industrial, and philosophical revolutions. Paul de Man writes, for instance, that after Romanticism, "the hierarchical world . . . becomes a world of means moving towards an end" (de Man 1979, p. 79). For inhabitants of Spain's nineteenth century, an awareness of living immersed in a world of "moving means" does seem more acute than ever, though that world's "end" is rarely clear. Whether we look at those writers who attribute the turmoil of their world to progress, or at more pessimistic writers, who see their world as a means without end, a farce or a "*farsa mercantil*" (Parlaverdades 1849, p. 26), what is clear in both cases is that fullness or presence is always elsewhere, either temporally displaced into the future or lost forever in the past.

Horkheimer and Adorno see modernity as characterized by the "leveling domination of abstraction and industry" (1972, p. 13); Simmel speaks of money as the "frightful leveler" of modern society "that hollows out the core of things" and forces them to "rest on the same level" (1971, p. 330). Subirats, following Marx, discusses the "leveling impetus of merchandise" (1979, pp. 96–97). These images of leveling, of collapsed hierarchies are equally common in nineteenth-century texts: many writers often attribute their confusion to a similar leveling process. For them, the city street becomes a "[a] confused and helter-skelter museum" in which the most heterogeneous of elements are forced into a relation of contiguity, the contiguity of the commodity showplace, the *escaparate* (shop window): "At the foot of Christ lie a pair of pistols, or . . . in front of the virgin you can find a couple of bottles of wine. . . ."[16] All of modern society is on exhibit in this "world of display windows and shelves."[17] Mesonero Romanos's words, for example, are typical of what have come to be called "the usual complaints about the leveling of Spanish life."[18] He blames the breakdown of social classes and their conventional dress codes for flattening distinctions; one can no longer look at a person and decide who he or she is: "the leveling overcoat and the black tie had not yet confused, as they later would, all classes, all ages, all conditions."[19] Modern politics, with its relentless display of reputations and its incessant production of rhetoric and of battling interpretations is especially susceptible to this kind of leveled description: "What is the Parliament if not an exquisite display case?" writes Antonio Flores.[20]

As early as 1849, the Barón de Parlaverdades was offering the completely leveled world of Madrid's flea market, the Rastro, as the ultimate emblem of his society: "That is where our politics and our customs should be studied. . . . The flea market composes eloquent phrases: [there you can find] the crutch of a crippled man beside a North Star. . . ."[21] "Eloquent phrases"—the linguistic metaphor is very telling. For many of these authors, the sentence or the combination of words is a privileged image of the leveled, confused syntagma that is modernity. As is often the case, it is Larra who provides one of the most striking examples of this topos; in his article "Cuasi," he offers a bird's-eye view of Paris, that modern city par excellence, in which the citizens become words and the city a baffling text: "Those figures which resemble men, and that you see swarming, pushing, squeezing, wriggling, colliding, and struggling to overcome each other . . . are not really men, but words. . . . [Later] I landed back in Paris, where I found myself roaming amidst the confusion of these words dressed in *fracs* and hats. . . ."[22] The *frac*, or tailcoat, that garment blamed throughout the nineteenth century for erasing class distinctions, is likened to the modern word or text, whose meaning is ultimately indeterminate—up for grabs.

Larra's description of all of modern history is strikingly similar in its imagery; as we have seen in chapter 1, he writes in his review of Godoy's *Memorias:* "We can compare modern History to an immense mirror in a masquerade ball, where kings and subjects, the rich and poor, victims and their executioners, the tyrants and the tyrannized mingle, stir, jostle and obstruct each other, and are all mixed up in a preposterous display of loud and annoying colors, without any kind of harmony or symmetry. . . ."[23] Susan Kirkpatrick (1977) has noticed how many of Larra's insights seem to announce the problems

that are later taken up by the realist novel in Spain; indeed, Mikhail
Bakhtin's characterization of the novel as a space of carnivalization,
of leveling—"people who are separated by impenetrable hierarchical barriers enter into free, familiar contact" (Bakhtin 1983,
p. 123)—would seem to make this genre (antigenre?) especially
appropriate for representing the world described by Larra. And
while some writers and many autobiographers do little but repeat
"the usual complaints," others, Pérez Galdós in particular, make
great use of this modern confusion.

For Pérez Galdós, arguably Spain's most important nineteenth-
century novelist, "the same evolutionary confusion which we witness in society" constitutes "the raw material of the art of the
novel."[24] Confusion, leveling, the disappearance of national and
class distinctions, of authority; all these things are advantages,
rather than handicaps, for the novelist: "But do not think that from
what has so far been exposed I will try to come up with a pessimistic
deduction, asserting that this social decomposition must bring
forth days of anemia and death for narrative art. [On the con-
trary] . . . the lack of unifying principles favors the flourishing of
literature."[25] The unity that has been lost—a unity between appearance and being, sign and meaning—is a unity supported by
faith in God (see Fernández-Cifuentes 1988). Pérez Galdós seemed
to realize that the novel is the epic of a godless world: "We indefati-
gable travelers trusted, no doubt, that a supernatural voice would
speak to us from above and say: this is the one and only way. But the
supernatural voice no longer reaches our ears and even the wisest
among us entangle themselves in endless controversies."[26] After the
abandonment or the death of God, "one is doomed, in Said's
vocabulary, to repetitive representational beginnings rather than
absolute origins" (Donato 1979, p. 40). The loss of unity and of
origin is responsible not only for the flourishing of novels like those
of Pérez Galdós, but also for a proliferation of discourse—endless
controversies—of all sorts. Larra had written many years earlier,
"On one side, voices with a certain version, on the other, voices
with the opposite version: a multitude of pamphlets and memoirs,
alleged materials for History, . . . [which] in fact [are] nothing but
sewage flowing into a river and mixing with the water, though not
without first polluting it and hindering its course."[27] "*La intriga*

comienza cuando aparta Dios su mano"—that is, "Intrigue starts up when God withdraws his intervening hand" (MG, I, p. 234); the words appear in Godoy's *Memorias,* and, as we have seen in chapter 1, one of the principal characteristics of this *intriga* is the proliferation of discourse. Of course Adam Smith's equally providential invisible hand was supposed to have appeared to guide this free market of discourse toward truth, though it too seems nowhere to be found. In this godforsaken, leveled world, a true account (the autobiographical one) is forced merely to take its place alongside the countless false versions in the *rastro del discurso* (the flea market of discourse), with no unequivocal distinguishing feature to guarantee that its authority will be recognized. A consummate, polyphonic novelist like Pérez Galdós documents, exposes, and exploits this situation to no end; the Spanish autobiographer typically resists or laments it.

Modernity is characterized by a proliferation of media—everything is a medium, everything a sign. Now; from Babylon forward, the city has been represented as the degraded space of unending, nonreferential discourse. In the sixteenth century Antonio de Guevara laments that "in the city everyone thinks he is a bishop to anoint and a priest to baptize and change names. . . ."[28] In the nineteenth century, Antonio Flores complains of the "shouts of street vendors. . . . This has become a true Babylon."[29] He goes on to note the irrelevance of origins in the city's place-names: "The Puerta del Sol [a central crossroads in Madrid] is not even a *puerta,* a door. But who cares anymore about etymologies, or noble ancestry, or historical traditions today, when by the time night has arrived anything born that same morning has already been declared old and outdated?"[30] The city, the scene of the modern novel—the space resisted by certain autobiographers—is the place in which everything is leveled, flattened. Everything is brought down to the level of a signifier; there is no pure signified, no origin to be found; there is nothing outside the text of the city.

Clearly, this poses a threat to pure experience because pure experience is conventionally defined as a subject's unmediated encounter with a signified. Not only is the modern subject run through with signification—Alonso Quijano, Emma Bovary, Isidora Rufete, Ana Ozores—but so is everything out there. Everything is a sign of something else, and something else is always elsewhere. Even people, like words, are equivocal, mobile signs in need of interpretation. Apparently solid, monumental things, like streets, buildings, and products are all provisional, soon to be obsolete. This chaos is the plight of men and women living in a world whose supposedly stable, immanent meaning has been replaced by a world order with a vested interest in crisis. It is the plight recorded, exemplified, and, more often than not, lamented in Spain's nineteenth-century autobiographical writing. The politicians I discussed in chapter 1, for example, try to resist this plight by means of a strategy of invocation: they apostrophize an authority above and beyond the leveled here and now. Others, like Zorrilla, Palacio Valdés, and, to a certain extent, Mesonero Romanos, deploy what we might call a strategy of evocation: they reminisce or fantasize about other moments, other places in which things had meaning.

Mesonero Romanos 1

Spain's fall into history, into modernity, would be impossible to date: it is announced throughout the centuries. Modernity, of course, is invariably contrasted with the timeless time of the good old days, and, as Raymond Williams has illustrated in the case of England, we could push these good old days all the way back to Eden, that calm before the storm of history (1973, pp. 9–12). In the sixteenth century Antonio de Guevara complains of the "horses that trample you . . . noises that scare you" and the "great confusion of business" of the city.[31] In the seventeenth century, Cervantes has don Quijote contrast the *tiempos ruines* (vile times) of his "now" with a golden age somewhere in the past. Torres Villarroel in the eighteenth century complains to Quevedo: "Deceased friend, what you are bound to see in this century is the progress of vice and foolishness. . . . No century has been more overrun by deception: because, you see, we are drowning in tailors, being flooded by shoemakers, there is a plague of men of letters and swarms of agents, scribes and *relatores*."[32] Once again, by the way, we see the contemporary moment characterized by a dangerous proliferation of words: several professional manufacturers of discourse figure prominently in this plaintive list. But it is in the nineteenth century and throughout the twentieth that representations and criticisms of modernity, of the city, abound more than ever. Chronicling modernity becomes one of the principal missions of the writer in these centuries. The constant movement of modernity comes to replace the movement of transgression or travel. In other words, whereas sins or voyages— personal movements—used to legitimate autobiographical texts, now a writer can experience tremendous difference while standing still (and growing old): "We should forgive the old for reminiscing about their good or bad times, just as we forgive the poor wretches who tell about their misfortunes."[33]

Conventional descriptions often locate the origin of modernity in France—more concretely, in the French Revolution. Alcalá Galiano sees fit to remind his reader that his birth coincided with the French Revolution, "in the exact month and year in which the world underwent its most important and grave transformation ever."[34] Clearly, if modernity is a product of the French Revolution, it might be exported to Spain with the arrival of Napoleon's soldiers in 1808.[35] Sure enough, Mesonero Romanos, in his *Memorias de un setentón,* has his figurative birth—his first memory—coincide with Spain's new beginning, the days leading up to the invasion:

> the first impression on my childhood imagination was also the cover, the prospectus, let us say, of the book of our contemporary history. I mean the nineteenth of March of 1808. A memorable date on which the bonds and traditions that united one generation to the other were broken, the ancient foundations of old Spanish society fell apart, and the nation was launched into a new, agitated, vertiginous life.[36]

The opening of Mesonero's *Memorias* is exemplary: this new beginning comes to intrude on the tranquility and the routine of a sacred, domestic scene, directed by the clearest of authorities, the paterfamilias. The family's nightly recitation of the holy rosary is violently interrupted by the shouts of a street throng, "Long live the king!"[37] Politics and history violate domesticity and routine; interrupting the circularity of the old days, modernity or modern political history snaps the string of the rosary and irretrievably scatters the beads. . . .

Once set in motion, this process cannot be stopped; the devastating march of modernity does not end with the withdrawal of Napoleon's troops: like original sin, it is inherited: "The foreign war was over: but at the same time a more gut-wrenching and obstinate war had been taking shape and was now emerging among the Spaniards themselves; a fatal struggle between the past and the future which is still going on; one that we inherited from our parents, and will transmit to our own children and grandchildren."[38] This new legacy is conflict, a "fatal struggle" that dissolves the traditional unities of the old time; it destroys and turns into ruins. In fact, Mesonero Romanos claims that the principal activity of the French invasion was the creation of ruins: "[their] government was incapable of doing anything but scheming improvement plans, lamentably transforming spaces into ruins, whenever they deemed it convenient to carry out their projects."[39]

After the withdrawal of the French, Mesonero Romanos visits his father's possessions near Salamanca: "Upon seeing them, my good father, his face bathed in tears and his voice drowned by the most profound sorrow, had us . . . climb those dangerous ruins, indicating the location and the remains of the monumental buildings which they represented. 'Here, he would tell us . . . lay the magnificent monastery of San Vicente; here that of San Cayetano . . . and through here used to run the streets of Larga, de los Angeles, de Santa Ana . . . and others which had completely disappeared.'"[40] Mesonero Romanos sees his inheritance transformed into a cemetery, a field fertile with death: "We walked around those famous but modest properties, finding them barren though they were sown with bones and skeletons of men and horses. . . . It was an immense cemetery. . . ."[41] Mesonero Romanos, throughout his *Memorias*—indeed, throughout his career as a writer—will more or less step into the shoes of his father, describing ruins, making a living by recording "the dialectics between what is and what was."[42]

Mesonero Romanos 2

As we have repeatedly seen, the parable of the Prodigal Son provides a paradigm for many autobiographies, beginning with Augustine.

The structure of these texts is simple and symmetrical—home, wandering, home—and the wandering is what gets narrated. (What would the Prodigal Son's older brother's life story be like? Would it be worth narrating? Could it become an autobiography?) Nevertheless, there are many texts that do not follow this model with its neat closure and return home. In book 1 of the *Confessions,* Rousseau offers an emblem of his open-ended life and his permanent homelessness: "In Geneva, gate closed, drawbridge pulled high, he sees in this event a turning point for his entire life. He could assign such meaning to the event only years later when the haunting feeling had taken hold of his awareness that he was destined to be the man who had lost his home and had never been permitted to find one" (Weintraub, 1975, p. 826). We might put forth another myth whose structure reflects the one we find in these texts: the myth of the Wandering Jew.

As the legend goes, when Christ was bearing his cross toward Calvary, he passed the house of a certain Jew, Ahasverus. He asks the Jew whether he might rest in his doorway; Ahasverus refuses, and, in some versions, he slaps Christ in the face. Christ looks at him and says, "You deny me rest, though I go unto my eternal resting place; you, however, shall never rest until I come again." From that moment on, the Wandering Jew is both unable to return home and unable to die. Throughout the centuries he will reportedly appear and reappear as he wanders around the world. The figure became enormously popular during the period of Romanticism and is explicitly evoked by many autobiographers, among them Zorrilla. For some, the wandering of Ahasverus even becomes an explicit image of the modern writer's losing battle with closure: "I write, write, write as the Wandering Jew walks, walks, walks" (Mme. Blavatsky, quoted in Hartman 1970, p. 51). Faust, with his open-ended quest for knowledge is one emblem of modernity; the Wandering Jew, another, though the two have often been conflated: "Their experience is the constant deferment of the unfulfilled goal. . . ."; the perpetual postponement of Presence.[43]

The figure of the Wandering Jew is especially appropriate for my purposes because it has lent itself to two interpretations that roughly correspond to the two stances toward modernity I wish to explore in this chapter. For many nineteenth-century writers, the homeless-

ness and the unending, pointless, progressless wandering of Ahasverus become an emblem of the human condition: "never nearer to
the goal" in the words of Wordsworth.[44] For others, though, the
Wandering Jew becomes, on the contrary, a witness to progress. He
witnessed the crucifixion of Christ—the beginning of new time—
and all human history from that point forward. In fact, he becomes
an important model for the historian in the nineteenth century:
Subirats argues that the figure of the wanderer can be related to some
of the fundamental premises of the bourgeois philosophy of history,
such as the notion of *perfectibilité continue* and the continuity of progress.[45] For some, Ahasverus witnesses time as it progresses toward
fullness, toward the second coming; he is the ultimate historian.

One of Ahasverus's outstanding characteristics is his age, which
makes of him a unique witness. The posture of the old man/unique
witness is frequently assumed by the autobiographer/chronicler of
modernity; the claim to authority based on age is often announced in
titles: *Recuerdos de un anciano* (Alcalá Galiano), *Recuerdos del tiempo
viejo* (Zorrilla), *Recuerdos de mi larga vida* (Conrado Roure), or the
Memorias de un setentón (Mesonero Romanos). In the twentieth century, González Ruano will speak of "that deferred death, postponed
yet again."[46] Roure interrupts his "octogenarian's retirement" in
order to "narrate all that I have seen in Barcelona."[47] Mesonero
Romanos, in his first *escenas costumbristas,* goes as far as to portray
himself as an old man, even though he was quite young when he
wrote them. And throughout the *Memorias* he is constantly remind-
ing the reader of his age and, consequently, of his power as eyewitness *(testigo presencial)* (MR, pp. 24, 26, et al.). "His already rusty pen
can only offer today the prosaic and candid narration of certain and
positive facts, with photographical portraits of real men which he
had the opportunity to observe throughout his long, contemplative
life . . . and we should remark that this is all narrated by an impartial
witness of that epoch, practically on the verge of the grave."[48]
Mesonero Romanos is a witness to change, to movement; his *Memorias* attempt to reflect "the historical march of our society," "the
material progress of the capital," and "the civilizing march of the
century."[49]

Movement, though, is not necessarily progress; there is a negative movement as well, a fall away from fullness, which Mesonero

Romanos is also obliged to record: "The march of civilization and culture, be it progressive or retrograde, is what I proposed to reflect in these Memoirs."[50] In any event, it is clear that movement, *la marcha*, is what gets narrated, and Mesonero Romanos assumes the responsibility of distinguishing the good movement from the bad.

Progress, the good kind of movement, has a price: although modernization, with its new divisions of labor, produces new occupations and types of people to be described—*tipos hallados* (found types)—it also makes obsolete another set of types—*tipos perdidos* (lost types).[51] "The ashes of this type, recently buried by the municipal government's latest law, are still smoking."[52] These ashes, ruins, or remains are privileged objects of representation for Mesonero Romanos, and for the autobiographer-witness of modernity in general. "And in the meantime, may God bless you and may He take us in His hand so that the objects that we are to examine do not fly out of our hands," quips Antonio Flores in *Ayer, hoy y mañana*.[53] These authors' objects of description are constantly in danger of disappearing: González Ruano calls himself "a melancholy expert on things that are in the process of becoming extinct."[54]

One gesture typical of this kind of autobiography is to rescue orality from oblivion. Many autobiographers, like Mesonero Romanos, take pains to transcribe songs sung to them as children.[55] Another related gesture is to recall friends who have passed away. Blanco White added notes to his narrative like the following: "He is one of my friends whom death has carried off since I began to write these memoirs" (BW, I, p. 217n). This type of annotation, rather incidental in Blanco White, is found in nearly every description Mesonero Romanos offers. When he gives a list of participants in a project, he writes some of the names in italics and explains in a note: "The italicized names correspond to those who have passed away." "Out of the 295 names that appear [in another list], only 12 of us are still alive."[56] This awareness of a before and after is especially evident in Mesonero Romanos's descriptions of urban space. Time after time, parenthetical statements are appended to descriptions of old Madrid in order to explain that the building or street in question no longer exists.[57] The remarks are repeated so often that the reader is left with the feeling that some cataclysmic event has taken place between the autobiographer's "now" and the past he is

describing—a flood, a devastating catastrophe, or simply, the onslaught of modernity.

It is neither surprising nor especially interesting that changing topography is frequently recorded in Spanish autobiographies.
What is interesting, however, is the attention often paid to changing toponymy. Any recent visitor to Spain has experienced the
confusion brought about by the restoration of traditional names to
the streets and plazas, the towns and counties that had been "patri-
otically" renamed or "Castilianized" under Franco. This kind of
name changing has gone on in Spain for years, and it is frequently
recorded in literature. At times, the writer's attitude toward changing place names is one of relative indifference: Conrado Roure, for
example, simply mentions, "Later the names of many streets and
plazas [were] changed."[58] For others, though, the changing of toponyms indicates an uncertainty about origins, or a fall away from
authenticity. Cecilia Boehl de Faber, for instance, in her 1849 reac-
tionary novel *La gaviota* uses changing toponyms to represent the
introduction of liberalism and political modernity in Spain as a kind
of grotesque transplantation of foreign ideas in Spanish soil (Boehl
de Faber 1977). She has don Perfecto Cívico, the ridiculous liberal
mayor of her fictional town, change the name of the venerable—and
signless—"Plaza de la iglesia" (Church Square) to "Plaza de la Con-
stitución" (Constitution Place), and a hastily composed, improvised
sign, complete with a misspelling, is painted on a wall. In many
autobiographies as well, name changing is regarded as an intrusion
of politics on the natural relationship between words and things,
place-names and places. Ruiz Contreras, for instance, complains:
"Not even the streets can live in peace with this City Government!
Now they have decided to take the name of A away so as to baptize it
with that of R . . . Ch . . . , a deceased politician."[59] Jacinto
Benavente y Martínez, writing his *Recuerdos y olvidos* in the midst of
the Civil War, will consistently and despairingly hesitate before
naming a place: "Today, who knows how that street might be called
today?"[60] As Pedro Agustín Girón would have it, "Political parties
cannot even agree on the names of things."[61]

Mesonero Romanos has frequently been called *el autor de Madrid*
(the author from/of Madrid), in reference to the fact that he was an
early cultivator, if not an inventor, of *madrileñismo*. We might take

this expression in a different way though, and propose that Mesonero Romanos not only writes of, and from Madrid, but also writes Madrid, he is its author. He does this in at least two different ways. First, in his autobiography, he makes Madrid the protagonist of a text; several readers have noticed this: "These are Memoirs in which Madrid finds itself." "His biography ends up being nothing but a piece of the great biography of the city. To talk about Mesonero, to write about Mesonero, is to talk and write about Madrid."[62] Second, as an urban planner, we see Mesonero Romanos throughout his *Memorias* proposing improvements, demolitions, and changes of names—those same things for which he criticizes the French invaders: "I also insisted on the complete reform of house numbering . . . adopting the system of even numbers on the right and odd on the left. . . . [I insisted on] the placement of new, clear and consistent signs, with the corresponding name at the beginning and end of each street. I proposed to change many names which were duplicated or triplicated, most of them ridiculous and even obscene, and substitute them with those of historical events and eminent men of the nation."[63] But what exactly is it that gives Mesonero Romanos the right or the authority to name Madrid, to write Madrid's autobiography? What gives him the right to change things—to level buildings and rename streets, for example—in an authentic way?

Certain ingenuous readers might consider Spain's principal *costumbrista* texts to be unproblematically mimetic or referential: verbal snapshots of a nation in flux. Nonetheless, it could be argued that *costumbrismo's* handling or presentation of fragments was a considerable factor in the articulation or fabrication of Spain's modern national identity. In her article "The Ideology of Costumbrismo," for example, Susan Kirkpatrick (1978) demonstrates how *costumbrismo* in general, and Mesonero Romanos in particular, through the choice, framing, and presentation of material, played an important role in the establishment of the following formula: the Spanish Nation = Madrid = the middle class. And as we have seen, one of Mesonero Romanos's principal autobiographical strategies is to link his personal history with the collective history of Madrid and, by extension, of Spain. His birth coincides with the birth of a new Spain. He tells us of his father's death—his own coming of age—in terms of the "notable coincidence" between his "entrance into life" and "the inauguration of a new epoch in the historical march of our society."[64] Madrid eventually becomes the protagonist of the *Memorias;* Mesonero Romanos sees fit to replace the words "I witnessed" with the words "Madrid witnessed." The autobiographer becomes the eyes and the voice of the city; moreover, the city becomes a person. Indeed, Madrid shares many characteristics with the protagonist of a novel, or perhaps better yet, of an epic. More particularly, Madrid and Spain come to be portrayed as a being whose natural, organic growth is hindered by a number of obstacles. The real Madrid, the true Spain, the one destined to fulfill itself in History is, from time to time, obstructed or incarcerated.[65]

If Madrid or Spain is an organic entity independent from politics, which is occasionally imprisoned by forces of reaction or revolution,—excess, in either case—Mesonero Romanos is the most appropriate person through which Madrid and Spain might speak. For, in the end, what seems to give Mesonero Romanos the right to name Madrid, to tell Madrid's story, to write its autobiography, is his independence, his truancy from the school of the world, politics:

> What significant interest can be inspired by the recollections of a man who, according to his own confession, has not in the least figured in the historical or political map of the nation, who has not lived what is usually called a public life; who has not participated in intrigues or in revolutionary conspiracies? . . . Hold it right there, dear sirs, the author will reply, everything you say is true, but it is also true that his political insignificance, combined with the independence of his position and character, offer him a greater gift of impartiality, and at the same time allow him to consider political events solely from their outside appearance and effect.[66]

In that most pervasive move of bourgeois ideology, Mesonero Romanos systematically attempts to naturalize his perspective by belittling or effacing himself as an interested and desiring subject. He claims to have no interests, no desires: "I am, in the end, independent . . . without commitments to anyone and without even desires of my own . . . I was nothing, I am nothing."[67]

Throughout the *Memorias,* Mesonero Romanos promises time and time again not to invade the limits of history, though he never quite manages to keep his promise. On the first page of his introduction he announces that his intention is not to write history (MR, p. 23), but some three hundred pages later he is still promising to bid "*adiós a la historia*," "penetrating (perhaps for the last time in these memoirs) into the domains of history [in order to] record some singular political '*peripecias*' or plights. . . ."[68]

Mesonero Romanos makes it clear that he would rather not narrate these *peripecias;* each incursion into history or politics is introduced by a distancing expression: "I return, not without repugnance, to the narration of the political events of that year."[69] This history, these *sucesos* or *peripecias* are produced by interested parties, covetous invaders, greedy politicians. For Mesonero Romanos, premodern life, the life of his father, that is, allowed one to lead a "tranquil and benign life, uninterrupted by political agitations or the peripeteias of history."[70] "Peripeteia" means "a fall" in Greek, and in fact, to take part in a certain history or politics is, for Mesonero Romanos, to fall; it is essentially negative: "Homage should be paid to the [Spanish] people, whose common sense, enlightenment and culture have managed to resist the terrible trials of three civil wars, without irrigating their countryside with the blood of their children, and without adding a single page to our lugubrious contemporary history (*nuestra lúgubre historia contemporánea*)."[71] We might notice the position of the adjective "*lúgubre*"; placed before "*historia*," it denotes essence rather than distinction: it is as if there were no other history. To this *lúgubre historia*—son's blood is to the battlefield as the historian's ink is to the page—Mesonero Romanos opposes a natural life, which is simply "fostered" and "administered" (MR, p. 386) by *independientes*. This natural life is characterized by expressions such as "the nation's businesses and its most natural activities . . ." and "the vitality proper to all modern nations."[72]

Here are the two kinds of movement that Mesonero Romanos chronicles: there is the negative movement of the *lúgubre historia* that tends to hinder or undo "*el progreso verdadero*" (MR, p. 396) or true progress, and that leads to farce; this negative movement is opposed to progress, the natural course of civilization and culture. The first is portrayed as a product of ambition, effort, politics; the second— which Mesonero Romanos consistently equates with the habits, interests, and aspirations of Madrid's middle class—is characterized as an original and natural progression toward fullness. Mesonero

Romanos, the exemplary independent, and moderate bourgeois, ordains himself as the observer capable of distinguishing between the two. It is this power of distinction, moreover, that allows Mesonero Romanos to write the autobiography of a nation.

The Family versus the City

"Now the city of man was first founded by a fratricide who was moved by envy to kill his brother. . . . 'With brother's blood the earliest walls were wet'" (Augustine 1958, p. 328). Augustine invokes these words of Lucan in order to remind us that Cain and Romulus, the paradigmatic founders of cities, were both fratricides. The remark is a clear example of a tendency, that has lasted throughout the centuries, which opposes a myth of the city to a myth of the family. This opposition becomes extraordinarily important in the nineteenth century. In fact, one could argue that this opposition structures the plots of a good many nineteenth-century novels. It is also a recurring opposition in autobiographies of that time. We have already seen how Mesonero Romanos represents modernity as something that violently interrupts domestic routine and introduces a fatal conflict between generations or between brothers.

The city, the polis, gives rise to politics, and according to a certain worldview, politics is the antifamiliar activity par excellence; it is the space of envy, ambition, greed, and artificial alliances. Curiously enough, there are several recent studies (Benjamin, Sennet, e.g.) that argue that it is precisely modernization, the boom of the city, that produces the private family as we know it today, and its sacred realm, that invention we call home. Nevertheless, throughout the nineteenth century, the sacred and united family is often evoked nostalgically as the origin, the timeless, natural state, whose existence is threatened by the new order of modernity.

When Ortega y Gasset analyzes the origins of the modern novel (of modern life?), he comments with a certain nostalgia, a certain homesickness:

The organism, which seemed to be an independent unit, capable of acting on its own, is inserted in the physical environment, like a figure in a tapestry. . . . There is no freedom, no originality. To live means to adapt: to adapt means to let the material surroundings penetrate within us and *evict or dislodge (desalojar)* us from ourselves. Adaptation is submission and renunciation. Darwin sweeps heroes off the face of the earth.[73]

I emphasize the word *"desalojar"* (to dislodge or evict); according to this view, to live in the modern world means to no longer be at home with ourselves, it means to abandon the world of being in order to enter the world of becoming, of doing: the city—to abandon un-mediated experience and to enter into representation. The epic hero—an object of nostalgia for many—*is* at the beginning just as he *is* in the end. Not so with the hero of the novel, although frequently, most clearly perhaps in the Quijote, the conflict of the novel seems to be a conflict of genres: the hero tries to reaffirm being and meaning in a world of becoming and signification, "epicness" in a novelistic world, virtue in the city.

In order to illustrate this move from the epic hero, "in whom the hammer of events shatters nothing and forges nothing" to the novel-istic hero (Bakhtin 1983, p. 107), permeated by his environment, forced to adapt, Ortega y Gasset evokes Darwin. And Darwin's thought, as many authors have argued, is at root, antiessentialist: he puts forth a kind of metonymizing of the world, a carnivalization of the natural order. The hierarchies of natural being are dissolved, and the world becomes a chain of constant adaptation, function, compe-tition, work. As one recent author has said, after Darwin, "living beings are always in process of transformation, and you can't go home again" (Levine 1986, p. 61). But we do not have to quote our contemporaries to illustrate this. Several nineteenth-century auto-biographers recognized the opposition. For Mesonero Romanos, "the bold aspirations of power, the frenzy of leadership and the contempt for authority" are clearly threats to "the sacred bonds of birth, family and property."[74] Julio Nombela writes in his memoirs: "Politics has no heart [*entrañas*]: it is selfish and greedy; it readily disguises iniquities as pseudo-patriotic sacrifices, and subordinates everything to the achievement of its ambitions. *Qua nominor leo* is its moral and slogan, and anticipating Darwin . . . it has made in the past, makes now, and will always make conventional superiority

into the weapon used to destroy inferior enemies. . . . I had frequently heard about politics, but I never realized what it meant in
the life of nations [and] . . . of families.[75] Or José Zorrilla: "Oh,
damned, antisocial and antichristian politics, whose ghost can di-
vide parents from their children . . ."[76]

Modernity and its quintessential activities—politics and business—dissolve unity; natural family ties are replaced by ambitious
societies of self-made men, essence by function, the old aristocracy
of blood by the new aristocracy of money. If modernity is characterized by a leveling of the old aristocracy, it is also characterized by a
shift from being to doing: "[The] center [of the aristocracy's basic
ethos] is in the being of the subject, whose value, like the value of
everything that arises directly from him is determined by the *terminus a quo*. However, labor is action that is eminently a means, that
is oriented towards something external, that is determined by the
terminus ad quem. It is on this point that Schiller distinguishes
between low natures, who pay with what they do, and noble natures, who pay with what they are" (Simmel 1971, p. 210). Antonio
Flores, with his characteristic insight and wit, describes the dichotomy in remarkably similar terms: "We would be in quite a fix if we
had to spend time trying to discover why things are the way they
are, these days when everyone is granted a title of what they ought to
be, simply by hiding any and all evidence of what they were, and by
presenting testimony of what they are currently doing."[77] Autobiography often records the shift from one nature to the other, or
rather, the tension between the two natures, between being and
doing.

This tension can be seen clearly if we look at the problematic role
played by the family and genealogy in the genre. Modern autobiography is supposed to have been born with the fall of the ancien
régime and with the rise of the ethos of the self-made man; yet many
autobiographers are profoundly interested in their lineage, their
genetic past. This contradiction can produce some surprising results: Blanco White, for example, whose autobiography narrates
one of the genre's most radical rejections of biological-cultural inheritance, wished to include a family tree in his memoirs. It is as if
there were a kind of unresolved ontological tension in these texts: is
my autobiography the story of who I am (my heritage, my geneal-

ogy, my blood) or is it rather the story of what I have made myself (my actions, my achievements, my curriculum vitae)? For some, modernity, liberalism or democracy even threatens familial or genealogical identity. Alcalá Galiano, for instance, writes in the nineteenth century: "When I speak of myself, I must say something about my family. This is not common nowadays, at least not in Spain, where democratic ideas predominate."[78] José Moreno Villa repeats the same hesitation in the twentieth century: "I spend time speaking about the family tree because my mother would remind me of it whenever I would put forth liberal and democratic ideas, rather dissonant in that domestic environment."[79]

This opposition—family and home versus politics and city— could be inscribed within the larger opposition we have already seen in a number of manifestations: on one side, essence, presence, being, nature, the family, and the home; on the other, functionality, representation, signification, artifice, politics, and the city. In *The Fall of Public Man,* Richard Sennet traces the development of this opposition—"the private and natural, on the one hand, and the public and conventional, on the other" (Sennet 1978, p. 73)— throughout the eighteenth and nineteenth centuries. We might recall also that throughout the nineteenth century, the home came to be defined as a kind of haven, a space of identity, of simple presences, in opposition to the ever-changing world of use, the world of work, ambition, and adaptation. Autobiography, or the need to write autobiographically, is invariably aligned with the negative side of this equation—with homelessness, the city, the impersonal, unfamiliar institutions of socialization, and, more concretely, the institution of writing.

José Zorrilla, Poetry versus Politics

When the curtain goes up on to the set of Zorrilla's *Don Juan Tenorio,* the spectator immediately enters the leveled world of carnival: "Don Juan, wearing a mask, sits at a table writing. . . . When the curtain rises, people in masks, students and townspeople are seen passing by. . . ."[80] The setting is appropriate; in fact, don Juan, "the first hero of modernity" (Serres 1982, p. 3), seems quite at home in this

world of carnival. We might even say that carnival, the carnivalesque, is his modus vivendi: When he boasts of his amorous and
bellicose exploits, he tells us that he would often resort to disguises.[81] Moreover, his entire life, like carnival, knows no boundaries, respects no hierarchies: "My love has spanned the whole of our
social scale . . . ; From the haughty princess to the wench who fishes
in a miserable boat . . . ; I descended to humble cabins, I rose to
palaces, I climbed the walls of cloisters and everywhere I left a bitter
memory of myself, I recognized the sacredness of nothing and my
audacity respected not a single place or occasion. Nor have I both-
ered to distinguish between the religious and the secular."[82]

Not quite as comfortable in this world are the two fathers who
make their appearance in this opening scene: don Gonzalo, and don
Diego, the father of don Juan.[83] These men are acutely aware of
social status, of those hierarchies violated by both don Juan and the
carnivalesque:

> *Gonzalo:* That a man like me should have to wait here, and put up
> with such a role! Oh well, I care for the tranquility of my home, and
> the good fortune of my pure and simple daughter.
> *Diego:* That a man of my lineage should descend to such a foul
> mansion. But there is no humiliation to which a father would not
> subject himself for the benefit of his son.[84]

It could be argued that the entire drama is centered on a conflict
between these two worldviews: fathers versus sons, a hierarchical
world versus a carnivalized world; a providential world ruled by a
divine hand versus a world abandoned by God, by truth, which has
become an arena for pleasure and adventure. As the father don Diego
leaves the scene, he reminds his son: "Farewell, then; but do not
forget that there is a God of justice."[85]

At first sight, a similar battle is waged on the pages of Zorrilla's
autobiography, *Recuerdos del tiempo viejo*. In this text, Zorrilla constantly harps on the irreconcilable differences between son and father: "My father was the last unbroken link in the broken chain of
the Royalist epoch, the living epitome, the personified memory of
formulaic absolutism, the good, syllogism-spewing student of the
old-fashioned Universities, doctor of both laws from the University
of Valladolid; convinced from his childhood that only the study of

law, theology, and the canons could produce men. . . . I was the first and weak link of the new literary epoch, the mad breaker of tradition and classical rules."[86] Not only was Zorrilla's father a lawyer, he was also the highest representative of the law, the superintendent of police, under Fernando VII. In the *Recuerdos* we see how he intended to make a man of Zorrilla by sending him to law school. The son, though, had other plans—plans that more or less follow the conventional design of the bohemian: "[The] young provincial sent . . . by his father to study procedural law and good manners, . . . after some time in the big city, renounces his career and finds himself both penniless and intellectually emancipated" (Graña 1964, p. 29). The son's decision to abandon law school coincides completely with his decision to *"fugarse del paterno hogar en brazos de su locura* (run away from the paternal home and into the arms of his madness)" (RTV, I, p. 228) and with his need to elude the long arm of the law. Zorrilla announces that he will not continue in school, and immediately "I was placed in a wagon that was headed for [my father's house in Lerma but] taking advantage of the driver's momentary distraction, I leapt on to a mare, which was not mine and was grazing around there, and I returned to Valladolid . . . along a different road."[87] After this escape, Zorrilla flees to Madrid and is forced to don a series of don Juan–esque disguises—passing himself off as the son of an Italian artist or dressing as a gypsy.[88]

Zorrilla develops his whole life story around this tension with authority, his father, and the law. "Woe to him whose first crime is a rebellion against paternal authority! [God] does not allow [his] conscience to have a moment's rest."[89] Almost every episode in these extensive *Recuerdos* is presented in terms of an irreducible opposition: between the man and the poet (RTV, I, p. 6), between "sacred duties" and "mad desires" (RTV, I, p. 27), between *"la voz de mi conciencia* (the voice of my conscience)" and *"la {voz} de mi desatinada locura* (the [voice] of my wayward madness)" (RTV, I, p. 27).

Desatino (waywardness) is a word Zorrilla frequently uses in reference to his character don Juan: *"como dice mi desatinado don Juan Tenorio* (as my wayward don Juan Tenorio says)" (RTVK, II, p. 175).[90] Zorrilla ends his version of don Juan, however, with a correction of this waywardness, with a *tino* (a hitting of the mark); there is a resolution of the tension between worldviews; knowledge, truth, and justice triumph over *libertinaje,* adventure, and pleasure; in other words, the fathers win. Zorrilla's Tenorio realizes the auto-biographer's dream—he witnesses his own death—and is allowed to hear that divine voice, to see that divine hand, which reestablishes order, meaning, truth: "so there is after all another life and another world besides this one."[91] If don Juan is the "first hero of modernity" because of the open-endedness of his quest, Zorrilla cancels the modernity of the myth with this final apotheosis, repentance, and salvation of the character.

José Luis Martín, in his prologue to the *Recuerdos del tiempo viejo* compares don Juan's postmortem conversion scene with Zorrilla's autobiographical project: "That is why, in the end, when in the 'Recuerdos' he turns back his gaze to lament his days, he wants to save them with the same weapons with which his don Juan was redeemed: the strength and courage of a noble and sincere heart."[92] This is an oversimplification, though; in fact, no final resolution takes place in the *Recuerdos;* there is no unequivocal repentance, no ultimate redemption. Instead, what we have is a constant wavering: Zorrilla alternately refers to the events of his life as "*mis viejos pecados* (my old sins)" (RTV, I, p. 5) or "*aquel buen tiempo viejo* (the good old days)" (RTV, I, p. 27); to write his autobiography means to "*saborear los recuerdos* (relish the memories)" (RTV, II, p. 112) as well as to "*llorar sobre {mis} días* (lament [my] days)" (RTV, I, p. viii); his text is both an account of his "*desatinos personales*" and a "return, following faint traces, down youth's flowery path . . ."[93]

Perhaps no scene better captures this irreducible tension, this constant wavering, than the one Zorrilla chooses as the matrix of his life story. As in the don Juan, this primal scene takes place in a cemetery. Zorrilla describes his now-legendary participation in the burial ceremonies of Mariano José de Larra. Larra's suicide in 1836 dealt a great blow to Spain's literary community, and some of the nation's most important intellectual figures gathered at the funeral. This gathering was the context of Zorrilla's poetic debut; there, at the foot of Larra's grave, he read a poem he had composed to honor the deceased author. Years later, when an editor invites Zorrilla to describe "what happened in the cemetery," this reminiscence serves as the catalyst, or as the matrix of the three volumes of the *Recuerdos del tiempo viejo.*[94]

While don Juan's experience in the cemetery results in a restoration of unity, this first memory, a birth in the space of death—
"*nací . . . al borde de la tumba . . .* (I was born on the edge of a grave)"
(RTV, I, p. 35)—is characterized by that same doubleness or lack of unity that will be sustained throughout the *Recuerdos*. On the one hand, Zorrilla is blessed with the opportunity to read his verses before such a distinguished audience; with this reading, he is born into the world of letters, the world of poetry: "As I read those rather sketchy verses of mine, I could read on the absorbed faces of those surrounding me, the amazement that my presence there and my voice was producing in them. I imagined that God had provided that strange setting for me, that audience which seemed to be in unison with my every word, and on such a suitable and exceptional occasion."[95] At the same time, though, this opportunity is a curse. Zorrilla's entrance into the world of poetry coincides with or, rather, brings about his irreversible separation from his father, a death of sorts—"as if God had taken away from him by natural death the son who for all civil matters died when he abandoned the paternal home."[96] "It was written, as the Arabs say, that the miserable genius which God bestowed on me was to serve me no other purpose than my own doom; my verses were cursed by my father."[97] This curse seems to be part of Zorrilla's destiny; in light of this destiny, his tendency at age twelve to write verses instead of attending to more serious studies (RTV, I, p. 23) comes to represent a miniature version of this more definitive entrance into the world of poetry, this "rebellion against paternal authority" (RTV, I, p. 36).

Writing, then—a career in writing—is both a blessing and a curse: it allows Zorrilla to fulfill his destiny at the same time that it separates him from his father and his home. It is, in other words, both a *destino* and a *desatino*. This doubleness helps explain the apparent superimposition of autobiographical models and the thorough, relentless ambivalence of the *Recuerdos*. At the moment when he sits down to write, is Zorrilla the cursed Wandering Jew or the blessed Prodigal Son? Is this the narration of a dismal failure or of a brilliant success? Zorrilla abandons his paternal home and the study of law in order to become a writer, a poet. From the point of view of his father, writing is a *desatino*, a transgression that brings about his homelessness and makes of him a "*poeta desheredado* (disinherited poet)" (RTV, I, p. 21). His parents die, he sells the family estate and "leaves for America because of his sins."[98] Apparently, these sins consist of his career in Spain as a writer: he portrays his departure from Spain as a kind of self-imposed penance for having become a poet.

From the point of view of the Nation, though—it is almost impossible to distinguish Nation from reading public—Zorrilla's rejection of the study of law and his career as a writer are both positive, for they represent the fulfillment of his natural and national destiny. In this light, his departure from Spain and his adventures in America constitute not his penance but, rather, his sin, his transgression: "I was fleeing from my Homeland as I had fled before from the paternal home. . . . In 1854 I turned my back on Spain, on Europe, on my beliefs and on my poetry."[99] Consequently, Zorrilla's return to Spain is portrayed as the return of the Prodigal Son: "This return of mine was the return of the Prodigal Son to the paternal home, and everything I said and did seemed to please people, and all doors were opened to me, and I was welcomed like a brother in every family, . . . [like] a brilliant son of the Nation."[100] For the Nation, Zorrilla's natural condition is that of a writer; his writing gives him a family, the family of the Nation.

It seems clear that Zorrilla is patterning his life story on one of Romanticism's fundamental antitheses: the Hegelian opposition between the law of the heart and the law of the world. José Luis Aranguren has written: "Man, upon breaking away from established society, becomes an outlaw, a 'bandit' in the original sense of that word. This situation of the out(side-of-an-always-unjust)law, has a certain romantic grandeur; the grandeur of he who, rejecting all conveniences, rises up against adaptation, against social integration."[101] In Zorrilla's case the elements of the opposition would be the following: poetry versus the law; *patria* versus politics; home versus society; the child versus the man. The question Zorrilla asks of his father early on in the *Recuerdos,* "Who would come forth definitively, the father or the magistrate?" can now be translated as, "By which law will the father abide?"[102]

The answer, as it unfolds in the autobiography, is the law of the world; Zorrilla is unable to remain or return home because, thanks to his father, home has been infiltrated by that law: even after inheriting his father's house, he considers himself homeless and *desheredado:* "If a son had inherited that house with the love and the blessings of his parents, it would have been a paradise; but for me, who inherited it as a necessary owner, only because of laws, which have rights, but no heart and no feelings, it was an uninhabitable cave."[103] Zorrilla's father—like so many fathers portrayed in the genre—comes to represent not natural identity but rather the voice of convention, of society; not private authenticity but rather public hypocrisy. He is constantly pushing his son toward the side of adaptation, politics, society, and the law and away from poetry, and the home, that warm refuge from the cold, impersonal *ley del mundo.* For many autobiographers, school provides the first sample of the cruel ways of the world; Zorrilla is no exception, and his father is clearly the one that enrolls him in the world: "I had lived very little time with my mother; when I was only eight years old, my father enrolled me in a school in Seville."[104]

If the father comes to embody the cold, impersonal law of the world, Zorrilla's mother comes to represent the law of the heart. In the *Recuerdos* she is systematically aligned with the home, child-hood, and poetry. Throughout the three volumes of the *Recuerdos,* the various elements invested with authenticity and related to the law of the heart—home, mother, childhood, poetry, and so on—inevitably cluster together in every permutation imaginable, with the mother often at the center.[105]

In the end, Zorrilla, the poet, the eternal child, is most proud of never having adapted, of never having bent to the law of the world: "I do not belong to any class of society because we poets are not classified under any social category; I have never belonged to any political party. . . ."[106] It is precisely this outsideness that allows Zorrilla to fulfill his destiny as the national poet of Spain, not a political poet—the poet not of a party, but rather, of the *Patria:* "A Poet formed within the soul of his people, his ideas, his feelings, though universal . . . are above all Spanish: so much so that, when he strums his lyre, we hear the accent of the Nation."[107] His greatest moments are those in which his writing transcends political divisions, the turbulent flow of history, and makes of Spain a unified home, a united family, prepared for the return of its Prodigal Son. He describes his return from Mexico in these terms: "Madrid was in a state of siege and the gathering of more than five persons was forbidden, yet more than four thousand people came together to accompany me from the station to my home on that October morning of 1866."[108]

And yet, even this triumphant return is tainted, thoroughly ambivalent: there is no rest for this weary Prodigal Son. Without a pension, and having sold the rights to his *Don Juan* many years before, Zorrilla is forced to *"descender a la prosa* (descend to prose)" to write an autobiography: *"a morir sobre el trabajo a lo que parece me condenan mis viejos pecados* (to die while working, something to which my old sins apparently condemn me)" (RTV, I, p. 6). "Now that old age burdens him and work fatigues him, they have taken away the modest pension with which he lived and have abandoned him to his misery, surely to put two crowns on his head at once: poetry's crown of laurels and martyrdom's crown of thorns."[109] Even though at times Zorrilla depicts the writing of autobiography as a pleasant act of reminiscence, it becomes clear that he ultimately aligns autobiography with work, prose, and penance. In other words, he, like countless autobiographers, would rather not be writing. He ends up inscribing the genre within the law of the world—that same law that makes of him a martyr. The cruel ways of the world are relentless; the images of Poet and martyr are superimposed to the bitter end.

Armando Palacio Valdés: Being versus the Law; or, There Is No Place like Home

During the nineteenth century, Spain's relative backwardness was responsible for a Spanish fad in European letters. This fad was characterized by "an idealization of Spain as one of those countries not yet contaminated by the commercialism and rationalism of modern life" (Graña 1964, p. 147). Passion, adventure, excitement; in short, Spain becomes a place for real, authentic experience, the kind of experience no longer available in the rarefied, modernized centers of Europe.

Toward the end of the century, Eusebio Blasco, a Spaniard who had been living in Paris, would portray Madrid as a placid lake when compared to Paris. Madrid, that same city we have seen described as Babylon, becomes in Blasco's eyes, a haven, a home: "All this makes me forget the dizzying life of Paris, the noise and racket of the Grand Boulevard, the hustle and bustle of modern life."[110] For Blasco, Madrid is a place of identity, of authenticity, and, as such, it is intimately associated with the Nation, the mother, and the home. It is precisely Madrid's or Spain's hesitation to enter the whirlwind of modernity that sets it apart; this is an authenticity founded on backwardness:

> The strength of its local color is in a relation of inverse proportion to its progress. But does that really matter in the case of the Mother-land [*Patria*]? Was there ever a defective mother? . . . If in Spain people were to do what is done in other countries, this simply would not be Spain anymore . . . Suppress the smell of olive oil in the stairwells of a Madrid household . . . and there is no Madrid left. And sounds and smells, and music and scents constitute nationality, which emanates and penetrates in waves of smells, and which makes us shiver with pleasure upon returning to the maternal home.[111]

Every north has its south, though, and within Spain we see the same lines being drawn, the same attempt to delimit a space of identity, insulated from the threatening onslaught of modernity, of history. For Palacio Valdés, according to the emplotment he gives his life in *La novela de un novelista,* that privileged space is the rural world of Asturias. Leaving that world for Madrid represents an expulsion from paradise or even a descent into hell. Madrid is to Paris, for Blasco, what Asturias is to Madrid for Palacio Valdés: a home, a place of identity—"not only a physical shelter but also a te-leological shelter . . . against the remorselessness of history" (Berger 1982, p. 105). The fact that one place—Madrid—can be portrayed as both paradise and hell—the refuge from crisis and crisis itself—is more evidence for the argument according to which crisis is a state of mind, not of events.

Conventional visions of the home and of the rural world—Asturias, in the case of Palacio Valdés—have several things in common. In both Zorrilla and Blasco, the home becomes associated with the mother. This linking of home, mother, and authenticity is an interesting byproduct of the nineteenth century's rigid codification

of gender roles: public man and private woman. As Bridget Aldaraca has written, "A perception of the public world as materialistic
and threatening provokes in turn an idealization of the supposedly
isolated sphere of female domesticity as a timeless, spiritual refuge,
a stable locus outside the turbulent flow of history" (1982, p. 62). A
similar association is often established between the countryside and
the feminine or the maternal. Leopoldo Alas's short story "Boroña,"
for instance (1989), tells of an Asturian *indiano* (a Spaniard that
emigrates to the New World and later returns to Spain) whose evocations of the *idilio* he left behind are obsessively focused on his
mother; in this text and many others, the region, in all its simplicity and lack of modernity, becomes virtually identified with the
mother. Palacio Valdés alludes to precisely this kind of association
when he emphasizes that his departure from Asturias coincided with
the death of his mother.

But even more important, perhaps, is the strong conventional association between both the home and the country, on one side, and
childhood on the other. "Country life has been seen repeatedly as the
life of the past, of the writer's childhood" (Williams 1957, p. 630).
While in many cases this coincidence of childhood and rusticity
is the result of concrete biographical circumstances—"for every
Victorian in the city had either grown up in the country or in a
town small enough for ready contact with the rural environment"
(Houghton 1957, p. 79)—in other cases, the coupling is of a more
conventional nature. The country life becomes associated not so
much with the childhood of a man as with the childhood of man-
kind. According to a certain view of history, civilization spent its
childhood in the country and its adult life in the city.

Palacio Valdés's experience of Asturias is described in both the
concrete and the conventional way. That is, his childhood was spent
in Asturias and his adult life in Madrid: when he plots his life story
as a fall from childhood, paradise, and Asturias into adulthood, *el
mundo,* and Madrid, he takes advantage of those concrete circumstances. At the same time, though, Asturias becomes not only the
place of his childhood, but also an essentially childish, or childlike,
place. Although he does make some distinctions between the countryside and the cities of Asturias, on the whole, the entire region—
its adults included—is portrayed as childlike or innocent: "A kind

and childish joviality rules over this village [Avilés]"; "as if this beautiful town wanted to put its joy and its innocence under the care of he who said 'Either children or like children'"; "the charm of Avilés lies in its infantile joy."[112] Even business and politics, those adult and urban activities par excellence are somewhat infantile in the remote world of Asturias: "Business itself, sordid by its very nature, had in our town a noble and tranquil temperament"; "politics, which is usually tragic and likely to ignite all kinds of passions . . . acquires in Oviedo a comical aspect."[113] Finally, the region, like the child's home, is supposedly undaunted by history: "The year was 1861. In Avilés we lived rather ignored but quite happy. Somewhere, far away, battalions could revolt, and in Madrid barricades could be erected, and all over Spain battles could take place followed by bloody repressions, massacres and mass executions. We did not worry about such trifles."[114]

Both the home and the countryside are not only refuges from history, but they are also places conventionally (and erroneously) defined by the absence of work, places distant from the modern world of offices, factories and their fabrications. Raymond Williams has shown how in countless pastoral portrayals of the rural world, what is conspicuously missing is *work:* "The actual men and women . . . who plant and manure and prune and harvest the fruit trees, these are not present; their work is all done for them by a natural order" (1973, p. 32). As Eduardo Subirats has contended, an ironic landscape painter like Turner disrupts the pastoral harmony of the rural world precisely "insofar as he shows the pain caused by the effort of work."[115] The child, once again, the inmate of both home and country, is often brought into this effortless, pastoral relation. George Simmel, like many others, sees fit to establish a certain identity between children and rustics or primitives in this respect: "The child lives in an insurmountable rhythm of sleeping and relaxation and something similar may be observed in rural areas" (Simmel 1978, p. 486).

In the first paragraph of his *La novela de un novelista,* Palacio Valdés writes:

"If you want to know what a cherry tastes like, ask a child or a bird"; so says a German proverb. I do not know how they might taste to birds, but they tasted so good to me sixty years ago that whenever I saw a basket full of cherries I would fall into ecstasy like Saint Teresa in the presence of the Sacrament.[116]

The tone of this passage is playful, but it reveals a number of interesting things. In the image, Palacio Valdés is presented with a basket of cherries; there is no sign of the effort behind the production of this fruit. Throughout the *Novela,* we see the child Palacio Valdés effortlessly provided with everything he might want; he is brought up in a world of servants who cater to his every need. He constantly portrays himself as being sent whatever he desires: "That summer God sent to earth the greenest foliage, the most perfumed breeze, the most crystalline waters and the reddest cherries of his infinite repertoire."[117] In the end, it would seem that God is responsible for the child's happiness: "All [my loved ones] had been sent by God to make me happy."[118]

This harmony, this lack of effort or passivity, is the key to the child's happiness, for the child has immediate access not only to fruit in a literal sense, but also to true, authentic, unmediated experience—to presence. The absence of work is, in other words, analogous to the absence of mediation. In the adult world, there are only signs that must be used, interpreted, and worked over; the child is able to experience things in and for themselves. In the prelapsarian world of childhood and Asturias, labor and use—as well as the problems of interpretation —are unknown; all things can be effortlessly enjoyed. It is in this respect that the child is compared to the mystic, Teresa; later on, Palacio Valdés again compares his experience of nature with the mystical experience: "My soul got in touch with nature. . . . It was as if the earth were nurturing me with love by offering me its gifts, and I partook of its happiness, living in mystical union with it."[119]

As we have seen, in the section of her *Vida* devoted to a description of her mystical experience, Teresa uses the sustained analogy of the garden and the four waters in order to describe the four levels of her prayer. According to this pastoral analogy, as she approaches the most perfect level of complete union with God, what steadily decreases is the amount of work: if the first, least perfect level corresponds to a garden whose keeper must cart water from a far-off stream, the last level corresponds to the garden being effortlessly provided with rainwater. Adam, on being expelled from paradise, was cursed to "labor by the sweat of his brow," and so it is fitting that Teresa's journey, a reversal of the Fall, is described as an elimination of work. This elimination of work represents, among other things, a suspension of the mind's discourse, a suspension of her cognitive faculties, an abandonment of representation. Meaning becomes Present: the mystic no longer needs to interpret, to work to read: "Like one who without learning or without working at all to learn how to read, were to find all of knowledge already within."[120]

Palacio Valdés explicitly evokes the expulsion from paradise in his *Novela.* The first chapter is called "Adam in Paradise"; the last, "Adam Expelled." Paradise is his childhood in Asturias. It is timeless and unified; it is eminently unnaratable, unautobiographical:[121] "The history of childhood is always identical to itself. It is happiness. Every child is happy unless a brutal hand intervenes between him and happiness."[122] In the case of Palacio Valdés, as in many cases, the first brutal hand seems to have been that of the school teacher: "I remember that the hazel-tree rod that the teacher don Juan de la Cruz used to correct us was not very pleasant."[123] The image almost seems like a literal version of the Spanish proverb: "*La letra con sangre entra* (literacy is inculcated by the schoolmaster's bloodied rod)." In any event, socialization (the assignment of conventional roles) and literacy—a metaphor for the imposition of an arbitrary and impersonal system through which the student must learn to see the world—very often contribute to the negative characterization of schooling so common in the genre.[124] Even within the confines of Asturias, it is school that interrupts Palacio Valdés's timeless, happy existence: "I was ready to spend eternity like the angels do, assuming angels do not attend school."[125]

As in the case of Zorrilla the first schooling is a miniature version of a greater fall, the author's entrance into law school and Madrid. "There was never a fifth-year student more eager to graduate. This grand achievement was, I thought, the key to Paradise. And in fact, it was the key, though not to open it, but rather to close it. . . . Such a vehement desire to become a graduate was not only due to the privileges that the glorious title carries with it. My parents had promised to send me to Madrid to continue with the career of jurisprudence."[126] The book ends with his departure/exile en route to Madrid: "But we are already starting to ascend the grandiose mountains of Pajares. . . . Farewell, sweet childhood! Farewell dreamy youth! The sordid boardinghouse, disdainful indifference, irrational hostility, hollow pleasures, and remorse all await me down there."[127] What characterizes this Fall or exile—what separates the man from the child—is, according to Palacio Valdés, mediation, an imposition between the subject and the world. The child has direct access; the man does not: "Many, many times have I asked myself . . . Which is in truth the real world, that which I used to see in my childhood, or this other one I can now contemplate through the veil woven of perfidy, treason, lowness and vileness that the years have placed before my eyes?"[128] The answer to this question is clear, at least for Palacio Valdés: "In reality we are wise only in childhood, for only then do we establish true relationships."[129] Childhood and Asturias become the place of authenticity, unity, identity, where *"el odio es odio, el orgullo es orgullo y la justicia, justicia* (hatred is hatred, pride is pride and justice, justice)" (PV, p. 10). Again, childhood and the rural world have been frequently described in similar, idealizing terms: For children and "primitives," according to Simmel, "the word and the object, the symbol and what it represents, the name and the person are identical, as has been shown in innumerable ethnological findings and by child psychology" (Simmel 1978, p. 486). Ethnology and child psychology; Simmel's pairing is yet another example of that powerful analogy: child is to adult as primitive is to civilized, country to city. Adult life and the city, with their proliferation of equivocal signs, are characterized by duplicity, or multiplicity. In the *Novela* the loss of unity, of immediacy, of unmediated perception, is at first connected to school and eventually to the study of law and the experience of politics, modernity, and Madrid. After these things, one can never experience the world—even, or especially the natural world—in a direct way:

> Nowadays I approach the sea as if it were the Puerta del Sol. I contemplate the silver curves of its waves with the same indifference with which I watch the spurts of a watering hose. Its frightful roar leaves me as indifferent as the noise from cars, and seagulls with

their squawking seem to me like street vendors selling the afternoon newspapers. [130]

Birds, children, and mystics have access to Presence. What the three have in common is the inability—or better, the lack of desire—to express that presence. The mute bird, the enraptured mystic and the *infans,* the one who does not speak. After the fall into adulthood and the acquisition of letters and the law, the bird becomes a proliferator of discourse and diffuses information, rather than being infused with experience; the mystic goes to the city and becomes a lawyer, a master of the law of the world; the natural child becomes an urban adult, and, alas, an autobiographer. Auto. Autobio. Autobiographer.

Conclusion:

Apostrophes Are

Forbidden . . .

The difficulty or the impossibility of closure is the subject of the most repeated lesson in the schoolroom of autobiography. And the critic who sits down to write a conclusion faces more or less the same options and dilemmas as the autobiographer seeking an end point for his or her life. My "marketplace of words"—the groves of academia—forbids (thank God) endless revisions, or the accumulation of provisional drafts à la Blanco White. But my own conscience also rules out the authoritative, definitive epilogue, which might "grant . . . retrospective coherence to the simple accumulation of ruins," subordinate every thought, every sentence, to the Idea, the apparently foregone Conclusion.[1]

Nonetheless, the genre obliges: I capitulate and recapitulate; I write and rewrite. My title—*Apology to Apostrophe*—pretends to represent succinctly a tension found in countless autobiographical narratives, between historicism and essentialism, between engagement with the here and now and detachment, unworldliness, and asceticism. The two words, as I use them in this study, aim to summon up two rather different images of the writing subject of autobiography. Apology—the writer, feet on the ground, eyes straight ahead, openly addresses a self-defense to his or her contemporaries, his or her neighbors. Apostrophe—amid the hustle and bustle, the unjust persecutions and the fallen contingencies of historical existence, the writer averts his or her gaze toward the heavens. Detached, at times even apparently indifferent to those degraded, contemporary realities, the apostrophic autobiographer invokes or evokes the noncontingent: some idyllic being, place, or time, in which, curiously enough, reflexivity, self-justification, autobiographical writing, or even speech would be unnecessary, inconceivable.

Throughout this study, I have argued repeatedly for the need to historicize autobiographical discourse. And yet I draw comparisons among texts written in different languages, in different nations, and even, in the case of Augustine, in different millennia. This apparent contradiction can, I think, be reconciled. The idea that truth or identity is always at odds with contingency, that historical existence can be an obstacle to true knowledge, is deeply ingrained in Western thought; from Paul to Marx, from Christ to Freud and beyond. This fact legitimizes, to my mind, some of the more removed comparisons I put forth in this study. It is when the critic or the historian wishes to identify and analyze those specific topoi that, at different moments, have been invested with the aura of truth, identity, and knowledge, that historicism becomes absolutely essential. What is it that allows a miragelike Public Opinion or History to be suddenly elevated to the status of Universal Judge? How is it that the rural countryside can, at a certain moment in history, come to be portrayed as the temple of Identity? What are the conditions that allow certain women—self-sacrificing domestic mothers, for example—to become represented, by men, of course, as vessels of Essence? Historical perspective is, I think, the only tool we have that allows us to strip these seductive constructs of their apparent force of Nature.

In the texts I have studied, I have seen a number of situations put forth as this privileged space of noncontingency: places or moments of identity, presence, authenticity, allegedly free from the struggles of historical, social, and political existence. The need to posit the existence of a home, a haven free from change, adaptation, signification, and interpretation, seems to be a constant among autobiographers throughout the centuries. In this study, I have tried, however, to maintain a historical perspective; I have tried to be relentlessly critical of these formulations and to take as a starting point the premise that these situations tend to have no objective existence; they are products not of History or Nature, but rather of the discursive characteristics and strategies of autobiographical writing. That impartial Public Opinion or History that political autobiographers so often appeal to is nowhere to be found, except in the rhetoric of apostrophe. The brutal injustice with which Blanco White has been treated is chilling proof of this. Zorrilla's natural Home and apolitical *Patria* are likewise rhetorical constructions, products of his wistful evocation. When Mesonero Romanos speaks of premodern life as a kind of peaceful bliss, uninterrupted by political turmoil, it is easy to forget that he is describing absolutism, despotism. And when he portrays a certain kind of progress—capitalism and the "emerging bourgeois lifestyle" of Madrid—as the "natural, national, character of Spain" (Kirkpatrick 1978, p. 34), we may lose sight of the millions of victims of modernization and centralism: Spain's brutally exploited lower classes and peripheral regions. Palacio Valdés unwittingly gives us a glimpse of this underside of progress when his idyllic portrait of an Asturias supposedly undaunted by history is suddenly and inexplicably slashed by a childhood memory of an industrial accident: the little boy watches drowned workers being fished out of the waters of Avilés.

Were it not so unwieldy, I might have used "From Apology to Apostrophe and Back Again" as the title for this book. Because all the appeals and invocations to the heavens, all the pleas to posterity and the evocations of nature, or of the natural, inexorably end up forming part of an apology; that is, a textual intervention addressed to one's fellow men and women, fallible and partial readers. Apostrophe, though it pretends to get beyond rhetoric, worldliness, and historical existence, is always enlisted into the service of rhetoric, persuasion, apology.

In other words, apostrophe, like many of the enabling tropes of autobiographical discourse, is a kind of spectacle or performance. And as a spectacle, it is an instance of what speech-act theorists call performative discourse. Rather than represent things, performative language *does* things. Like the shaman's invocation or the priest's "I now pronounce," performative statements are governed not so much by the criterion of truth or falsity as by the criterion of effectiveness or ineffectiveness. This performative aspect leads me to maintain that in many instances, particularly throughout the nineteenth century, the truly interesting question is often not whether an autobiography is factual or fictional, but rather whether it is effective, successful, and felicitous. Is the autobiographer granted the last word?

Before having my illusory last word, I would like to address a potentially problematic issue raised by my critical approach. I recognize that, by concentrating on these autobiographical texts as figures of rhetoric or as performances, I seem to grant an equal status to all the texts, to level them all into mere instances of discourse. And yet certainly, some of these autobiographies are bound to be more or less truthful, more or less accurate than others. By refusing to shuttle back and forth between the autobiographical accounts and the consensus of the historical record I do end up eschewing the categories of sincerity and truthfulness, of honesty, and perhaps even of morality. Recently, after giving a lecture on the material of this book, I was confronted by a perplexed and somewhat angry scholar, who thought it was inappropriate, and, I presume, ultimately amoral, to talk about the autobiographies of Manuel de Godoy (who was, I was told, a "*sinvergüenza*") and Blanco White (who was an "honest man") without remarking from the outset that one was a scoundrel and a liar and the other an admirable figure. I am not sure I can adequately address this criticism. I do think that my reading for rhetoric has been productive. In fact, the widely held notion that Godoy was a scoundrel has probably prevented many people from even opening his autobiography. The contingencies of my locus of enunciation—Hispanism, academic literary criticism of the late 1980s, and poststructuralism, with its keen interest in questions of textuality—all these things have allowed me to find and open these neglected books, and to have these books finally speak to us. Perhaps it is ironic, or perhaps it is inevitable, that they seem to speak to us precisely of the problems of contingency, textuality, and transcendence. Nonetheless, my listener's objection, though somewhat crudely formulated, is well taken, for it points to the impasse faced by a good deal of contemporary literary criticism: if everything is performance or discourse, then what? I am convinced that in my future endeavors to find a meeting ground for morality and poststructuralism, I will be in good company.

And so, benevolent reader, there will be no apostrophe in my conclusion. No attempt to have the last word.

Abbreviations of
Frequently Cited
Works

The following is a list of abbreviations used throughout this book to identify quotations. In multivolume works, the roman numeral "I" always indicates the first volume of the series. In other words, in the case of Alcalá Galiano, the roman numeral "I" refers to volume 83 of the *Biblioteca de autores españoles,* and "II" refers to volume 84. In the case of Blanco White (BW), a lower case "n" means that the quotation appears in a footnote.

AG   Alcalá Galiano, Antonio. 1955. *Obras escogidas.* Vols. 83–84, *Biblioteca de autores españoles.* Madrid: Atlas.

BW   Blanco White, Joseph. 1845. *The Life of the Reverend Joseph Blanco White. Written by Himself.* London: Chapman.

CEM   de la Vega, Juana (Condesa de Espoz y Mina). 1977. *Memorias.* Madrid: Tebas.

FdC   Fernández de Córdoba, Fernando. 1966. *Mis memorias íntimas.* Vols. 193–94, *Biblioteca de autores españoles.* Madrid: Atlas.

FEM   Espoz y Mina, Francisco. 1962. *Memorias.* Vols. 146–47, *Biblioteca de autores españoles.* Madrid: Atlas.

GLP   García de León y Pizarro, José. 1953. *Memorias.* 2 vols. Madrid: Revista de Occidente.

JdE   Escoiquiz, Juan de. *Memorias.* 1915. Madrid: Revista de Archivos, Bibliotecas y Museos.

JG   Goytisolo, Juan. 1974. "Prólogo." In *Obra inglesa de don José María Blanco White.* Barcelona, Seix Barral.

JHT   Thom, John Hamilton. 1867. "Archbishop Whately and the Life of Blanco White." *Theological Review* 4:173–92.

MG   Godoy, Manuel de. *Memorias*. 1956. Vols. 88–89, *Biblioteca de autores españoles*. Madrid: Atlas.

MP   Menéndez y Pelayo, Marcelino. 1932. "Blanco White." Vol. 7, *Historia de los heterodoxos españoles*. Madrid: Victoriano Suárez.

MR   Mesonero Romanos, Ramón de. 1975. *Memorias de un setentón*. Madrid: Tebas.

PAG   Girón, Pedro Agustín. 1978. *Recuerdos de la vida de don Pedro Agustín Girón, escritos por él mismo*. Pamplona: Ediciones de la Universidad de Navarra.

PM   Palafox y Melzi, José de. 1966. *Autobiografía*. Madrid: Taurus.

PV   Palacio Valdés, Armando. 1965. *La novela de un novelista*. Buenos Aires: Espasa-Calpe.

RTV   Zorrilla y Moral, José. 1961. *Recuerdos del tiempo viejo*. 2 vols. Madrid: Publicaciones Españolas.

RW   Whateley, E. Jane, ed. and comp. 1866. *The Life of Archbishop {Richard} Whately*. London: Longman.

TV   Torres Villarroel, Diego de. 1984. *Vida*. Madrid: Clásicos Castalia.

WEG   Gladstone, William Ewart. 1879. "Blanco White." In *Gleanings of Past Years*, vol. 1, 1–64. New York: Scribners.

Notes

Introduction

1. "No hay en España lo que es común intitular Memorias" (AG, I, p. 35).

2. "En nuestra literatura escasean obras de este género" (Benavente y Martínez 1958, p. 491).

3. "Es un género poco abundante entre nosotros" (González Ruano 1979, p. 14).

4. "Los españoles se muestran singularmente reticentes a la idea de exponer [. . . la vida] por escrito" (JG, p. 14).

5. "Je forme une entreprise qui n'eut jamais d'exemple" (Rousseau 1959, p. 8).

6. "Las Memorias son un síntoma de complacencia en la vida. . . . ¡No puede extrañar la escasez de Memorias [en España] si se repara que el español siente la vida como un universal dolor de muelas!" (Ortega y Gasset 1947, p. 585).

7. "Hemos vivido la mitad del siglo XIX en una sociedad de perseguidores y perseguidos, emigrando por tandas al extranjero, para que el mundo no ignorara nuestras fraternales disensiones" (Flores 1968, p. 19).

8. "*Memoria Rota: Exilios y Heterodoxias:* Con este título significativo se inicia una colección de libros cuyo objeto es recuperar la continuidad cultural de España y sus gentes, quebrada por la guerra civil y los distintos infortunios que la perpetuaron." The series is being published by Anthropos, of Barcelona.

9. "Ese torrente sin diques de memorias" (Larra 1969, p. 904).

10. Because my analysis of these texts is, for the most part rhetorical,

and because the number of memoirs is relatively large, I have decided to dispense with a description of the historical roles of these figures in my text. The reader interested in the history of these figures and their texts is referred to app. 1.

11. "[Una] expansión del Memorial de Servicios" (Levisi 1985, p. 129).

12. "Apego al orden y la mentalidad jurídica" (Pope 1974, p. 101).

13. "Documento oficial" (Pope 1974, p. 210).

14. "La structure judiciaire inquisitoriale lui organise . . . [un] espace concret ou le je . . . peut s'inscrire comme personnage principale" (Schizzano Mandel 1980, p. 163).

15. "Escuchando y registrando las deposiciones autobiográficas de los galeotes" (Rico 1970, p. 83).

16. "Con criterio estrictamente legal inserta en su *Vida* un Memorial de agravios" (Levisi 1985, p. 131).

17. "La situación comunicativa propia del discurso autobiográfico convencional" (Gómez-Moriana 1980, p. 61).

18. See Roberto González Echevarría (1980, 1987) and Antonio Gómez-Moriana (1980, 1983).

19. "Tomo a mis confesores en lugar de Dios" (Teresa de Jesús 1963, p. 341).

20. "Morir casi del todo a todas las cosas del mundo" (ibid., p. 118).

21. "[La mentira] se encuentra sólidamente anclada en la realidad biográfica del sujeto individual. Junto al aspecto de hacer tábula rasa de los contenidos de la conciencia, de la purificación del sujeto intelectual y de cualesquiera axiomas o conceptos recibidos, y la anti-historicidad a la que este principio le obliga, es importante también . . . una ruptura con el conjunto de la cultura anterior" (Subirats 1983, pp. 171, 182).

22. "Desconfianza hacia la realidad empírica del mundo, de sus costumbres, de la vida cotidiana, de los valores prácticos" (ibid., p. 187).

23. "Dios me ha condenado a vivir entre miserias, pequeñeces y mezquindades" (RTV, II, p. 221).

24. "El cumplimiento de un deber" (CEM, p. 15).

25. "Un encargo solemne y sagrado" (AG, I, p. 252).

26. "Vuelvo, no sin repugnancia, a la narración . . ." (MR, p. 219).

27. "Descender a la prosa" [y a] "morir sobre el trabajo, a lo que parece que me condenan mis viejos pecados" (RTV, I, pp. 7, 5).

28. "Si mi vida militar y política hubiera sido siempre feliz, me abstendría de este trabajo" (PM, p. 7).

29. "Espero . . . la indulgencia de mis lectores . . . que disimularán la poca elegancia de mi estilo y la naturalidad de mis expresiones. Aproveché poco las sabias lecciones de mis maestros, mi natural impaciencia desde niño me hizo aplicarme poco a las reglas de la retórica" (ibid., p. 47).

30. "Yo como hombre de la naturaleza más que del arte, acostumbro a

decir las cosas ingenuamente, y mis acciones siguen el impulso de este carácter natural" (FEM, I, p. 45).

31. "La honradez y hombría de bien, vinculada más bien que en esas clases elevadas, en la humilde y más útil de la sociedad a que pertenezco por nacimiento" (ibid., I, p. 46).

32. "Estas desaliñadas *Memorias* . . ." (FdC, I, p. 111).

33. "Aprendí a aborrecer las cosas del mundo" (GLP, I, p. 24).

34. "Me lo hacían más y más parecido a aquellos hombres de la antigüedad . . . Se hacía notar la severidad de sus costumbres en medio de los atractivos de aquella voluptuosa capital" (CEM, pp. 35–37).

35. "La incipiente máquina política y burocrática del Estado" (Pastor 1975, p. 11).

36. "Sin cuidarme ni poco ni mucho del artificio retórico" (MR, pp. 23, 372).

37. "Obra de cronológica ilación, de continuidad lógica y progresiva, de bien enlazados sucesos y de uniforme estilo" (RTV, I, p. 167).

38. "¿Cuál será el mundo verdaderamente real, aquél que yo veía en mi infancia, o este otro que ahora contemplo a través del velo tejido de perfidias, traiciones, bajezas y ruindades que los años colocaron ante mis ojos?" (PV, 64).

39. "Jamás hubo un estudiante de quinto año más ansioso de hacerse bachiller. Este magno acontecimiento era, a mi modo de ver, la llave del Paraíso. En efecto, fue la llave, mas no para abrirlo, sino para cerrarlo" (ibid., p. 234).

1   Addressee Unknown

1. "En vida está claro que no se ha de decir de lo bueno" (Teresa de Jesús 1963, p. 71).

2. "Los de caballerías y otras . . . obras llenas de vanidades y lascivias" (de León 1959, p. 1326).

3. "Esa morada en el centro y mitad" (Teresa de Jesús 1963, p. 584).

4. "Quédanse las letras a un cabo"; "llamo ruido andar con el entendimiento, buscando palabras, . . . trastornando la retórica" (ibid., pp. 111, 113).

5. "Es disparate pensar que tiene semejanza lo uno con lo otro . . . no más ni menos que la tiene una persona viva a su retrato" (ibid, p. 232).

6. "Pone el Señor lo que quiere que el alma entienda en lo muy interior del alma y allí lo representa sin imagen ni forma de palabra" (ibid., p. 219).

7. "Ne pouvant plus me confier à aucun homme qui ne me trahît, je résolus de me confier uniquement à la Providence, et de remettre à elle

seule l'entière disposition du depôt que je desirois laisser en de sûres mains"
(Rousseau 1959, pp. 977–78).

8. "Je voulus entrer par une des portes latérales, par laquelle je comptois
pénetrer dans le choeur. Surpris de la trouver fermée, j'allai passer plus bas,
par l'autre porte laterale qui donne dans la nef. En entrant, mes yeux furent
frappés d'une grille que je n'avais jamais remarqué . . . les portes de cette
grille etoient fermées . . . et . . . il m'était impossible d'y pénétrer" (ibid.,
pp. 979–80).

9. "On ne me laisse de communication, . . . qu'avec des gens apostés par
mes persecuteurs" (ibid., p. 984).

10. "Es otro libro nuevo de aquí adelante, digo, otra vida nueva" (Teresa
de Jesús 1963, p. 182).

11. "El deseo de cosas semejantes abre puerta en las mujeres, que son
crédulas, para que el demonio las engañe con ilusiones" (de León 1959,
p. 1324).

12. "Esto de dar recaudo a tercera persona—como he dicho—es lo que
más siento siempre, en especial a quien no sabía como lo tomaría"; "¡Cómo
no son menester terceros para Vos!" (Teresa de Jesús 1963, pp. 305, 342).

13. "Fáltame todo, Señor mío; mas si Vos no me desamparáis, no os
faltaré yo a Vos. Levántense contra mi todos los letrados, persíganme todas
las cosas criadas, atorméntenme los demonios. . . ." (ibid., p. 208).

14. "Rompa vuestra merced esto que he dicho—si le pareciere—y
tómelo por carta para sí, y perdóneme, que he estado muy atrevida" (ibid.,
p. 123).

15. "¿Qué aseguraba en la filosofía occidental que las cosas a conocer y el
propio conocimiento estaban en relación de continuidad? ¿Qué era lo que
aseguraba al conocimiento el poder de conocer bien las cosas del mundo y
de no ser indefinidamente error, ilusión, arbitrariedad? ¿Quién sino Dios
garantizaba esto en la filosofía occidental?" (Foucault 1984, p. 24).

16. "Occidente será dominado por el gran mito de que la verdad nunca
pertenece al poder político, de que el poder político es ciego, de que el
verdadero saber es el que se posee cuando se está en contacto con los
dioses. . . ." (ibid., p. 59).

17. "No hay tal yo de conjunto" (Borges 1925, p. 87).

18. See Fernández-Cifuentes (1987, 1991).

19. "Se trata . . . de un conflicto entre un YO generalmente identificado
con la felicidad secular y ese OTRO portavoz exterior de la vida miserable y
de la muerte continua" (Fernández-Cifuentes 1991, p. 25).

20. "Entre las cortaduras del papel y los rollos del pergamino" (TV,
p. 69).

21. "Ahora voy apuntando las desdichas del sexto [trozo de mi *Vida*] y si
Dios quiere que lo cumpla, lo echaré a la calle con los demás" (ibid., p. 228).

22. "Tu dirás, (como si lo oyera) luego que agarres en tu mano este papel. . . ." (ibid., p. 49).

23. "[Responda] con la pluma o la conversación" (ibid., 180); "hable o escriba" (ibid., pp. 183, 232, 250, et al.).

24. "[Deseaba] desmentir, con mis verdades, las acusaciones, las bastardas novelas y los cuentos misteriosos que se voceaban de mi en las cocinas, calles y tabernas, entresacadas de 500 pliegos de maldiciones y sátiras que corren a cuatro pies por el mundo" (ibid., p. 180).

25. "La ausencia del dicente deja ante nosotros la palabra escrita descoyuntada del complejo expresivo que era el cuerpo de aquél" (Ortega y Gasset 1981, p. 142).

26. "Aconsejo a todos . . . que examinen con recato y quietud la opinión de los hombres famosos y aplaudidos, especialmente la de las dos castas de doctos y de santos, que las más veces se hallará debajo de una reputación desmesurada de sabiduría y experiencia, un idiota terco, un hablador vacío, un misterioso extravagante, un impertinente, . . . un bergante, *comilón, ocioso,* repleto de *avaricia* y de *lujuria*" (TV, p. 234).

27. "Los libros gordos, los magros, los chicos y los grandes son unas alhajas que entretienen y sirven en el *comercio de los hombres*" (ibid., p. 71).

28. "Estudiaban los médicos en los capítulos de sus libros, disculpas para sus disparates. . . . Conocían las burlas que de sus recetas, sus aforismos y sus discursos, les hacía mi naturaleza y mi dolor, y, con todos estos desengaños, jamás los oí confesar su ignorancia" (ibid., p. 208).

29. "Día catorce de abril de 1744 confesé general y particularmente los vicios, ocasiones próximas y actuales pecados de mis humores a los catedráticos de Salamanca. Fue el confesionario una de las aulas de Leyes del patio de la Universidad, y allí les desabroché mis delitos, y sujeté a su absolución todas mis venialidades, reincidencias y pecados gordos. Hice puntual acusación de mi vida pasada y mi estado presente . . . y quedé satisfecho de la diligencia que envidiaba mi alma, y apetecía, para las confesiones de sus enfermedades, el examen, la claridad y la expresión con que había declarado las del cuerpo" (ibid., pp. 204–5).

30. "Descubro, entre poquísimas felicidades, las persecuciones . . . , las miserias a que me condenó mi altanería, los precipicios adonde me asomaron mis costumbres y los más de los errores que dieron justamente a mi vida el renombre de mala vida" (ibid., p. 47).

31. "*Hallábame* ligero, fácil en las acciones, sin remordimientos ni escrúpulos en la salud y sin la más leve alteración en el espíritu, porque ni yo me *acordaba* de que había justicia, ladrones, cárceles, médicos, calenturas, críticos, maldicientes, ni otros fantasmas y cocos que nos tienen continuamente amenazados. . . . *Duróme* este sosiego hasta el mes de agosto. . . ." (ibid., pp. 193–94).

32. "Salieron de la ciudad de Soria, no sé si arrojados de la pobreza o de alguna travesura de mancebos Francisco y Roque de Torres" (ibid., p. 61).

33. The second *trozo,* where he recounts his picaresque years of study, is punctuated with rupture: "Era grave delito en mi tiempo romper de noche la clausura y tomar de día la capa y la gorra y todas las noches y los días quebrantaba a rienda suelta estos preceptos" (ibid., p. 82). The most extensive example of transgression in this *trozo* is Torres's abandonment of the paternal home, the *lance* (p. 109) of his trip to Portugal: "tomé una camisa, el pan que pudo caber debajo del brazo izquierdo . . . y sin pensar en paradero, vereda ni destino, me entregué a la majadería de mis deseos" (p. 86). The third section is centered on yet another *salida* or exit: after a spell in jail, Torres explains "determiné dejar para siempre a Salamanca y buscar en Madrid mejor opinión" (p. 120). The fourth *trozo* revolves around Torres's exile to Portugal—"[ese] libro de mis desgracias" (p. 147). The fifth describes his run-in with the Inquisition and his *accidente,* the incident of his illness.

34. The ambivalence is abundantly clear in Torres's contradictory depictions of the journey. "Y al año siguiente, que fue el de 1736, después de finalizadas mis tareas, empecé a satisfacer varios votos que había hecho por mi libertad y mi vida en el tiempo de mi esclavitud y mis dolencias. Fue el más penoso el que hice de ir a pie a visitar el templo del apóstol Santiago. . . ." (ibid., p. 166); "en medio de estar ocupado con los deleites, las visitas y los concursos, no dejaba de escoger algunos ratos para mis tareas. . . . Cinco meses me detuve en este viaje, y fue el más feliz, el más venturoso y acomodado que he tenido en mi vida. . . ." (ibid., p. 169).

35. "Debiendo haber jubilado a los veinte años de residencia, no pudo lograr este descanso, porque esa Universidad dudaba en pasarle los años de 732, 33 y 34, que en virtud de orden de la Majestad del señor Rey D. Felipe V, estuvo en Portugal, quien, usando de su Real clemencia, se sirvió restituirle al reino, a la patria y a todos los honores de su cátedra y claustro: . . . pidió que se le concediese el indulto de dichos tres años y el de otras faltas que había tenido por sus enfermedades e infortunios" (ibid., p. 247).

36. "Yo confesé . . . todas las faltas que había cometido, producidas de las barrumbadas de mi genio, de mis infortunios y de mis perezas y mis enfermedades . . . [y] supliqué a su Alteza me absolviese de las idas y venidas . . . concediéndome en la jubilación . . . la quietud y el reposo" (ibid., p. 229).

37. "Suplico a Vuestra Excelencia se digne de recibir la vida que gozo y la Vida que escribo, pues sobre una y otra han puesto las honras de V.E. un dominio apetecible y una esclavitud inexcusable" (ibid., p. 48); "Y si te parece que te engaño, arrímate a mí, que juro ponerte de manera que no te conozca la madre que te parió" (p. 50).

38. "Confieso que escribo estas escusadas noticias por darles un poco de

pesadumbre y un retazo de motivo para que recaigan sobre mí sus murmuraciones y blasfemias. . . . No me faltan algunos enemigos veniales y maldicientes de escalera abajo, aunque ya tengo pocos y malos, y siento mucho que se me haya hundido este caudal, porque a estos tales he debido mucha porción de fama, gusto y conveniencia, que hoy hace feliz y venturosa mi vida" (ibid., p. 171).

39. "Todo lo debo a su Majestad y al respeto con que he mirado a sus sustitutos en la tierra" (ibid., p. 109).

40. "Porque nada me importaba tanto como salir de mis errores, aborrecer mis disparates y rendir toda mi obediencia a sus determinaciones y decretos. Examinaron los piadosos ministros mi sencillez, mi cristiana intención y las ansias de mi católico deseo, y a los 15 días me volvieron el libro, el que imprimí segunda vez, juntamente con el memorial presentado y un nuevo prólogo, lo que podrá ver el incrédulo o el curioso en la reimpresión hecha en la imprenta de la Merced de Madrid . . . y no se quedará sin él el que lo buscare, pues aún duran algunos ejemplares en casa de Juan de Moya, frente a San Felipe el Real. . . . Ahora deseo con ansia que mis producciones sufran y se mejoren con sus avisos" (ibid., p. 197).

41. "La de presentar una autodefensa ante un Juez, quizá más temible que el del rey, el Juez omnipresente y multiforme, delegado por la sociedad, sin hablar del que espera al cristiano en el más allá" (ibid., p. 23).

42. "Resistíme poderosamente a esta novedad, diciendo con cautelosa soberbia que no había examinadores tan oportunos que pudiesen sentenciar en nuestras habilidades y aptitudes; además de que mi intención no era la de ser catedrático, sino la de hablar en público" (ibid., p. 136).

43. "Remitimos a Sevilla . . . trescientos memoriales a diferentes señoras, señores, ministros y agentes para que solicitasen el buen despacho de nuestras súplicas" (ibid., p. 154).

44. "El fiscal y el informante menos apasionado y más verdadero que cuantos andan trompicando por el mundo" (ibid., p. 230).

45. "Aquella mal entendida máxima de que Dios se explica en la voz de el pueblo, autorizó la plebe para tiranizar el buen juicio, y erigió en ella una potestad tribunicia, capaz de oprimir la nobleza literaria. Es éste un error de donde nacen infinitos; porque asentada la conclusión de que la multitud sea regla de la verdad, todos los desaciertos del vulgo se veneran como inspiraciones del Cielo. Esta consideración me mueve a combatir el primero este error, haciéndome la cuenta de que venzo muchos enemigos en uno solo, o a lo menos de que será más fácil expugnar los demás errores quitándoles primero el patrocinio que les da la voz común en la estimación de los hombres menos cautos" (Feijoo y Montenegro 1958, p. 85).

46. "La voz del pueblo está totalmente desnuda de autoridad, pues tan frecuentemente la vemos puesta de parte del error" (ibid., p. 102).

47. "En 1820, a juzgar por Pérez de Camino, la benéfica fuerza de la

opinión pública resultaba admirable. La opinión podía destronar tiranos, restablecer el régimen liberal y democrático ('el imperio de la ley'), y expresarse libremente" (Glendinning 1984, p. 157).

48. "Antes de que se defina en las Cortes de Cádiz la 'soberanía nacional,' . . . el pueblo actúa como soberano, recogiendo y asumiendo . . . la soberanía que sus reyes han dejado en el arroyo. Y a ese nuevo soberano se dirigen los innumerables escritos que tratan de ilustrarle, adoctrinarle, prevenirle. Un factor nuevo y ya fundamental ha hecho su aparición, la 'opinión pública,' y a formarla, encauzarla, dirigirla se dedica esta prensa auroral del siglo. . . ." (Seoane Couceiro 1977, p. 25).

49. "El libre mercado en el que los intereses del público al parecer aseguran el éxito del mejor producto" (Kirkpatrick 1977, p. 126).

50. "Faltaba dar a conocer y denunciar a todo el mundo el duro monopolio que, como en todas las cosas, en punto de escribir había ejercido la facción tiránica . . . que por tantos años, a fuerza de mentiras, de rigores y violencias [ha estado] . . . *corrompiendo la opinión*" (MG, II, p. 418).

51. "Podría acaso oponerse a esta pintura de sus ventajas la de [sus desventajas, como, por ejemplo] la de las injurias que afectan contra los objetos de su parcialidad y su encono. Pero éste es un abuso que todos los hombres prudentes condenan y que . . . no puede ahogar la estimación debida a los papeles dignamente desempeñados. ¿Qué importa con efecto que algunos piratas escandalicen el mar cuando tantos navegantes llevan a todas partes el alimento y la vida?" (Quintana, cited in Seoane Couceiro 1977, p. 23).

52. "¿Dónde está ese público tan indulgente, tan ilustrado, tan imparcial, tan justo, tan respetable, eterno dispensador de la fama, de que tanto me han hablado; cuyo fallo es irrecusable constante, dirigido por un buen gusto invariable . . . ?" (Larra 1969, p. 36).

53. "Esa voz *público*, que todos traen en boca, siempre en apoyo de sus opiniones [es el] . . . comodín de todos los partidos, de todos los pareceres." "No existe un público invariable, juez imparcial, como se pretende; . . . cada clase de la sociedad tiene su público particular . . . éste es caprichoso, y casi siempre tan injusto y parcial como la mayor parte de los hombres que le componen" (ibid., pp. 31, 38).

54. "La luz de la verdad disipa, por fin, tarde o temprano las nieblas en que quieren ocultarla los partidarios de la ignorancia; y la fuerza de la opinión, que pudiéramos llamar, moralmente hablando, *ultima ratio populorum*, es, a la larga más poderosa e irresistible que lo es momentáneamente la que se ha llamado *ultima ratio regum*" (quoted in Kirkpatrick 1977, p. 11).

55. "No nos toca a nosotros decidir tan importante cuestión; la lectura de las Memorias del príncipe y los demás datos que la opinión pública tiene a la vista son los autos de este gran pleito entre el favorito y la sociedad. La

opinión pública . . . [aquel supremo tribunal] es quien debe hacer recaer su fallo" (Larra 1969, p. 1,053).

56. "[Ya] no se trata de una rectificación ante Dios o la conciencia, sino ante la opinión pública que ahora se manifiesta en las sociedades patrióticas, en pasquines murales, en pliegos, en periódicos y en libros" (Sánchez Blanco 1983, p. 39).

57. "[Pero] la opinión pública con la que se enfrenta la conciencia de sí mismo traspasa los límites de la corte o la ciudad y se presenta bajo la dimensión de la Nación o de la Historia" (ibid., p. 40).

58. "De la que se declaraban únicos intérpretes legítimos" (FEM, I, p. xxiii).

59. "Esa multitud de folletos, de libelos, de memorias, de biografías y de artículos de gaceta" (MG, I, p. 9).

60. "Hay españoles, y no españoles que se ocupan en publicar hechos parciales de mi vida política y militar, desfigurándolos a su antojo por la influencia apasionada de que están dominados" (FEM, I, p. 45).

61. E.g., "me propongo sólo decir lo que a la Historia no compite" (AG, I, p. 64); "Es de la Historia y no de mi propósito. . . ." (PAG, II, p. 79).

62. "La Historia ha publicado todo lo que es oficial a esta misión" (FdC, I, p. 65).

63. "La Historia, a que corresponde, no callará este extraño suceso" (PAG, II, p. 28).

64. "Mas la Historia . . . juzgará—me decía yo a mi mismo—esta reina de la opinión no recoge las brozas que las olas de las pasiones amontonaron en la orilla mientras bramaba la tormenta: no, la Historia no es nunca el órgano de las iras ni el grito de algazara de las parcialidades y los bandos: ella observa, ella ve, ella compara, ella pesa y pronuncia sus fallos sin someterse a las facciones" (MG, I, p. 9).

65. "[Al hombre del Estado] pocos lo juzgan con imparcialidad: los unos claman porque temen, los otros porque esperaban y no reciben, y entre los gustos interesados del mayor número, se oye mal la voz, en tales casos débil y apagada, de la razón, que enumera los aciertos o recuerda los beneficios para transmitirlos, en días más serenos, a la Historia" (PAG, II, p. 166).

66. "Siento molestar al lector repitiéndole unas mismas cosas . . . pero así lo exige la verdadera narración de los hechos" (FEM, I, p. 289). Another example: "Dejando estas particularidades, si propias de mis *Memorias,* nada a propósito para entretener a mis lectores. . . ." (AG, II, p. 188).

67. "Yo como hombre de la naturaleza más que del arte, acostumbro a decir las cosas ingenuamente, y mis acciones siguen el impulso de este carácter natural" (FEM, II, p. 45).

68. "No es mi intención fatigar a mis lectores" (MG, I, p. 113); "la verdad histórica, como la judicial, está compuesta de la totalidad de datos que concurren a formarla y a ilustrarla" (II, p. 221).

69. "Estos pobres recuerdos" (AG, I, p. 23); "mi pobre persona" (II, p. 84).

70. "Dejemos todas estas pequeñeces . . . y volvamos a la gravedad de los negocios políticos" (GLP, I, p. 247).

71. "Voy a referir los sucesos de mi vida, con los cuales están eslabonados muchos de los más importantes de mi Patria" (AG, I, p. 255).

72. "Sólo puede inducirles a sus publicaciones debilidades de hombres pequeños, pasiones e intereses mezquinos, envidia, soberbia, vanidad y acaso, acaso, resentimientos injustos, por no haberme hallado siempre tan dócil como ellos quisieran" (FEM, II, p. 45).

73. "Vivía yo en el seno de la más profunda paz y una tranquilidad perfecta, cuando las revueltas y convulsiones de la Patria, en los principios del año 1808, vinieron a robarme esta felicidad de que gozaba" (ibid., I, p. 7). "De esta dulce tranquilidad me sacó . . . el aviso inesperado de haberme elegido el Rey para Maestro del Príncipe de Asturias don Fernando . . . Hablando pocos días antes . . . con unos parientes míos . . . les dije que verdaderamente debíamos agradecer mucho a Dios la vida tranquila y agradable que disfrutábamos en Madrid, y que yo, por mí, no la trocaría por cuantos empleos pudieran darme en Palacio, como no fuesen tales que me proporcionasen ser de utilidad a la Patria, pues a ésta la antepondría a todas mis conveniencias" (JdE, pp. 15–16).

74. "Los que han querido detractarme y deprimirme por todos medios han hablado de mí como de un aventurero" (MG, I, p. 12).

75. "Doy estas particularidades sobre mi parentela porque muchos me tienen por un aventurero político de los que se elevan con las revoluciones, cuando, al revés, la revolución me ha sido funesta" (AG, II, p. 284). García de León y Pizarro claims, "Yo jamás he mirado en mis empleos principalmente en los Ministerios al interés de mi conservación, sino al bien del Estado" (GLP, I, p. 210).

76. "Como objeto de poco tamaño, propio para hacer medir, de pronto, con el cotejo, las dimensiones de las superficies" (AG, I, p. 329).

77. Girón exclaims at one moment, "¡Pobre España, si tan pequeños son todos tus grandes hombres!" (PAG, II, p. 178).

78. "—Señora—le dije—está reducida a que V.M. tenga la bondad de darme y cumplirme la palabra de no conferirme jamás renta alguna, honor ni empleo, ni a ningún pariente mío, a lo menos en consideración mía, segura de que, por mi parte, jamás pediré cosa alguna para mi ni para ellos" (JdE, p. 31).

79. "Referidos con la sencillez del hombre de la naturaleza . . ." (CEM, p. 15).

80. "Estos detalles que dan a conocer lo que era Mina, a quien solamente se conoce como guerrero y patriota, pero no como el individuo particular,

adornado de tantas dotes especiales para vivir en el hogar doméstico"
(ibid., p. 60).

81. "Y aun cuando a primera vista parezca que no tiene conexión con lo
que voy relatando lo que sigue, que es la relación de los medios con que he
contado para poder subsistir con mi familia durante mi emigración, se verá
que la tiene, porque no sólo destruye insinuaciones calumniosas . . . sino
que también prueba que hasta mi posición particular fuera de mi patria no
tiene los atractivos que pudieran suponerse para que no desee regresar a
ella" (FEM, II, p. 124).

82. "Yo, sin perjudicar a [la religión santa de mis padres] tenía que llenar
además los dogmas de otra religión patriótica" (ibid., I, p. 56).

83. "Pues . . . yo no era capaz de faltar a los deberes de buen español y
patriota por ninguna consideración del mundo" (ibid., I, p. 60).

84. "Forzosa separación a que el bien de la Patria me condenaba" (CEM,
p. 68).

85. "Empeoraba nuestra situación diariamente, y la mía en proporción a
la de la Patria" (ibid., p. 72).

86. "El descubrimiento de la interioridad en este siglo tiene unas carac-
terísticas especiales. El sujeto olvida las categorías teológicas y pierde el
horizonte de la transcendencia al observarse inmerso en el curso imparable
de los cambios históricos. La identidad individual no se puede hallar en la
continuidad del carácter, de las opiniones, de la posición social, sino en la
experiencia misma de las guerras internas, las transformaciones de las
instituciones y de las innovaciones que tienen lugar en las ciudades. El
mundo interior es el reflejo de la turbación que surge al derrumbarse el
fundamento del Antiguo Régimen" (Sánchez Blanco 1983, p. 46).

87. "Independencia que se manifiesta sobre todo frente a la incipiente
máquina política y burocrática del Estado" (Pastor 1975, p. 11).

88. "Veréis lo poco que vale el mundo" (GLP, I, p. 1). More examples
from the same text: "Yo callaba, sufría, y aprendía a aborrecer el mundo" (I,
p. 24); "empieza aquí mi carrera pública, o, por mejor decir, la historia de
lo que son las cosas del mundo" (I, p. 17).

89. "Sin papeles, sin noticias . . . me pareció estar en la gloria" (PAG, II,
p. 189).

90. "Y cuando menos lo pensaba me encontré de nuevo en medio de la
corte, y por consiguiente blanco otra vez de todos los chismes y de todas las
calumnias de mis enemigos" (ibid., II, p. 189).

91. "Las acusaciones, las bastardas novelas y los cuentos misteriosos"
(TV, p. 180).

92. "La tropa de los médicos chicos y grandes, [que] ha blaterado
horrores contra mi nombre, ha escupido sapos, ha vomitado culebras, ha

regoldado venenosas savandijas, y embidiosas desvergüenzas" (Gómez Arias 1744, prologue).

93. "La turba de copistas y hacedores de diccionarios y biografías . . . que les dan boga a estos errores" (MG, I, p. 12).

94. "Fábulas . . . , mentiras y basuras de pasiones" (ibid., I, p. 12).

95. "Injurias y amenazas . . . vomitad[as] contra [ellos]" (PAG, II, p. 171).

96. "La vulgarización de la imprenta [hace posible] la mentira a la orden del día y al alcance de todos" (Larra 1969, p. 906).

97. "Multitud de folletos y memorias, supuestos materiales para la Historia, . . . [que] en realidad [son] verdaderos albañales que corren hacia un río para perderse en él, ensuciándole y entrabando su curso" (ibid., p. 905).

98. "Mis enemigos . . . multiplicaban los enredos y los chismes de palacio para indisponerme de mil modos" (MG, I, p. 249).

99. "Afligido de la inutilidad de mis esfuerzos a favor de la Patria, pero contentísimo de verme fuera de Babilonia y restituído a mi antigua libertad y ocio" (JdE, p. 37).

100. "Fáltame todo, Señor mío; mas si Vos no me desamparáis, no os faltaré yo a Vos. Levántense contra mí todos los letrados, persíganme todas las cosas criadas, atorméntenme los demonios. . . ." (Teresa de Jesús 1963, p. 208).

101. "¡Adorada patria mía, yo te amé, yo te serví, con mi vida, con mi corazón, con mi alma; . . . y, sin embargo, este hombre mismo, calumniado de muchos . . . no encuentra tu justicia!" (MG, I, p. 167).

102. "La Historia, cuando aparte la basura que han esparcido las pasiones, *dirá* mejor y *dirá* más. . . ." (ibid., II, p. 484).

103. "La historia y el público *juzgarán* a todos" (FEM, II, p. 45).

104. "España *verá*, en fin, en mis desgracias, no común en las historias . . . *verá* la víctima inocente del error que le infundieron sus enemigos y los míos" (MG, II, p. 485).

2 A Life of Reading, the Readings of a *Life*

1. "En este tiempo me dieron las *Confesiones* de San Agustín que parece el Señor lo ordenó"; "Mucho me aprovechó . . . haber leído la historia de Job en los *Morales* de San Gregorio, que parece previno el Señor con esto" (Teresa de Jesús 1963, pp. 64, 29).

2. "Je ne sais comment j'appris à lire: je ne me souviens que de mes premières lectures et de leur effet sur moi; c'est le temps d'ou je date sans interruption la conscience de moi même" (Rousseau 1959, p. 5).

3. "Je forme une entreprise qui n'eut jamais d'exemple" (ibid., p. 8).

4. "Análisis clínicos de quienes resuelven en histeria y sensualidad los raptos y deliquios de Teresa de Avila" (Castro 1972, p. 44).

5. "Ce texte n'est pas lu"; "un refus deliberé d'écouter"; "refuser de le lire"; "le lecteur non-averti"; "le choix arbitraire de [ce lecteur]" (Lejeune 1975, pp. 51, 51, 56, 59, 70).

6. "L'episode de la fessée y retrouv[er] sa place fondatrice" (ibid., p. 70).

7. "Jusqu'ici j'ai essayé de rien dire que ce que Rousseau dit lui même. J'ai adopté sinon son langage, du moins sa problematique et son point de vue" (ibid., p. 77).

8. "Fai[re] de l'énonciation le lieu de sa recherche"; "evolution des systemes des contrats de lecture" (ibid., p. 8).

9. *Sous rature* is a practice used by both Heidegger and Derrida: "this is to write a word, cross it out, and then print both word and deletion. (Since the word is inaccurate, it is crossed out. Since it is necessary, it remains legible)" (Spivak 1976, p. xiv).

10. "As Augustine's soul is suffused with the Christ-logos, the narrative of his own origins returns to the narrative of universals, to the source of narrativity itself" (Vance 1973a, p. 13). "It is as though he dare not undertake anything so risky as the interpretation of Scripture until he has brought himself to an awareness of where he stands and where he has come" (Burrel 1970, p. 334).

11. "Así pasó sus trabajosos e infelices días, como nave sin piloto en ruda tempestad, entre continuas apostasías y cambios de frente, dudando cada día de lo que el anterior afirmaba, renegando hasta su propio entendimiento, levantándose cada mañana con nuevos apasionamientos que él tomaba por convicciones y que venían a tierra con la misma facilidad que sus hermanas a la víspera. . . ." (MP, p. 174).

12. "Vanamente pedía a la ciencia lo que la ciencia no podía darle, la serenidad y templanza de espíritu" (ibid.).

13. "Católico primero, enciclopedista después, luego partidario de la iglesia anglicana, y a la postre unitario y apenas cristiano . . . , tal fue la vida teológica de Blanco, nunca regida sino por el ídolo del momento y el amor desenfrenado del propio pensar, que con ser adverso a toda solución dogmática, tampoco en el escepticismo se aquietaba nunca, sino que cabalgaba afanosamente, y por sendas torcidas, en busca de la unidad" (ibid.).

14. "Perdió definitivamente [la serenidad] desde que el orgullo y la lujuria le hicieron abandonar la benéfica sombra del santuario" (ibid.).

15. See Vicente Lloréns (1971, p. 22).

16. "Tenía varios hijos y amando entrañablemente a aquellos frutos de sus pecados, quería a toda costa darles nombre y consideración social" (MP, p. 185).

17. "La esperanza de honores y estimación social para él y para sus hijos" (ibid., p. 191).

18. "Aprenda [mi lector] a qué atenerse sobre las teologías y liberalismos de Blanco. Que siempre han de andar faldas de por medio en este negocio de herejías" (ibid., p. 184).

19. "¿Y no sería absurdo invocar argumentos de unidad, autoridad y tradición dogmática en favor de la Iglesia anglicana, es decir, de una Iglesia nacida ayer, rebelde y cismática, y desestimar la misma unidad y la misma tradición aplicadas a la Iglesia de Roma, la más antigua y robusta institución del mundo moderno, fundada sobre la roca incontrastable de los siglos? [Eso sería] . . . otorgar a la hija rebelde lo que negaba a la madre. . . ." (ibid., pp. 194–95).

20. "Nacida ayer de mañana por torpe contubernio de la lujuria de un rey, de la codicia de una aristocracia y del servilismo de un clero opulento y degradado" (ibid., p. 195).

21. "Que sois un puñado de rebeldes, y no os llaméis herederos de la primitiva Iglesia, que os hubiera arrojado de su seno" (ibid., p. 200).

22. "No nos indignemos con Blanco: basta compadecerle. Ni una idea robusta, ni un afecto sereno había atravesado su vida. Era el renegado de todas las sectas, el leproso de todos los partidos, y caminaba al sepulcro sin fé en la misma duda" (ibid., p. 209).

23. "Sólo esta flor poética crece, a modo de siempreviva, sobre el infamado sepulcro de Blanco. Cuando acabe de extinguir el último eco de sus polémicas y de su escandalosa vida, la Musa del Canto conservará su memoria vinculada en catorce versos de melancólica armonía" (ibid., p. 212).

24. "Sus ideas, su sensibilidad, su lenguaje tenían que ser incomprensibles para quienes seguían aferrados a una tradición que él había abandonado hacía años" (JG, p. 5).

25. "Predicaba en el desierto" (ibid., p. 26); "era el chivo emisario de nuestros calenturientos patriotas" (p. 38); "recibe palos de todas partes y apenas encuentra un alma que se lo agradezca" (p. 44).

26. "El imperdonable delito de pensar y escribir por su cuenta" (ibid., p. 43).

27. "Al hablar de Blanco White no he cesado de hablar de mí mismo" (ibid., p. 98).

28. "Una fraternidad de outsiders, parias y marginales" (ibid., p. 97).

29. "La voz extinguida de España, voz que en 1971 reconocemos *nuestra*—voz descondicionada, profética, libre que brota del infierno en donde para vergüenza de todos, permanece todavía enterrada" (ibid., p. 32).

3 The Experience of Crisis, the Crisis of Experience

1. "Mi vida, [no] . . . merece más honras ni más epitafios que el olvido y el silencio" (TV, p. 52).

2. "La identidad individual no se puede hallar . . . sino en la experiencia misma de las guerras internas, las transformaciones de las instituciones y de las innovaciones que tienen lugar en las ciudades" (Sánchez Blanco 1983, p. 46).

3. "La fabricación más importante de la villa capital, ya se considere como materia prima para aplicaciones sucesivas, ya como producto elaborado y de uso cómodo e inmediato es la fabricación de reputaciones: fabricación tan amplia, que no solamente sirve al surtido de la corte y sitios reales, sino que extiende su comercio y abastece por lo general todos los mercados del reino. Esta poderosa industria, explotada en grande en Madrid, tiene por ricos veneros y por activos talleres la tribuna, la imprenta y la plaza pública" (Mesonero Romanos 1925, vol. 2, pp. 39–40).

4. "El vapor, que es el motor del siglo, tiene los pulmones de hierro y no se cansa de dar carreras" (Flores 1968, p. 168).

5. For a fascinating look at the impact of the railroad on nineteenth-century culture, see Schivelbusch (1986). The short stories of Clarín (Leopoldo Alas, 1989) are a rich source of images of the conflicts of modernity in Spain.

6. "Veleidoso" or "fickle" (MP, p. 178); "móvil, arrebatado y violento" (ibid., p. 173); "constant to nothing but mutability" (WEG, p. 17).

7. "Principio constante de inquietud, de veleidad y agitación" (Martínez de la Rosa 1835, p. 18); "siglo agitado, agitador" (MR, p. 257).

8. "Los que han alcanzado otra época" (AG, I, p. 266).

9. "Hoy existen pocos que hayan sido testigos presenciales: pocos y que parecemos ruinas en pie, pero en quienes no está mal cuando podamos, que hablemos, pues no somos de piedra" (ibid., p. 64).

10. "Por algo y para algo sobrevivo y espero sobrevivir mucho tiempo. To tell my story, como le decía Hamlet a Horacio al impedirle que se diera muerte. Así viviré yo . . . to tell my story" (Benavente y Martínez 1958, p. 806).

11. "Asómate a París, Emilio, y medita dos horas; ¡dime en seguida si camina el siglo hacia la perfección o se precipita hacia la locura!" (Alarcón 1943, p. 114).

12. "Todo por allí es desorden, confusión . . ." (Parlaverdades 1849, p. 17).

13. "Época de confusión" (Pérez Galdós 1972, p. 218).

14. "Verdadera imagen de la primera confusión de los elementos" (Larra 1969, pp. 127–28).

15. "Vida[s] agitada[s . . .], vertiginosa[s]" (MR, 28).

16. "Museo amalgamado y confundido"; "Al pie de Cristo hay un par de pistolas, o . . . delante de la virgen hay un par de botellas de vino. . . ." (Flores 1968, p. 200).

17. "Mundo de escaparates y de andenes" (ibid., p. 192).

18. "Las consabidas quejas sobre la nivelación de la vida española" (Montesinos 1983, p. 116).

19. "El gabán nivelador y la negra corbata no habían aún confundido como después lo hicieron, todas las clases, todas las edades, todas las condiciones" (MR, p. 259). The complaint is echoed throughout the nineteenth century. Cf. Alarcón (1943), for example: "Antes de que el implacable nivel revolucionario reduzca el suelo español, como ya redujo el de otras naciones, a una monótona llanura cubierta de ciudades uniformadas . . . , antes de que en todas las villas y aldeas de la península se vistan los señores y los labriegos con arreglo a un mismo figurín y dejen de hablar los patuás, perseguidos ya como el contrabando . . . ; antes, en fin, de que la explanación, la alineación, la perforación y la expropiación forzosa hayan terminado su sacrílega tarea . . . deber es de los escritores y de los artistas de nuestro tiempo apresurarse a recoger y archivar. . . ." (Montesinos 1977, p. 196).

20. "¿Qué es el parlamento sino un armario exquisito?" (Flores 1968, p. 192).

21. "Allí se deben estudiar nuestra política y nuestras costumbres. . . . El rastro compone frases elocuentes: la muleta de un cojo junto a una estrella del norte. . . ." (Parlaverdades 1849, p. 33).

22. "Esas figuras que semejan hombres, y que ves bullir, empujarse, oprimirse, retorcerse, cruzarse y sobreponerse . . . no son hombres tales, sino palabras. [. . . Al rato] volví a caer en París, donde me encontré rodando entre la confusión de palabras vestidas de frac y de sombrero. . . ." (Larra 1969, p. 510).

23. "Podemos comparar a la Historia moderna con una inmensa luna colocada en un salón de máscaras y donde mezclados rebullen y se codean, se obstruyen y confunden en un disparatado conjunto de colores chocantes y chillones, sin juego ni armonía, reyes y vasallos, ricos y pobres, víctimas y verdugos, tiranos y tiranizados. . . ." (ibid., p. 905).

24. "La misma confusión evolutiva que advertimos en la sociedad" [constituye] "la primera materia del arte novelesco" (Pérez Galdós 1972, p. 180; cited in Fernández-Cifuentes 1988, p. 291).

25. "Pero no creáis que de lo expuesto intentaré sacar una deducción pesimista, afirmando que esta descomposición social ha de traer días de anemia y de muerte para el arte narrativo. [Al contrario] . . . la falta de principios de unidad favorece el florecimiento literario" (Pérez Galdós 1972, p. 178).

26. "Contábamos, sin duda, los incansables viajeros con que una voz sobrenatural nos dijera desde lo alto: por aquí se va y nada más que por aquí. Pero la voz sobrenatural no hiere aún nuestros oídos y los más sabios de entre nosotros se enredan en interminables controversias" (ibid., p. 177).

27. "Voces por un lado con una relación, voces por otra con la contraria: multitud de folletos y memorias, supuestos materiales para la Historia en realidad verdaderos albañales que corren hacia un río para perderse en él, ensuciándole y entrabando su curso" (Larra 1969, p. 905).

28. "En la corte todos son obispos para crismar y curas para baptizar y mudar nombres. . . ." (Guevara 1915, pp. 144–45).

29. "Gritos de los pregones . . . Esto se ha convertido en una verdadera Babilonia" (Flores 1968, p. 24).

30. "La puerta del Sol no es una puerta. ¡Pero quién hace caso de etimologías, ni de abolengos, ni de tradiciones históricas, hoy que al anochecer se declara viejo y caduco lo que nació aquella misma mañana!" (ibid., p. 34).

31. "Cavallos que te atropell[a]n, . . . ruidos que te espant[a]n . . . [y la] gran confusión de negocios" (Guevara 1915, p. 129).

32. "Amigo difunto, lo que has de ver en este siglo es adelantado el vicio y la necedad. . . . Ningún siglo ha rebosado más embustes: porque has de entender que nos anegamos en sastres, llueven zapateros, hay langosta de letrados y a enjambres andan los agentes, escribanos y relatores" (Torres Villarroel 1966, p. 24).

33. "Hay que perdonar a los viejos que conmemoren sus buenos o malos tiempos, como a los desdichados que cuentan sus desdichas" (Nombela 1909, vol. 1, p. v).

34. "En el mes y año en que empezó en el mundo la más importante y grave mudanza que han visto todas la edades" (AG, I, p. 259).

35. Cf. Antonio Flores: "El cañón de los invasores nos hizo brincar sobre el lecho en que dormíamos con el sueño de los inocentes la siesta de los cándidos; desde la cama, y sin más ropa que la puesta, pasamos al carro de la revolución, y arrastrados de precipicio en precipicio, hicimos en pocas horas las jornadas que debimos haber hecho en muchos años" (Flores 1968, p. 7).

36. "La primera impresión en mi infantil imaginación fue también la portada, el prospecto, digámoslo así, del libro de nuestra historia contemporánea. Me refiero al 19 de marzo de 1808. Fecha memorable en que, rotos los lazos y tradiciones que unían una y otra generación, y quebrantados los antiguos cimientos de la antigua sociedad española, la lanzó a una vida nueva, agitada, vertiginosa" (MR, p. 27).

37. "Hallábase reunida toda la familia en la sala de la casa, . . . y rezando en actitud religiosa el Santo Rosario, operación cotidiana que dirigía mi padre, y a que contestábamos todos los demás . . . Cuando nos hallábamos todos más o menos místicamente entregados a tan santa ocupación, vino a interrumpirla un desusado resplandor, que entraba por los balcones, una algazara inaudita que se sentía en la calle . . . ¡Viva el Rey! ¡Viva el Príncipe de Asturias!" (ibid., p. 29).

38. "Concluía la guerra extranjera: pero surgía al mismo tiempo la más intestina y porfiada de los españoles entre sí; lucha fatal entre lo pasado y lo porvenir, que dura todavía; que nosotros heredamos de nuestros padres, y transmitimos a nuestros hijos y nietos" (ibid., p. 104).

39. "Ni tampoco [su] gobierno pudo hacer otra cosa que preparar proyectos de mejoría, convirtiendo, por de pronto en ruinas, siempre lamentables, los espacios que consideraban oportunos para efectuarlos" (ibid., p. 144).

40. "A su vista, mi buen padre, bañado en lágrimas el rostro y con la voz ahogada por la más profunda pena, nos hacía engolfar por aquellas sombrías encrucijadas, encaramarnos a aquellas peligrosas ruinas, indicándonos la situación y los restos de los monumentales edificios que representaban. 'Aquí, nos decía . . . era el magnífico monasterio de San Vicente; aquí el de San Cayetano . . . y por aquí cruzaban las calles Larga, de los Angeles, de Santa Ana . . . y otras que habían desaparecido del todo' " (ibid., p. 109–10).

41. "Pisamos pues, aquellas célebres aunque modestas heredades, hallándolas casi yermas, si bien sembradas de huesos y esqueletos de hombres y caballos . . . Era un inmenso cementerio. . . ." (ibid., p. 110).

42. "La dialéctica de lo que es y lo que fue" (Sánchez Blanco 1983, p. 41).

43. "Su experiencia es el constante aplazamiento de la incumplida meta. . . ." (Subirats 1979, p. 65).

44. William Wordsworth, "The Song of the Wandering Jew": "Day and night my toils redouble / never nearer to the goal."

45. "La determinación de la figura del errante debe remitirse a los orígenes de la filosofía burguesa de la historia y dentro de ella a dos momentos fundamentales e inter-relacionados. Uno de ellos es el primado epistemológico del perfectibilismo, de la *perfectibilité continue* . . . el segundo es el de la continuidad del progreso" (Subirats 1979, p. 64).

46. "Aquella muerte aplazada siempre, pospuesta una vez más" (González Ruano 1979, p. 9).

47. "Reposo de octogenario"; "narrar cuanto he visto en Barcelona." (Roure 1925, vol. 1, pp. 6–7).

48. "Su ya oxidada pluma sólo puede brindar hoy con prosaica y descarnada narración de hechos ciertos y positivos, con retratos fotográficos de hombres de verdad que le fue dado a observar en su larga vida contemplativa. . . ." (MR, p. 23) ". . . y cuenta que todo esto lo dice, casi al borde del sepulcro, un testigo imparcial de aquella época" (p. 290).

49. "La marcha histórica de nuestra sociedad" (ibid., p. 175); "el progreso material de la capital" (p. 381); "la marcha civilizadora del siglo" (p. 316).

50. "La marcha, ya progresiva o ya retrógrada de la civilización y de la

cultura es lo que bien o mal me propuse reflejar en estas Memorias" (ibid., p. 130).

51. "Tipos hallados" and "tipos perdidos" are Mesonero's categories. See vol. 3 of his *Obras completas* called *Tipos y caracteres*. For his pose as an old man, see the "nota del autor" appended to the article "El retrato" in the same vol.: "Este artículo fue el primero que publicó el autor con la firma de Un Curioso Parlante, en la revista titulada *Cartas españolas* del 12 de enero de 1832. Leyéndole hoy no puede menos de sonreir al observar el empeño que en su primera edad juvenil parece que formaba en aparecer viejo ante sus lectores. . . . Achaque es este natural y propio de los escritores de costumbres que anhelando siempre proceder por comparación con épocas anteriores, van a buscarlas, cuando muchachos, a las sociedades que no alcanzaron" (Mesonero Romanos 1925, p. 35).

52. "Todavía humean las cenizas de este tipo recientemente sepultado por la novísima ley de Ayuntamientos" (Flores, 1968, p. 21).

53. "Y mientras tanto, Dios te guarde y a nosotros nos tenga de su mano para que no se escapen de entre las nuestras los objetos que hemos de examinar" (ibid., p. 21).

54. "Un melancólico perito en cosas en trance de extinción" (González Ruano 1979, p. 10).

55. "No puedo menos de repetir que todas estas canciones (que no creo llegasen a ser impresas) las retengo desde entonces en mi memoria, con su música respectiva, a la manera que el novísimo invento del fonógrafo diz que conserva los sonidos . . . Yo he aplicado al fonógrafo de mi memoria el registro del año 1808 y encuentro reproducidos con música y letra estos cantos patrióticos que escuché en mi tierna edad" (MR, p. 61).

56. "Los nombres subrayados son los de los fallecidos" (ibid., p. 294); "de los 295 que en [la lista] constan, sólo sobrevivimos 12" (p. 364).

57. "La casa y el jardín (hoy suprimidos)" (ibid., p. 33); "la reducida calle de Olivo Bajo (que así se llamaba)" (p. 34); "la casa hoy derribada" (p. 43); "en la casa que hoy lleva el número dos, inmediata a la capilla . . . después derribada" (p. 182); "en la manzana frontera (que hoy no existe)" (p. 293).

58. "Luego [se les] cambió el nombre a muchas calles y plazas" (Roure 1925, vol. 3, p. 103).

59. "¡Ni las calles pueden vivir tranquilas con este Ayuntamiento! Ahora se trata de quitarle a la de A su nombre para bautizarla con el de R . . . Ch . . . , difunto ex-concejal" (Ruiz Contreras 1917, p. 37).

60. "Hoy, ¿quién sabe cómo se llamará hoy esta calle?" (Benavente y Martínez 1958, p. 563).

61. "Hasta en los nombres de las cosas disienten los partidos" (PAG, I, p. 181).

62. "Memorias son estas en las que Madrid se encuentra a sí mismo"

(Pastor, p. 22); "su biografía acaba por no ser otra cosa que un trozo de la gran biografía de la ciudad. Hablar de Mesonero, escribir de Mesonero, es hablar y escribir de Madrid" (Seco Serrano 1973, p. 141).

63. "Insistí también en la reforma completa de la numeración de las casas . . . adoptando el sistema de los números pares a la derecha e impares a la izquierda . . . La fijación de nuevas lápidas claras y consistentes con el nombre de cada calle a la entrada y salida de ella y la variación de muchos nombres duplicados y aun triplicados, ridículos y hasta obscenos, sustituyéndolos con los de hechos históricos y personajes notables del país" (MR, p. 343).

64. "No creo inoportuno hacer mención de la notable coincidencia que ofrecía mi entrada en la vida con la inauguración de una época nueva en la marcha histórica de nuestra sociedad" (ibid., p. 174).

65. "Reducido el vecindario de Madrid a la estrecha esfera de una triste cautividad. . . ." (ibid., p. 73); "cuatro años mortales de cautiverio" (p. 73); "un largo y penoso cautiverio" (pp. 117–18).

66. "¿Qué interés de novedad han de podernos inspirar los recuerdos de un hombre que, según confesión propia, no ha figurado para nada en el mapa histórico ni político del país, no ha vivido lo que suele llamarse la vida pública; no ha entrado jamás en intrigas cortesanas ni en conspiraciones revolucionarias? . . . Alto ahí, señores míos, contestará el autor, todo eso que Uds. dicen es verdad, pero también lo es que esta misma insignificancia política de su persona, combinada con su independencia de posición y carácter, le brindan con mayor don de imparcialidad, al mismo tiempo que le reducen a considerar los sucesos políticos únicamente bajo su aspecto exterior" (ibid., p. 24).

67. "Soy en fin, independiente/de hecho y también de propósito/sin compromisos ajenos/y hasta sin deseos propios. . . . Nada era, nada soy" (ibid., p. 404). Other self-effacing expressions found throughout the Memorias: "mi impolítica personilla" (p. 218); "mi humilde persona" (p. 295); "mi insignificante persona" (p. 385).

68. "Penetrando (acaso por última vez en estas Memorias) en el dominio de la historia [para] consignar las singulares peripecias políticas. . . ." (ibid., p. 325).

69. "Vuelvo, no sin repugnancia, a la narración de los sucesos políticos en aquel año" (ibid., p. 219).

70. "Vida tranquila y bonacible, no interrumpida por las agitaciones políticas ni por las peripecias de la historia" (ibid., p. 26).

71. "Habrá al menos que rendir el debido homenaje a un pueblo cuya sensatez, ilustración y cultura ha sabido resistir a las terribles pruebas de tres guerras civiles, sin haber regado sus campiñas con la sangre de sus hijos, ni añadido una página sola a nuestra lúgubre historia contemporánea" (ibid., p. 115).

72. "Sus negocios y sus expansiones más naturales. . . ." (ibid., p. 72); "la vitalidad propia de los pueblos modernos" (ibid., p. 211).

73. "El organismo, que parecía una unidad independiente, capaz de obrar por sí mismo, es inserto en el medio físico, como una figura en un tapiz. . . . No hay libertad, originalidad. Vivir es adaptarse: adaptarse es dejar que el contorno material penetre en nosotros, nos *desaloje* de nosotros mismos. Adaptación es sumisión y renuncia. Darwin barre los héroes de sobre el haz de la tierra" (Ortega y Gasset 1921, pp. 193–94).

74. "Las osadas aspiraciones del poder, el frenesí del mando y el menosprecio de la autoridad" (MR, p. 262); "los sagrados vínculos de la cuna, de la familia y de la propiedad" (p. 347).

75. "La política no tiene entrañas: es egoista, codiciosa, convierte por conveniencia las iniquidades en sacrificios pseudo-patrióticos, todo lo supedita al logro de sus ambiciones, el *Qua nominor leo* es su moral y divisa y anticipándose a Darwin . . . ha hecho, hace y hará de la superioridad convencional el arma con que destruye a los enemigos inferiores. . . . Había oído hablar con frecuencia de política, pero sin enterarme de lo que significaba en la vida de los pueblos y . . . en la de las familias" (Nombela 1909, vol. 2, pp. 7, 340).

76. "Oh, maldita, antisocial y anticristiana política, cuyo fantasma puede separar en vida a los padres de sus hijos . . ." (RTV, I, p. 263).

77. "¡Medrados estábamos si perdiéramos el tiempo en averiguar el porqué de las cosas, cuando cada cual recibe el título de lo que debe ser con solo ocultar las pruebas de lo que ha sido y presentar el testimonio de lo que está haciendo!" (Flores 1968, p. 34).

78. "Al hablar de mí, debo decir algo de mi familia. Esto no está al uso ahora, al menos en España, donde las ideas democráticas predominan" (AG, I, p. 255).

79. "Me detengo en genealogías porque mi madre me las recordaba siempre que yo aventuraba ideas liberales y democráticas, disonantes en aquel ámbito doméstico" (Moreno Villa 1944, p. 27).

80. "Don Juan, con antifaz, sentado a una mesa escribiendo. . . . Al levantarse el telón se ven pasar por la puerta del fondo máscaras, estudiantes y pueblo" (Zorrilla 1987, p. 79).

81. "Salí de Roma, por fin / . . . / Con un disfraz harto ruin / y a lomos de un mal rocín" (ibid., p. 100).

82. "Ha recorrido mi amor / toda la escala social . . . ; Desde la princesa altiva / a la que pesca en ruin barca . . . ; Yo a las cabañas bajé / yo a los palacios subí / yo a los claustros escalé / y en todas partes dejé / memoria amarga de mí / No reconocí sagrado / ni hubo ocasión ni lugar / por mi audacia respetado / ni en distinguir me he parado / el clérigo del seglar" (ibid., pp. 106, 100, 223).

83. My reading of the Tenorio owes a great deal to seminars and discus-

sions with Luis Fernández-Cifuentes. Gustavo Pérez Firmat, in his *Literature and Liminality: Festive Readings in the Hispanic Tradition* (1986) makes a number of interesting observations on the relationship between the don Juan, fathers, and carnival.

84. "*Gonzalo:* ¡Que un hombre como yo tenga / que esperar aquí, y se avenga / con semejante papel! / En fin, me importa el sosiego / de mi casa, y la ventura / de mi hija sencilla y pura" (ibid., p. 89). "*Diego:* ¡Que un hombre de mi linaje / descienda a tan ruin mansión / Pero no hay humillación / a que un padre no se baje / por un hijo!" (Zorrilla, 1987, p. 91).

85. "Adiós, pues; mas no te olvides / de que hay un Dios justiciero" (ibid., p. 109).

86. "Mi padre era el último eslabón entero de la rota cadena de la época realista, la cifra viviente, el recuerdo personificado del formulista absolutismo, el buen estudiante ergotista de las Universidades de sotana y manteo, el doctor en ambos derechos por el claustro de la de Valladolid; convencido desde su niñez de que solo el estudio del derecho, la teología y los cánones podría producir hombres. . . . Yo era el primero y débil eslabón de la nueva época literaria, el atropellador desaforado de la tradición y de las reglas clásicas" (RTV, p. 206).

87. "Metiéronme, pues, en una galera que iba para [la casa paterna en Lerma . . . pero] en un descuido del conductor eché a lomos de una yegua, que no era mía, y que por aquellos campos pastaba, y me volví a Valladolid por . . . otro camino del que la galera había traido" (ibid., I, p. 27).

88. "Sirviéndome de infalible seña gitanesca mi trenzada melena, que, riza y suelta, servía de seña personal a los que me buscaban, de parte de mi familia, para volverme a casa" (ibid., I, p. 29).

89. "¡Desventurado aquel cuyo primer delito es una rebelión contra la autoridad paterna! . . . [Dios] no deja que repose [su] conciencia" (ibid., I, p. 36).

90. "Don Juan desatina siempre; doña Inés encauza siempre las escenas que él desborda" (ibid., I, p. 153).

91. "Conque hay otra vida más / y otro mundo que el de aquí" (Zorrilla 1987, p. 221).

92. "Por eso, al final, cuando en los 'Recuerdos' vuelve su mirada para llorar sobre sus días, quiere rescatarlos con las mismas armas con que su don Juan se redimiera: con la fuerza y el arrojo de un corazón noble y sincero" (RTV, I, p. vii).

93. "Viaje de vuelta por el casi borrado rastro del florido camino de la juventud. . . ." (ibid., I, p. 121).

94. "La primera carta del bravo Velarde me dio pie para contar lo pasado en el cementerio al borde de la tumba de Larra: y por este recuerdo, como

quien tira de un hilo de una madeja enredada, fui yo tirando de mis pobres recuerdos del tiempo viejo" (ibid., I, p. 7).

95. "Según iba leyendo aquellos mis tan hilvanados versos, iba leyendo en los semblantes de los que absorptos me rodeaban, el asombro que mi aparición y mi voz les causaba. Imaginé que Dios me deparaba aquel extraño escenario, aquel auditorio tan unísono con mi palabra, y aquella ocasión tan propicia y excepcional" (ibid., I, p. 36).

96. "Como si Dios le hubiera quitado por muerte natural al hijo que civilmente murió al fugarse del paterno hogar" (ibid., I, p. 229).

97. "Estaba escrito, como dicen los árabes, que el miserable ingenio que Dios me dio no me había de servir más que para mi perdición; mis versos estaban malditos por mi padre" (ibid., II, p. 9).

98. "Se va a América por sus pecados" (ibid., II, p. 226).

99. "Me fugaba de mi patria como en otro tiempo me había fugado del hogar paterno . . . volví yo en 1854 la espalda a España, a Europa, a mis creencias y a mi poesía" (ibid., I, p. 273).

100. "Esta vuelta mía fue la vuelta del hijo pródigo al paterno hogar, y cayó en gracia cuanto hice y dije, y se me abrieron todas las puertas, y me recibieron como a hermano en todas las familias (ibid., I, p. 10) [. . . como] el esclarecido hijo [de la patria]" (I, p. 15).

101. "El hombre, al romper con la sociedad establecida se pone fuera de la ley, se convierte, en el sentido primario de la palabra en "bandido." . . . Esta situación de fuera-de-la-ley-injusta siempre, y cuando menos falsa . . . ostenta su propia grandeza romántica, la del que, despreciando todas las conveniencias, se alza contra la *adaptación,* contra la *integración social*" (Aranguren 1966, p. 80).

102. "¿Quién se iba a revelar definitivamente, el padre o el magistrado?" (RTV, I, p. 208).

103. "Era un paraíso para heredado por el hijo con el amor y la bendición de sus padres: pero era un antro inhabitable para el que a heredarle venía como poseedor forzoso, amparado no más por la ley, que no tiene entrañas, ni sentimientos, sino derechos" (ibid., I, p. 251).

104. "Había yo vivido poquísimo tiempo con mi madre; a los ocho años me había metido mi padre en un colegio de Sevilla"; ". . . [un] resultado inevitable de la educación fuera de la familia [es que] se pierde uno para ésta tanto cuanto se gana para la sociedad: yo me gané para el mundo y me perdí para mi familia" (ibid., I, p. 182).

105. "Era aquel rincón [la casa] un nido de recuerdos, un manantial de poesía, donde se encerraban los de mi madre y la de mis primeros amores" (ibid., I, p. 23); "aquella mansión con la cual había soñado siempre y la cual me había siempre imaginado como un oasis en el desierto de mi vida de trabajo y abnegación" (I, p. 116); "Mi carácter había conservado siempre la infantil alegría del niño en medio de los trabajos y las vicisitudes de la

existencia del hombre" (II, p. 111). Finally, poetry itself, "l'enfance retrouvée a volonté," is consistently portrayed as being antithetical to work and to "laws."

106. "Yo no pertenezco a ninguna clase de la sociedad porque los poetas no estamos clasificados en ninguna categoría social; no he pertenecido jamás a ningún partido político. . . ." (ibid., I, p. 18).

107. "Poeta formado de las entrañas de su pueblo, sus ideas, sus sentimientos, aunque universales . . . son ante todo españoles: tanto que, al vibrar su lira, nos parece escuchar el acento de la patria." The words are Velarde's. They appear in a letter included in Zorrilla's *Recuerdos* (ibid., I, p. 13).

108. "Madrid, declarado en estado de sitio y prohibida en él la reunión de más de cinco personas, reunió más de cuatro mil para acompañarme a mi casa desde la estación una mañana de octubre de 1866" (ibid., II, p. 19).

109. "Hoy que la edad le agobia y el trabajo le fatiga, le ha[n] retirado la modesta asignación con que vivía y le ha[n] abandonado a la miseria, sin duda para que ciña a un tiempo a sus sienes la corona de laurel de la poesía y la de espinas del martirio" (José Velarde in ibid., I, p. 16).

110. "Todo esto me hace olvidar la vida vertiginosa de allá, el ruido y la balumba del Gran Boulevard, la prisa de la vida moderna" (Blasco 1894, p. 7).

111. "La fuerza de su color local está en razón inversa de su progreso. Pero ¿qué importa si es la patria? ¿Acaso hay madre defectuosa? . . . si en España se hiciera lo que en otros países, ya no sería España . . . Suprimid en las escaleras de una casa de Madrid el olor del aceite . . . y no hay tal Madrid. Y sones y olores, y músicas y aromas constituyen la nacionalidad, que surge y penetra en ondas de olor y dan escalofrío de placer al tornar al hogar materno" (ibid., pp. 113–14, 128, 44, 118).

112. "Reina en este pueblo [Avilés] una amable jovialidad infantil" (PV, p. 55); "como si la hermosa villa quisiera poner su alegría y su inocencia bajo la guardia de aquel que dijo 'O niños o como niños'" (p. 57); "el encanto de Avilés consiste en su alegría infantil" (p. 166).

113. "El comercio mismo, que por su naturaleza es sórdido, tenía en nuestra villa un temperamento noble y tranquilo" (PV, p. 118); "la política que suele ser trágica en los pueblos y encender las pasiones . . . reviste en Oviedo un aspecto cómico" (p. 167).

114. "Corría el año 1861. En Avilés vivíamos ignorados pero felices. Allá lejos podrían sublevarse los batallones y en Madrid alzarse barricadas y en todas partes encenderse la lucha y venir en pos de ella las sangrientas represiones, matanzas y fusilamientos. Nosotros no nos ocupábamos en semejantes bagatelas" (PV, p. 153).

115. "En la medida en que muestra el dolor del esfuerzo del trabajo" (Subirats 1979, p. 33).

116. " 'Preguntad a los niños y a los pájaros cómo saben las cerezas' dice un proverbio alemán. Ignoro como sabrán a los pájaros, pero en cuanto a mí me sabían tan bien hace sesenta años que cuando veía una cesta de ellas caía inmediatamente en éxtasis como Santa Teresa en presencia del Sacramento" (PV, p. 9).

117. "Aquel verano envió Dios a la tierra el más verde follaje, las brisas más perfumadas, las aguas más cristalinas y las cerezas más encarnadas de su infinito repertorio" (ibid., p. 24).

118. "Todos [mis seres queridos] habían sido enviados por Dios para hacerme dichoso" (ibid., p. 159).

119. "Mi alma se puso en contacto con la naturaleza . . . Parecía que la tierra me sustentaba con amor ofreciéndome sus dones, que participaba de su felicidad y vivía en mística unidad con ella" (ibid., p. 231).

120. "Como uno que sin deprender ni haver travajado nada para saber leer, hallase toda la ciencia sabida ya en si" (Teresa de Jesús 1963, p. 220).

121. Lejeune has written on the alleged "unautobiographical character" of the rural world in similar terms: "L'absence d'autobiographie paysanne était previsible: le monde rural traditionel constitue par définition un espace culturel anti-autobiographique: insularité, temps cyclique, oralité, vie communitaire" (Lejeune 1983, p. 210).

122. "La historia de la infancia es igual siempre a sí misma. Es la felicidad. Todo niño es feliz si una mano brutal no se interpone entre él y la felicidad" (PV, p. 9).

123. "Recuerdo que la vara de avellano que usaba el maestro don Juan de la Cruz no me inspiraba simpatía" (ibid., p. 78).

124. Alfonso Camín, in his *Entre manzanos* takes a completely different stance toward the Asturias he left behind. It seems that leaving Asturias and acquiring culture or letters is precisely what enables him to see the region for what it is: "[me refiero al paisaje asturiano de la Peñuca,] paisaje que sólo comprendí cuando, a los 18 o 20 años, leí en la Habana las obras de Mauricio Maeterlinck" (Camín 1952, p. 12).

125. "Yo me dispuse a pasar la eternidad como la pasan los ángeles, suponiendo que los ángeles no tengan colegio" (PV, p. 19).

126. "Jamás hubo un estudiante de quinto año más ansioso de hacerse bachiller. Este magno acontecimiento era, a mi modo de ver, la llave del Paraíso. En efecto, fue la llave, mas no para abrirlo, sino para cerrarlo. . . . Tal deseo vehemente de hacerme bachiller no era sólo por las preeminencias que tan glorioso título lleva consigo. Mis padres me habían prometido enviarme a Madrid a seguir la carrera de jurisprudencia. . . ." (ibid., p. 234).

127. "Pero ya comenzamos a escalar las grandiosas montañas de Pajares. . . . ¡Adiós dulce infancia! ¡Adiós adolescencia soñadora! Allá abajo me esperan la casa de huéspedes sórdida, la indiferencia desdeñosa, la hostilidad irracional, el placer sin alegría, el remordimiento" (ibid., p. 239).

128. "Muchas, muchísimas veces me he preguntado. . . . ¿Cuál será el mundo verdaderamente real, aquel que yo veía en mi infancia, o este otro que ahora contemplo a través del velo tejido de perfidias, traiciones, bajezas y ruindades que los años colocaron ante mis ojos?" (ibid., p. 64).

129. "En realidad sólo en la niñez somos sabios, sólo entonces establecemos las verdaderas relaciones" (ibid., p. 10).

130. "Ahora me acerco al mar como si fuese a la Puerta del Sol. Contemplo las volutas argentadas de sus olas con la misma indiferencia que los chorros de las mangas de riego. Su estruendo temeroso me deja impasible como el ruido de los coches, y me parece que las gaviotas con sus graznidos pregonan los periódicos de la tarde" (ibid., p. 9).

Conclusion

1. "Otorgar . . . posterior coherencia a la simple acumulación de ruinas" (Goytisolo 1985, p. 193).

Works Cited

Alarcón, Pedro A. de. 1943. *Juicios literaios y artísticos*. Madrid: Victoriano Suárez.

Alas, Leopoldo. 1989. *Narraciones breves*. Barcelona: Anthropos.

Alcalá Galiano, Antonio. 1955. *Obras escogidas*. Vols. 83–84, *Biblioteca de autores españoles*. Madrid: Atlas.

Aldaraca, Bridget. 1982. "El ángel del hogar: The Cult of Domesticity in XIXth Century Spain." In *Theory and Practice of Feminist Literary Criticism,* edited by G. Mora and K. S. Van Hooft, 62–87. Ypsilanti, Mich.: Bilingual.

Amato, Joseph A. 1982. *Guilt and Gratitude: A Study of the Origins of Contemporary Conscience.* Westport, Conn.: Greenwood.

Anonymous. 1845. "Life of the Reverend Blanco White." *Eclectic Review* 19:200–216.

Anonymous. 1846. "Autobiography of the Rev. Josef Blanco White." *Dublin Review* 20:346–86.

Aranguren, José Luis. 1966. *Moral y sociedad: Introducción a la moral social española del siglo XIX.* Madrid: Edicusa.

Athanasius, Saint. 1980. *The Life of St. Anthony.* New York: Paulist.

Augustine, Saint. 1943. *The Confessions.* New York: Sheed and Ward.

———. 1958. *The City of God.* Garden City, N.Y.: Doubleday.

Bakhtin, Mikhail. 1981. *The Dialogic Imagination.* Austin: University of Texas Press.

———. 1983. *Problems of Dostoevsky's Poetics.* Minneapolis: University of Minnesota Press.

Barthes, Roland. 1967. "Le discours de l'histoire." *Information sur les sciences sociales* 6:65–75.

Benavente y Martínez, Jacinto. 1958. *Recuerdos y olvidos (Memorias)*. In *Obras completas*, vol. 11. Madrid: Aguilar.

Benjamin, Walter. 1978. *Reflections*. New York: Schocken.

Berger, John. 1980. *About Looking*. New York: Pantheon.

————. 1982. *Another Way of Telling*. New York: Pantheon.

Berman, Marshall. 1982. *All That Is Solid Melts into Air*. New York: Simon & Schuster.

Bersani, Leo. 1977. "The Subject of Power." *Diacritics* 7:1–10.

Blanco White, Joseph. 1845. *The Life of the Reverend Joseph Blanco White. Written by Himself*. 3 vols. London: Chapman.

Blasco, Eusebio. 1894. *Recuerdos: notas íntimas de Francia y España*. Madrid: Fernando Fé.

Bloom, Harold, ed. 1970. *Romanticism and Consciousness*. New York: Norton.

Boehl de Faber, C. 1977. *La gaviota*. Madrid: Castalia.

Borges, Jorge Luis. 1925. *Inquisiciones*. Buenos Aires: Proa.

Burrel, David. 1970. "Reading the *Confessions* of Augustine." *Journal of Religion* 50:327–51.

Camín, Alfonso. 1952. *Entre manzanos*. México: Revista Norte.

Campo Alange, Condesa de. 1983. *Mi atardecer entre dos mundos: Recuerdos y cavilaciones*. Madrid: Planeta.

Castro, Américo. 1972. *Teresa la santa y otros ensayos*. Madrid: Alfaguara.

Certeau, Michel de. 1987. *Heterologies*. Minneapolis: University of Minnesota Press.

Chacel, Rosa. 1972. *Desde el amanecer*. Madrid: Revista de Occidente.

Cochrane, C. N. 1940. *Christianity and Classical Culture*. Oxford: Clarendon.

Culler, Jonathan. 1981. *The Pursuit of Signs*. Ithaca, N.Y.: Cornell University Press.

de Ferrari, R. 1952. Introduction to *Early Christian Biographies*. New York: Fathers of the Church: i–xiv.

de la Vega, Juana (Condesa de Espoz y Mina). 1977. *Memorias*. Madrid: Tebas.

Delhez-Sarlet, C., ed. 1983. *Individualisme et autobiographie en Occident*. Bruxelles: Université de Bruxelles.

de Man, Paul. 1979. *Allegories of Reading*. New Haven, Conn.: Yale University Press.

————. 1983. *Blindness and Insight*. Minneapolis: University of Minnesota Press.

————. 1984. *The Rhetoric of Romanticism*. New York: Columbia University Press.

Derrida, Jacques. 1976. *Of Grammatology*. Translated by G. C. Spivak. Baltimore, Md.: Johns Hopkins University Press.

Donato, Eugenio. 1979. "Historical Imagination and the Idioms of Criticism." *boundary 2* 8:39–56.

Eagleton, Terry. 1981. *Walter Benjamin; or, Towards a Revolutionary Criticism.* London: Verso.

Escoiquiz, Juan de. 1915. *Memorias.* Madrid: Revista de Archivos, Bibliotecas y Museos.

Espoz y Mina, Francisco. 1962. *Memorias.* Vols. 146–47, *Biblioteca de autores españoles.* Madrid: Atlas.

Feijoo y Montenegro, Benito J. 1958. *Teatro crítico universal.* Madrid: Espasa-Calpe.

Fernández, James D. 1990. "Teresa de Jesús y la salvación del discurso." *MLN* 105:283–302.

———. 1991a. "A Life of Readings; the Readings of a Life: Joseph Blanco White." *Revista de estudios hispánicos* 14:121–42.

———. 1991b. "La novela familiar del autobiógrafo: Juan Goytisolo." *Anthropos* 125:54–60.

Fernández-Cifuentes, L. 1987. "Torres Villarroel: Seducción y escándalo en la Biblioteca." *Confluencia* 2:22–33.

———. 1988. "Signs for Sale in the City of Galdós." *MLN* 103:289–311.

———. 1991. "Tirando con gusto por la vida." *Anthropos.* 125:24–31.

Fernández de Córdoba, Fernando. 1966. *Mis memorias íntimas.* Vols. 193–94, *Biblioteca de autores españoles.* Madrid: Atlas.

Fish, Stanley. 1980. *Is There a Text in This Class?* Cambridge, Mass.: Harvard University Press.

Flores, Antonio. 1968. *La sociedad de 1850.* Madrid: Alianza.

Foucault, Michel. 1978. "The Eye of Power." *Semiotext(e)* 3:6–19.

———. 1983. Afterword to *Michel Foucault: Beyond Structuralism and Hermeneutics,* by H. L. Dreyfus and P. Rabinow, 208–26. Chicago: University of Chicago Press.

———. 1984. *La verdad y las formas jurídicas.* México: Gedisa.

Freccero, John. 1975. "The Fig Tree and the Laurel: Petrarch's Poetics." *Diacritics* 5:34–40.

Gallagher, C., and T. Laqueur, eds. 1987. Introduction to *The Making of the Modern Body: Sexuality and Society in the XIX Century,* vii–xv. Berkeley: University of California Press.

García de León y Pizarro, José. 1953. *Memorias.* 2 vols. Madrid: Revista de Occidente.

Girón, Pedro Agustín. 1978. *Recuerdos de la vida de don Pedro Agustín Girón, escritos por él mismo.* 3 vols. Pamplona: Ediciones de la Universidad de Navarra.

Gladstone, William Ewart. 1879. "Blanco White." In *Gleanings of Past Years,* vol. 1, 1–64. New York: Scribners.

Glendinning, Nigel. 1984. "Cambios en el concepto de la opinión pública a fines del siglo XVIII." *Nueva revista de filología hispánica* 33:157–64.

Godoy, Manuel de. 1956. *Memorias.* In vols. 88–89, *Biblioteca de autores españoles.* Madrid: Atlas.

Gómez Arias. 1744. *Vida y sucessos del astrólogo Gómez Arias.* Madrid.

Gómez-Moriana, Antonio. 1980. "La subversión del discurso ritual." *Imprevue* 2:37–67.

———. 1983. "Autobiographie et discours rituel; La confession autobiographique au tribunal de l'Inquisition." *Poetique* 56:444–60.

González Echevarría, Roberto. 1980. "The Life and Adventures of Cipión and Berganza: Cervantes and the Picaresque." *Diacritics* 10:15–26.

———. 1987. "The Law of the Letter: Garcilaso's *Commentaries* and the Origins of the Latin American Narrative." *Yale Journal of Criticism* 1:107–31.

González Ruano, César. 1979. *Mi medio siglo se confiesa a medias.* Madrid: Tebas.

Goytisolo, Juan. 1974. "Presentación Crítica." In *Obra inglesa de don José María Blanco White.* Barcelona: Seix Barral.

———. 1985. *Coto vedado.* Barcelona: Seix Barral.

Graña, César. 1964. *Bohemian versus Bourgeois: French Society and the French Man of Letters in the XIX Century.* New York: Basic.

Greenblatt, Stephen. 1979. "Dialectics of Being, Self, Family and Society" (Review of Weintraub). *Clio* 8:275–78.

———. 1980. "Improvisation and Power." *Literature and Society,* edited by E. Said. Baltimore, Md.: Johns Hopkins University Press.

Griggs, E. H. 1908. *Ten Great Autobiographies.* New York: Huebsch.

Guevara, Antonio de. 1915. *Menosprecio de corte y alabanza de aldea.* Madrid: La Lectura.

Halsted, J. B., ed. 1969. *Romanticism.* New York: Walker.

Hartman, G. 1970. "Romanticism and Anti-Self-Consciousness." In *Romanticism and Consciousness,* edited by Harold Bloom, 46–56. New York: Norton.

Heine, Heinrich. 1969. "The Romantic School." In *Romanticism,* edited by J. B. Halsted, 60–71. New York: Walker.

Heller, T. et al., eds. 1986. *Reconstructing Individualism: Autonomy, Individuality and the Self in Western Thought.* Stanford, Calif.: Stanford University Press.

Horkheimer, M., and T. Adorno. 1972. *The Dialectic of Enlightenment.* New York: Seabury.

Houghton, W. E. 1957. *The Victorian Frame of Mind.* New Haven, Conn.: Yale University Press.

Howarth, William. 1974. "Some Principles of Autobiography." *New Literary History* 2:363–81.

Jay, Paul. 1984. *Being in the Text: Self-Representation from Wordsworth to Roland Barthes.* Ithaca, N.Y.: Cornell University Press.

Kermode, Frank. 1979. *The Genesis of Secrecy: On the Interpretation of Narrative.* Cambridge, Mass.: Harvard University Press.

Kirkpatrick, Susan. 1977. *Larra: El laberinto inextricable de un romántico liberal.* Madrid: Gredos.

————. 1978. "The Ideology of Costumbrismo." *Ideologies and Literature* 7:28–44.

Labov, William. 1972. *Language in the Inner City.* Philadelphia: University of Pennsylvania Press.

Larra, Mariano José de. 1969. *Artículos.* Barcelona: Planeta.

Lejeune, Phillipe. 1975. *Le pacte autobiographique.* Paris: Seuil.

————. 1983. "Autobiographie et histoire sociale au XIXe siècle." In *Individualisme et autobiographie en Occident,* edited by Delhez Sarlet, 209–34. Bruxelles: Université de Bruxelles.

de León, Luis. 1959. *Obras completas.* Madrid: Biblioteca de Autores Cristianos.

Levin, Harry. 1931. *The Broken Column.* Cambridge, Mass.: Harvard University Press.

Levine, George. 1986. "Darwin and the Evolution of Fiction." *New York Times Book Review.* 5 October, 61.

Levisi, Margarita. 1985. *Autobiografías del siglo de oro.* Madrid: MSGEL.

Llorens, Vicente. 1971. "Introducción." In *José María Blanco White: Antología de obras en español.* Barcelona: Labor.

Lukács, G. 1983. *The Theory of the Novel.* Cambridge: MIT Press.

Lukacs, John. 1985. *Historical Consciousness.* New York: Schocken.

Martínez de la Rosa, M. 1835. *El espíritu del siglo.* Vol. 1. Madrid: Jordán.

Mellor, Anne, ed. 1988. *Romanticism and Feminism.* Bloomington: Indiana University Press.

Menéndez y Pelayo, Marcelino. 1930–32. *Historia de los heterodoxos españoles.* 7 vols. Madrid: Suárez.

Mercadier, G. 1972. "Introducción." In *Vida de Torres Villarroel.* Madrid: Clásicos Castalia.

Mesonero Romanos, Ramón de. 1925. *Obras completas.* 3 vols. Madrid: Renacimiento.

————. 1975. *Memorias de un setentón.* Madrid: Tebas.

Meyer, John. 1986. "Myths of Socialization and of Personality." In *Reconstructing Individualism: Autonomy, Individuality, and the Self in Western Thought,* edited by T. Heller et al., 208–21. Stanford, Calif.: Stanford University Press.

Misch, G. 1950. *A History of Autobiography in Antiquity.* 2 vols. London: Routledge & Kegan Paul.

Molloy, Sylvia. 1985. "At Face Value: Autobiographical Writing in Span-ish America." *Dispositio* 6:1–18.

Montesinos, José F. 1977. *Pedro Antonio de Alarcón*. Madrid: Castalia.

———. 1983. *Costumbrismo y novela*. Madrid: Castalia.

Mora, G., and K. S. Van Hooft. 1982. *Theory and Practice of Feminist Literary Criticism*. Ypsilanti, Mich.: Bilingual Press.

Moreno Villa, José. 1944. *Vida en claro*. México: Colegio de México.

Mozley, J. B. [1845] 1874. "Blanco White." *Christian Remembrancer* 10 (1845):144–212. Reprinted in *Essays Historical and Theological*. New York: Dutton.

Newman, John Henry. 1956. *Apologia pro vita sua*. Boston: Houghton Mifflin.

Nombela, Julio. 1909. *Impresiones y recuerdos*. 4 vols. Madrid: La Última Moda.

Olney, J. 1972. *Metaphors of Self: The Meaning of Autobiography*. Princeton: Princeton University Press.

———. 1980a. "Autobiography and the Cultural Moment." In *Auto-biography: Essays Theoretical and Critical*, ed. James Olney: 3–27. Prince-ton: Princeton University Press.

———, ed. 1980b. *Autobiography: Essays Theoretical and Critical*. Prince-ton: Princeton University Press.

Ortega y Gasset, José. 1921. *Meditaciones del Quijote*. Madrid: Espasa-Calpe.

———. 1947. "Sobre unas memorias." Vol. 3, *Obras completas*, 584–96. Madrid: Revista de Occidente.

———. 1981. *Historia como sistema y otros ensayos de filosofía*. Madrid: Alianza-Revista de Occidente.

Palacio Valdés, Armando. 1965. *La novela de un novelista*. Buenos Aires: Espasa-Calpe.

Palafox y Melzi, José de. 1966. *Autobiografía*. Madrid: Taurus.

Parlaverdades, El Barón de. 1849. *Madrid al daguerrotipo*. Madrid: Im-prenta de L. García.

Pastor, Enrique. 1975. "Prólogo." In *Memorias de un setentón*, by Ramón Mesonero Romanos. Madrid: Tebas.

Pérez Firmat, Gustavo. 1986. *Literature and Liminality: Festive Readings in the Hispanic Tradition*. Durham, N.C.: Duke University Press.

Pérez Galdós, Benito. 1972. *Ensayos de crítica literaria*. Barcelona: Edi-ciones Península.

Pope, Randolph. 1974. *La autobiografía española hasta Torres Villarroel*. Bern: Lang.

Powell, Baden. 1845. "Life of the Reverend Joseph Blanco White." *The Westminster Review* 44:273–325.

Prieto, Adolfo. 1966. *La literatura autobiográfica argentina.* Rosario: Filología y letras.

Rico, Francisco. 1970. *La novela picaresca y el punto de vista.* Barcelona: Seix Barral.

Rorty, Richard. 1979. *Philosophy and the Mirror of Nature.* Princeton: Princeton University Press.

Ross, Marlon R. 1988. "Romantic Quest and Conquest: Troping Masculine Power in the Crisis of Poetic Identity." In *Romanticism and Feminism,* edited by Anne Mellor, 26–51. Bloomington: Indiana University Press.

Roure, Conrado. 1925. *Recuerdos de mi larga vida.* 3 vols. Barcelona: Biblioteca el Diluvio.

Rousseau, Jean-Jacques. 1959. *Oeuvres completes.* Vol. 1. Paris: Pléiade.

Ruiz Contreras, Luis. 1917. *Memorias de un desmemoriado.* Madrid: Sociedad Española de Librerías.

Sánchez Blanco, Francisco. 1983. "La concepción del 'yo' en las autobiografías españolas del siglo XIX." *Boletín de la asociación de profesores de español* 15:29–36.

Schivelbusch, Wolfgang. 1986. *The Railway Journey: The Industrialization of Time and Space in the 19th Century.* Berkeley: University of California Press.

Schizzano Mandel, A. 1980. "Le proces inquisitoriale comme acte autobiographique." In *L'autobiographie dans le monde hispanique,* 155–70. Provence: Université de Provence.

Seco Serrano, Carlos. 1973. *Sociedad, literatura y política en la España del siglo XIX.* Madrid: Biblioteca Universitaria Guadiana.

Sennet, Richard. 1978. *The Fall of Public Man.* New York: Vintage.

Seoane Couceiro, M. C. 1977. *Oratoria y periodismo en la España del siglo XIX.* Madrid: Castalia.

Serres, Michel. 1982. *Hermes: Literature, Science and Philosophy.* Baltimore, Md.: Johns Hopkins University Press.

Simmel, George. 1971. *On Individuality and Social Forms.* Chicago: University of Chicago Press.

———. 1978. *The Philosophy of Money.* London: Routledge & Kegan Paul.

Spengemann, William C. 1980. *The Forms of Autobiography.* New Haven, Conn.: Yale University Press.

Spivak, Gayatri C., trans. 1976. Preface to *Of Grammatology,* by Jacques Derrida, ix–xc. Baltimore, Md.: Johns Hopkins University Press.

Starobinski, Jean. 1980. "The Style of Autobiography." In *Autobiography: Essays Theoretical and Critical,* edited by J. Olney: 73–83. Princeton: Princeton University Press.

Subirats, Eduardo. 1979. *Figuras de la conciencia desdichada.* Madrid: Taurus.

———. 1983. *El alma y la muerte.* Barcelona: Anthropos.

Tarr, F. Courtney. 1940. "Romanticism in Spain." *PMLA* 55:35–46.

Teresa de Jesús, Santa. 1963. *Obras completas.* Madrid: Editorial de Espiritualidad.

Thom, John Hamilton. 1867. "Archbishop Whately and the Life of Blanco White." *Theological Review* 4:173–92.

Torres Villarroel, Diego de. 1966. *Visiones y visitas de Torres con d. Francisco de Quevedo por la corte.* Madrid: Espasa-Calpe.

———. 1984. *Vida.* Madrid: Clásicos Castellanos.

Vance, Eugene. 1973a. "Augustine's *Confessions* and the Grammar of Selfhood." *Genre* 6:1–23.

———. 1973b. "Le moi comme langage." *Poetique* 14:163–77.

Vilar, Pierre. 1986. *Historia de España.* Barcelona: Editorial Crítica.

Weintraub, Karl Joachim. 1975. "Autobiography and Historical Consciousness." *Critical Inquiry* 1:821–48.

———. 1978. *The Value of the Individual: Self and Circumstance in Autobiography.* Chicago: University of Chicago Press.

Whately, E. Jane, ed. 1866. *The Life of Archbishop Whately.* London: Longman.

Williams, Raymond. 1957. "Literature and Rural Society." *Listener* 16:630.

———. 1973. *The Country and the City.* London: Oxford University Press.

———. 1983. *Culture and Society: 1780–1950.* New York: Columbia University Press.

Zambrano, María. 1942. *La confesión: método y género literario.* México: Luminar.

Zorrilla y Moral, José. 1961. *Recuerdos del tiempo viejo.* 2 vols. Madrid: Publicaciones Españolas.

———. 1987. *Don Juan Tenorio.* México: Red Editorial Iberoamericana.

Appendix 1

Principal Autobiographical Texts

Analyzed in This Study

Alcalá Galiano, Antonio (1789–1865). Liberal conspirator, writer, brilliant speaker, and politician. Exiled to England at the end of the *trienio constitucional,* he returned to Spain in 1832 and eventually came to repudiate the liberal fervor of his youth. I quote from 3 autobiographical texts:

Memorias. Written between 1847 and 1849, parts of the text were published serially in the periodical press. First published as a book by his son in Madrid, 1886. Republished in vol. 83 of the *Biblioteca de autores españoles* (BAE) (Madrid: Atlas, 1955).

Recuerdos de un anciano. First published in the journal *La América* between 1862 and 1864. Published as a book by the Biblioteca Clásica, vol. 7, Madrid, 1878, 1890, 1913, and 1927. Reprinted in vol. 83 of the BAE (Madrid: Atlas, 1955).

Apuntes para la biografía. First published in Madrid, 1865. Reprinted in vol. 84 of the BAE (Madrid: Atlas, 1955).

Blanco White, Joseph (1775–1841). Spanish dissident and exile. A Catholic priest in Spain, he fled to England during the French invasion; eventually became an Anglican minister, only later to renounce Anglicanism. A fascinating figure, Blanco White rubbed elbows with, and influenced, many of nineteenth-century Europe's most important figures.

The Life of the Reverend Joseph Blanco White. Written by Himself (London: Chapman, 1845). Translations into Spanish of parts of the *Life* have been published by Juan Goytisolo in *Obra inglesa de don José María Blanco*

White (Barcelona: Seix Barral, 1974) and A. Garnica in *Autobiografía de Blanco White* (Sevilla: Universidad de Sevilla, 1975).

Escoiquiz, Juan de. (1762–1820). Intriguer; tutor of the young Fernando VII; he had been handpicked by Godoy, though he proved to be one of Godoy's fiercest enemies.

   Memorias. Written around 1820, the *Memorias* were not published until the early twentieth century (Madrid: Revista de Archivos, Bibliotecas y Museos, 1915).

Espoz y Mina, Francisco (1781–1836). Liberal general in the War of Independence. Exiled to England, then France during the ominous decade; he returned to Spain in 1833 and fought in the Carlist wars.

   Memorias del general Espoz y Mina, escritas por él mismo. First published by his wife, Juana María de la Vega, in Madrid, 1851–52, 5 vols. Mina's wife not only published these memoirs, she also actively collaborated in their composition. They are reprinted in vols. 146–47 of the BAE (Madrid: Atlas, 1962).

de la Vega, Juana (Condesa de Espoz y Mina) (1805–72). Galician liberal. Married the General Espoz y Mina in 1821. Served as *Aya* and *Camarera Mayor* to the young Isabel II.

   Apuntes para la Historia del tiempo que ocupó los destinos de Aya de S. M. y Aya y Camarera Mayor de Palacio. Written between 1841–43. Published in the BAE (see Francisco Espoz y Mina). I used the more recent ed. (Madrid: Tebas, 1977).

   En honor de Mina (Memorias íntimas). This text was included in the BAE's edition of her husband's memoirs. Miguel Artola writes in his "Estudio preliminar": "la unión entre las . . . obras es tan estrecha que ha decidido a la BAE a publicarlas juntas." The first ed. of *En honor de Mina* and *Apuntes de la historia* appeared in 1910, with a long "prólogo" by Juan Pérez de Guzmán y Gallo (Madrid: Hijos de Hernández, 1910). They can both be found in a recent 1-vol. ed. prologued by the Condesa de Campo Alange (Madrid: Tebas, 1977).

Fernández de Córdoba, Fernando (1809–33). Distinguished soldier in the war against the Carlists. He occupied several government and military posts before retiring from public life in 1873. Even though his memoirs are from much later in the century than the rest of the texts studied in chap. 1, they resort to many of the same rhetorical strategies found in the other texts.

   Mis memorias íntimas. First published serially in *La ilustración española y americana* and later in 3 vols. Republished in vols. 193–94 of the BAE (Madrid: Atlas, 1966).

García de León y Pizarro, José (1770–1835). Important diplomat; was a minister under Fernando VII, until palace intrigues made him fall out of favor.

Memorias. Originally addressed "a mis hijos." Published as a 3-vol. book in Madrid between 1894 and 1897. I quote from a 2-vol. ed. prepared by Alvaro Alonso-Castrillo (Madrid: Revista de Occidente, 1953).

Girón, Pedro Agustín (1778–1842). Liberal politician and soldier in the War of Independence. Accused of nepotism, he was forced to resign from his post as minister of war in 1835.

Recuerdos de la vida de don Pedro Agustín Girón, escritos por él mismo. Written between 1830–35, they remained unedited until Ana María Berazaluce prepared a 3-vol. ed. (Pamplona: Ediciones de la Universidad de Navarra, 1978).

Godoy, Manuel de (1767–1851). Relatively enlightened favorite of Carlos IV, he came to rule Spain almost as a dictator in the years preceding the French invasion. Exiled in France after his fall; there he wrote his memoirs.

Memorias. Published first in French (1836–38) and then in Spanish; 6 vols. (1836–42). Reprinted in vols. 88–89 of the BAE (Madrid: Atlas, 1956).

Mesonero Romanos, Ramón de (1803–82). One of the "founders" of *costumbrismo* in Spain. Urban planner, author of travel books, and publishing entrepreneur.

Las memorias de un setentón. First published serially in 1879 in *La Ilustración Española y Americana*. The following year in book form (Madrid: La Ilustración Española y Americana, 1880). I have used the recent ed. (Madrid: Tebas, 1975).

Palacio Valdés, Armando (1853–1938). Prolific turn-of-the-century novelist who achieved a considerable international readership. Probably best known for the novels he situated in his beloved region of Asturias.

La novela de un novelista. First ed. (Madrid: Suárez, 1921). I have used the more recent ed. (Buenos Aires: Espasa-Calpe, 1965).

Palafox y Melzi, José de (1776–1847). Aragonese hero of the War of Independence.

Autobiografía. Written on "sesenta hojas de papel de oficio del año 1826," according to the editor of the recent ed. (Madrid: Taurus, 1966).

Torres Villarroel, Diego de (1693–1770). Arguably Spain's first professional writer in the age of print, Torres was also an astrologer, university professor, popular hero, dance instructor, and incessant autobiographer, among many other things.

Vida, ascendencia, nacimiento, crianza y aventuras del doctor don Diego de Torres Villarroel. Originally published in 6 "*trozos*" between 1743 and

1758. I have worked with Guy Mercadier's recent ed. (Madrid: Clásicos Castalia, 1984).

Zorrilla y Moral, José (1817–93). Probably Spain's most important Romantic poet and dramatist. Author of *Don Juan Tenorio.*

Recuerdos del tiempo viejo. First published serially in *El lunes del Imparcial,* beginning in October of 1879. As a book in 3 vols. shortly thereafter, and then again in 2 vols. (Madrid: Publicaciones Españolas, 1961).

Cossío, Francisco de. 1959. *Confesiones: Mi familia, mis amigos, mi época.* Madrid: Espasa-Calpe.

Cruz Ebro, María. 1952. *Memorias de una burgalesa.* Burgos: Diputación Provincial.

de Pombo, Ana. 1971. *Mi última condena: Autobiografía.* Madrid: Taurus.

Díaz Plaja, Guillermo. 1978. *Retrato de un escritor.* Madrid: Pomaire.

Escalas Real, Jaime. 1978. *Recuerdos de mi pasado.* Palma de Mallorca: Diputación Provincial.

Estévanez y Murphy, N. 1903. *Fragmentos de mis memorias.* Madrid: Hijos de R. Alvarez.

Figueroa, A. de. 1955. *Dentro y fuera de mi vida: capítulos de pequeña historia 1910–1936.* Madrid: Guadarrama.

Gómez Arias. 1744. *Vida y sucessos del astrólogo Gómez Arias.* Madrid.

Gómez de la Serna, Ramón. 1948. *Automoribundia.* Buenos Aires: Editorial Sudamericana.

———. 1957. *Nuevas páginas de mi vida: Lo que no dije en mi "Automoribundia."* Alcoy: Editorial Marfil.

González Ruano, César. 1979 [1951]. *Mi medio siglo se confiesa a medias.* Madrid: Tebas.

Goytisolo, Juan. 1985. *Coto vedado.* Barcelona: Seix Barral.

———. 1986. *En los reinos de taifa.* Barcelona: Seix Barral.

Gutiérrez Gamero, Emilio. 1926. *Mis primeros ochenta años: Memorias.* Madrid: Atlántida.

———. 1928. *Lo que me dejé en el tintero (Memorias).* Madrid: Librería y Editorial Madrid.

———. 1932. *El ocaso de un siglo: Continuación de "Mis primeros ochenta años."* Barcelona: Mentora.

Ibarruri, Dolores. 1984. *Memorias de Pasionaria 1939–1977: Me faltaba España.* Madrid: Planeta.

Insúa, Alberto. 1952. *Memorias.* 2 vols. Madrid: Tesoro.

———. 1959. *Amor, viajes y literatura: memorias.* Madrid: Siglo XX.

León, María Teresa. 1970. *Memoria de la melancolía.* Buenos Aires: Losada.

Llorente, Juan A. 1982 [1818]. *Noticia biográfica: Autobiografía.* Madrid: Taurus.

Manresa, Josefina. 1980. *Recuerdos de la viuda de Miguel Hernández.* Madrid: Editorial de la Torre.

Marquerre, Alfredo. 1971. *Personas y personajes: Memorias informales.* Barcelona: Dopesa.

Martín Vigil, J. Luis. 1969. *Los tallos verdes: Un hombre, una memoria.* Oviedo: R. Grando.

Martínez O'Connor, J. D. 1983. *Recuerdos de antaño.* Almería: Diputación provincial.

Martínez Olemedilla, A. 1908. *Memorias de un afrancesado*. Madrid: Librería de Pueyo.

———. 1952. *Nuevas memorias de un afrancesado*. Madrid: Sáez.

Martínez Ruiz, José. 1967. *Memorias inmemoriales*. Madrid: Biblioteca Nueva.

Martínez Sierra, María. 1989. *Una mujer por caminos de España*. Madrid: Castalia.

Mendaro, Eduardo. 1958. *Recuerdos de un periodista de principios de siglo*. Madrid: Prensa Española.

Menéndez Pelayo, Enrique. 1922. *Memorias de uno a quien no sucedió nada*. Santander: Librería Nacional y Extranjera.

Mihura, Miguel. 1948. *Mis memorias*. Barcelona: Janés.

Miranda, Sebastián. 1973. *Recuerdos y añoranzas: Mi vida y mis amigos*. Madrid: Prensa Española.

Montoliu, Manuel de. 1958. *Memorias de infancia y adolescencia*. Tarragona: Diputación Provincial.

———. 1975. *Segundo libro de recuerdos y añoranzas*. Madrid: Prensa Española.

Mor de Fuentes, J. 1981 [1836]. *Bosquejillo de la vida y escritos*. Zaragoza: Guara Editorial.

Moreno Villa, José. 1944. *Vida en claro*. México: Colegio de México.

Muñoz Ruiz, Joaquín. 1958. *Recuerdos de antaño*. Barcelona: Rumbos.

Nombela, Julio. 1909. *Impresiones y recuerdos*. 4 vols. Madrid: La Última Moda.

Ossorio y Gallardo, A. 1946. *Mis memorias*. Buenos Aires: Editorial Losada.

Palacio, Carlos. 1984. *Acordes en el alma: Memorias*. Alicante: Diputación Provincial.

Pardo Bazán, Emilia de. 1973 [1886]. "Apuntes autobiográficos." In *Obras completas*, vol. 3. Madrid: Aguilar.

Pérez Galdós, Benito. 1920. *Memorias de un desmemoriado*. Madrid: Alhambra.

Posada, José. 1964. *Vida corriente*. Madrid: Editorial Nacional.

Posse, J. Antonio. 1984. *Memorias del cura liberal don J. Antonio Posse*. Madrid: Centro de Investigaciones Sociales.

Pulido Martín, A. [1962] 1966. *Recuerdos de un médico*. Barcelona: Fauna.

Ramón y Cajal, Santiago. 1923. *Mi infancia y juventud*. Madrid: Imprenta de Pueyo.

Roca Buades, Ignacio. 1963. *Mis recuerdos*. Barcelona: Industria Gráfica Barcino.

Roig Rosello, A. 1977. *Todos los parques no son un paraíso: Memorias de un sacerdote*. Barcelona: Planeta.

Roure, Conrado. 1925–27. *Recuerdos de mi larga vida.* 3 vols. Barcelona: Biblioteca El Diluvio.

Ruiz Castillo Basal, J. 1986. *Memorias de un editor: El apasionante mundo del libro.* Madrid: Sánchez Rupérez.

Ruiz Contreras, Luis. 1917. *Memorias de un desmemoriado.* Madrid: Sociedad Española de Librerías, Diarios, Revistas y Publicaciones.

Sagarra, José M. de. 1957 [1954]. *Memorias.* Madrid: Noguer.

Sainz de Robles, F. 1949. *Madrid: Autobiografía.* Madrid: Aguilar.

Sainz Rodríguez, Pedro. 1978. *Testimonios y recuerdos.* Barcelona: Planeta.

Sanromá, J. M. 1887–94. *Mis memorias.* 2 vols. Madrid: Hernández.

Santillán, Ramón de. 1960. *Memorias 1815–1856.* Pamplona: Eunsa.

Sassone, Felipe. 1939. *España, nuestra madre: Notas autobiográficas.* Lima: Torres Aguirre.

———. 1958. *La rueda de mi fortuna: Memorias.* Madrid: Aguilar.

Sopeña, Federico. 1985. *Escrito de noche.* Madrid: Espasa-Calpe.

Torres Rioseco, Arturo. 1963. *Autobiografía.* Palma de Mallorca: Papeles Son Armadans.

Urales, Federico. 1930. *Mi vida.* Barcelona: La Revista Blanca.

Valero de Tornos, Juan. 1901. *Crónicas retrospectivas (recuerdos de la segunda mitad del siglo XIX) por un portero del observatorio.* Madrid: Ricardo Rojas.

Villalonga, Miguel. 1947. *Autobiografía.* Barcelona: Janés.

Villanueva, Joaquín L. 1825. *Vida literaria.* 2 vols. London: Dulau.

Zamacois, Eduardo. 1964. *Un hombre que se va . . .* Barcelona: AHR.

Index

About the Author

James D. Fernández is Assistant Professor
in the Department of Spanish and Portuguese
at Yale University.

Library of Congress Cataloging-in-Publication Data

Fernández, James D, 1961—
    Apology to apostrophe : autobiography and the rhetoric of self-
representation in Spain / James D. Fernández.
        p.   cm.
    English and Spanish.
    Includes bibliographical references and index.
    ISBN 0-8223-1254-9 (alk. paper)
    1. Autobiography—Spanish authors.   2. Biography as a literary
form.   3. Spain—Biography—History and criticism.
4. Autobiographies—Spain—History and criticism.   5. Self in
literature.   I. Title.
CT34.S7F47   1992
860.9'492—dc20   92-4879
                                                     CIP